S0-AYI-658

362.82
G36c

131452

WITHDRAWN

DATE DUE			

A Cry for
HELP

Also by Mary Giffin, M.D.
HER DOCTOR, WILL MAYO

Also by Carol Felsenthal
THE SWEETHEART OF THE SILENT MAJORITY:
The Biography of Phyllis Schlafly

A Cry for
HELP

Mary Giffin, M.D.

MEDICAL DIRECTOR, NORTH SHORE (ILL.)
MENTAL HEALTH ASSOCIATION

and Carol Felsenthal

CARL A. RUDISILL LIBRARY
LENOIR RHYNE COLLEGE

DOUBLEDAY & COMPANY, INC.
GARDEN CITY, NEW YORK
1983

362.82
G 36c
131452
apr. 1985

Library of Congress Cataloging in Publication Data
Giffin, Mary Elizabeth.
    A cry for help.
    Bibliography.
    Includes index.
    1. Youth—Suicidal behavior. 2. Parent and child.
I. Felsenthal, Carol. II. Title.
HV6546.G53   1983   362.8'2
        ISBN: 0-385-15599-9

  Library of Congress Catalog Card Number: 82-45395

Copyright © 1983 by Mary Giffin, M.D., and Carol Felsenthal
ALL RIGHTS RESERVED
PRINTED IN THE UNITED STATES OF AMERICA

Grateful acknowledgment is made to the following for permission to reprint their copyrighted material:

Excerpts from "Good Morning America" program of October 29, 1981 © American Broadcasting Companies, Inc. 1981.

Excerpts from ABC News "Directions" programs of December 6, 1981 and December 13, 1981, © American Broadcasting Companies, Inc. 1981.

Excerpts from ABC News "Nightline" program of April 24, 1982 © American Broadcasting Companies, Inc. 1982.

"Donahue" quotes courtesy of Multimedia Program Productions, Inc.

Excerpts from "NBC Nightly News" with Bob Jamieson, program of May 2, 1981 © 1982 National Broadcasting Company. All Rights Reserved.

Excerpts from *Live or Die* by Anne Sexton. Copyright © 1966 by Anne Sexton. Reprinted by permission of Houghton Mifflin Company.

Excerpts from "Teenage Suicide: Don't Try It" © Alan Landsburg Productions, 1981.

(Six lines) from "Lady Lazarus" in *The Collected Poems*—Sylvia Plath—edited by Ted Hughes
Copyright © 1963 by the Estate of Sylvia Plath
Reprinted by permission of Harper & Row, Publishers, Inc.

Specified excerpts from *The Bell Jar* by Sylvia Plath
Copyright © 1971 by Harper & Row, Publishers, Inc.
Reprinted by permission of Harper & Row, Publishers, Inc.

Lyrics excerpted from "Nowhere Man" by John Lennon and Paul McCartney, copyright © 1965 by Northern Songs, Ltd. Lyrics excerpted from "Strawberry Fields Forever" by John Lennon and Paul McCartney, copyright © 1967 by Northern Songs, Ltd. All rights for the U.S.A., Mexico, and Philippines controlled by Maclen Music, Inc., % ATV Music Corp., 6255 Sunset Blvd., Los Angeles, CA 90026. Used by permission. All Rights Reserved.

Suicide Is Painless
By Altman and Mandel
Copyright © 1970 by WB Music Corp.
All Rights Reserved. Used by permission.

Excerpts from "Straight Talk," with Bruce DuMont, courtesy of WFYR, RKO Radio for Chicago, Broadcast October 25, 1981.

Excerpts from *Baltimore Magazine,* "Suicide Ends Four Young Lives," by John Reisfeld, June 1980.

This book is dedicated to those whom we have known who found no other course except to kill themselves. Only they realize the horror, the agony, and the indecision of choosing the course that became theirs. They struggled with lives that found no other answer. Their sacrifice should not have been necessary. It is our hope that some lives may be saved by the material included in this book. If any lives are spared, our book will have had its ultimate confirmation.

Contents

Contents

Introduction

This book arose from the ashes of a string of adolescent suicides that struck the affluent North Shore suburbs of Chicago—an area that *Time* magazine promptly dubbed "the suicide belt" in recognition of a teen suicide rate three times the already burgeoning national average. We of the Irene Josselyn Clinic, a community mental health center serving the North Shore, had been minding our own case loads when the local chief of police called seeking help in handling what seemed to him to be growing into the most grotesque of fads.

In a few short months we were catapulted into offering seminars, lectures, and media interviews. As our visibility increased, we were unable to keep up with the demand. We realized the need for a guide that would lay bare the myths, the facts, and the plans for action against this apparent epidemic.

It was impossible for me to find the time to write a book, much less to find the writing skills. I was pondering this dilemma when Carol Felsenthal, a professional writer, asked me to collaborate on a book. I eagerly agreed. (Several months earlier Carol had interviewed me for an article on teen suicide she was writing for *Seventeen*.)

Ours has been a joyous and enriching collaboration. Carol's has been the task of research and writing; mine has been that of critic and clinician.

Our book reflects the fact that suicide rates are increasing among youngsters of all ages. The youngest person we describe is two and a half years old; the oldest is twenty-four. We cover these grim statistics in the first of the book's four sections. We also describe, in that section, the deadly myths that many of even the most enlightened parents believe—for example the myth that a person who threatens suicide is only looking for attention and so it is best to ignore him. The section ends with a description of the distress signals—the behavior that most young people exhibit in the months and weeks before they attempt suicide.

In the second section, "Why Do They Do It?" we have generalized about the reasons for what is, in one sense, a highly individual act. We feel comfortable in generalizing because we see, over and over, the same destructive dynamics, values, expectations, and environments in the families that produce suicidal children.

In the third section we cover two of the most common conditions present in suicidal children. In a startlingly high proportion of attempted or completed suicides, there has been a problem in the parent/child relationship from the beginning—literally. The mother and child failed to bond; they never developed a sense of attachment and trust. Next we discuss depression in children, an affliction that seems to strike most often those who suffered a bonding deprivation. Childhood depression is a disorder that until recently psychiatrists thought was a contradiction in terms— childhood is supposedly a carefree, innocent time. We now know that depression is sickeningly prevalent among children and that, if not treated, it can be fatal.

Finally, we offer a section of practical advice. What can parents do in the moment of crisis—when their child is threatening suicide or exhibiting several of the distress signals? Where can they find help in the community? How can they find a good—and an affordable—therapist? The book's last chapter is by no means the least in importance: How can we help the survivors? When a young person kills himself he invariably wounds his entire family. In too many cases that wound proves chronically debilitating, even fatal. (People who have had a suicide in their families are nine times as likely to commit suicide themselves as those who have not.)

We hope that parents will find our book helpful as they navigate through the developmental shoals of their adolescent children. We hope that educators will use the book in formulating programs in detection and referral of potentially suicidal young people. We hope that all readers will identify with the plight of those driven to suicide and especially with the survivors of this tragedy. This book is based upon the premise that adolescent suicide patterns can be altered if the myths and the facts are clarified and their implications for action applied.

My personal contact with suicide began forty-five years ago

when a high school friend killed herself. I will never forget the
shocked but uniform response: "Oh, no! Not a girl like her." She
was a successful and humorous person with no trace of depression
or mental illness. Similarly, what so impressed my colleagues and
me in our conversations with the police was that they were calling
our attention to regular kids, children who looked and thought
like your children, and parents who could have been our friends.
These were not obviously deviant children. These were children
who could have come from any family on the North Shore. These
were children who, for the most part, were not seeing a psychiatrist. They had not even sought the help of other mental health
professionals, such as school social workers.

It is with a sense of indebtedness that we assure our patients
that their individual material has been carefully disguised. If many
of the family interchanges and predicaments sound familiar, it is
because families are very much alike, even as they are also infinitely unique.

Mary Giffin, M.D.
Medical-Executive Director

Irene Josselyn Clinic
Northfield, Illinois
May 1982

PART I

The Facts

1
The Grim Statistics

It was seven o'clock on a warm, still bright, July evening in 1981. The street was tree-lined, lush, with almost an embarrassing bounty of riches—both natural and acquired. Suburbia, U.S.A.— good smells from Weber grills, sun setting on roofs of highly polished Mercedes not yet garaged for the night, two little girls sitting on a front lawn dressing their Barbie dolls, two teenage boys astride fifteen-speed bicycles.

The ambulance was eight blocks away when its siren was first audible, but it wasn't until it hit the next street that children and then their parents started peering out front windows. Sirens were a rare sound in this community and as an ambulance screeched into the street, the residents were still more surprised. For there were no old people on this block and no one knew of any sick ones. It was a street of few emergencies—a street on which people's lives were as well designed as their kitchens and their grounds.

The ambulance stopped outside the Bentley house. Three paramedics rushed inside. Neighbors now clustered on the sidewalk in front, some half smiling to others whom they hadn't seen in weeks or even months. The maid opened the massive oak doors to let out the paramedics, two of whom carried on a stretcher fifteen-year-old Bobby Bentley, who was obviously unconscious. The ambulance driver held a blood-soaked cloth to Bobby's head.

"I just saw him yesterday on his bike," commented one neighbor. "What happened?" asked a second. "Suicide?" whispered a third. The maid reappeared at the door. "Mr. and Mrs. would like that you all leave now."

"Can't we do anything?" asked the next-door neighbor, as the garage door opened and Robert and Judith Bentley, looking straight ahead, drove out, presumably to the hospital.

To find out what happened, the neighbors had to wait three hours until the late evening news. The news report was as follows:

> Robert Bentley, fifteen, a resident of the affluent North Shore (of Chicago) shot himself through the left temple with a gun from his father's valuable antique collection. The Lake County Coroner said young Bentley, who was found in his bedroom by the family maid, was unconscious almost immediately. He died en route to the hospital.
>
> The boy's father refused comment, but issued a statement through his attorney that the death was a "tragic accident" that occurred as the boy was polishing one of the rare pistols—part of a collection that dates back to the American Revolution. It was unclear at this time how the death would be ruled, although the coroner stated that there "apparently was no suicide note." An inquest will be held next week.
>
> Robert III is the eldest of the three Bentley children. His father, a LaSalle St. attorney, is described by a law partner as "extremely hard working and talented." A teacher at Robert's high school, who insisted on remaining anonymous, described the teenager as "almost the classic perfectionist. He gave 200 percent to everything and he responded very poorly when the results were less than perfect." The Bentleys have two other children, both girls, who attend elementary school.
>
> Neighbors, uniformly, refused to comment on the tragic death.

On that summer evening, at approximately six-thirty, while his parents downed their second martini, Robert Bentley III became another of the grim statistics of suicide—and we'll see very shortly just how grim those statistics are.

But at the same time that his death is a ghastly fact of life in the 1980s, it is also an as yet unexplored opportunity. For suicide is a cry for help that has backfired—a cry that we, the survivors, can heed.

We can prevent our children from killing themselves, and the purpose of this book is to show parents how—how to recognize signs that their children are "down" and, perhaps, preparing to end their lives; what exactly the Bentleys might have done had they realized at five-thirty that their son was preparing to blow his brains out; or what they might have done in the weeks and months before that July night had they noticed the boy's distress.

But first, the grim statistics, in the hope that these numbers—these "lives with the tears washed away"—will prod, indeed shock, parents into recognizing that suicide among their children is a huge and growing problem.

Every day, an average of 18 young Americans kill themselves—6,500 every year. Every *hour,* 57 children and adolescents in the United States attempt to destroy themselves—well over 1,000 attempts every day.

Obviously, young people, who we like to believe have everything to look forward to, do not share our optimistic view of their futures. At the Chicago-Read Mental Health Center, 300 of the 475 suicides committed by Read patients in 1976 were young people. At a Chicago-area suicide hotline, the phone rings every twenty seconds. Dr. Michael Peck, one of the country's leading suicidologists,* estimates that each year in the United States "somewhere in the neighborhood of a million or more children move in and out of suicidal crises . . ."

In researching their book *Teenage Rebellion,* Rev. Truman E. Dollar and psychiatrist Grace H. Ketterman surveyed 100 teens. Thirty-four percent answered yes to the question, "Have you ever seriously considered suicide?" Thirty-two percent said yes to, "Did you make specific plans to take your life?" When the authors asked, "Have you actually attempted suicide?" a whopping 14 percent said yes.[1]

In a recent study of 7,000 high school students, one of every five reported severe problems with self-esteem, feelings of failure, alienation, loneliness, lack of self-confidence, low self-regard, and thoughts of suicide. Three Chicago researchers who surveyed 1,385 teens in the late 1970s and in 1980 found 20 percent feeling emotionally empty, confused most of the time, and that they would rather die than go on living.[2]

Many more young people die of suicide than of cancer. Every year the death rate for childhood cancers falls (43 percent since

* A specialist in the study of and research into suicide's causes and prevention.

1950) and the suicide rate rises (a shocking 300 percent in the last two decades).

Today, only accidents and homicides claim more young lives than suicide. And anyone with even a passing knowledge of the subject agrees that a great many of the deaths that go down in the records as accidents or homicides are really suicides. As the late Dr. Gregory Zilboorg, psychiatrist-in-chief of the United Nations, put it, "Statistical data on suicides as compiled today deserves little credence. All too many suicides are not reported as such." The number of suicides is, *at the very least,* twice what is reported.

For, even in these nearly tabooless times, there are few more grotesque skeletons in the family closet than that of a son or daughter who has committed suicide. It is the most personal, the most terrible of rebukes, and parents will go to outrageous lengths to hide it. Dr. Dominick DiMaio, former Medical Examiner for New York City, explained, "Families sometimes will tell you all kinds of stories to make a suicide look like an accident. A kid blows his brains out with a gun, or jumps off a building. The parents come in and tell us he was playing Russian roulette, or that he slipped while playing on the roof"—or, as in the case of Bobby Bentley, that he was "cleaning" one of his father's guns.

The suicide stigma is so shattering that officials, whose public trust it is to ascertain the cause of death, frequently offer to disguise the truth. In a book about the suicide of his son Michael, journalist James A. Wechsler described how the police volunteered to hide the real circumstances. "Even in the numbness of those hours," Wechsler wrote, "we were astonished at the prevalence of the view that suicide was a dishonorable or at least disreputable matter, to be charitably covered up to protect Michael's good name and the sensibilities of the family."[3] †

† Peter Meyers, a reporter with the Suburban *Tribune* covering Chicago's North Shore suburbs, including the suburb where Bobby Bentley lived, explained that the paper "has a policy against reporting suicides, out of respect for the family." When three students at a North Shore high school committed suicide within a five-week period in late 1981, the paper broke its policy, but then only because of the "extremely unusual circumstances" of the second and third suicides. One boy shot himself to death and his friend, despondent over the death, also fatally shot himself, within hours of returning from his friend's funeral. Bobby Bentley's suicide, on the other hand, was reported only as a death, with no information on the circumstances surrounding it. When Ted, whose case is described in Chapter 6, hanged himself, the North Shore paper reported that he had "died suddenly at home."

This attitude should not surprise. In eight states, suicide is still a crime. It was not so long ago that English common law prescribed that a suicide be carried nude through the streets, to be buried at a crossroads with a stake driven through his heart. (Although the stake-through-the-heart practice was discontinued in 1823, suicide was a felony in Britain until 1961.)

It is not only the shame attached to suicide that keeps the real numbers so inaccurately low. Officials at the National Center for Health Statistics do not record a death as suicide unless there is proof that suicide was intentional; that it was a case of premeditated self-destruction. A suicide note is normally required, but only 15 percent of suicides leave notes. Thus, in the absence of a note, the person who drinks Drano, "falls" out a window, or shoots himself in the head while "cleaning" a gun will probably be omitted from the statistics.

Suicide: The Number One Killer of Young People

Suicide, the statisticians remind us, is the third-biggest killer of young people, *behind* accidents and homicides. Many of us believe that suicide is really the number one killer; that many of the homicide and accident victims are really suicides in disguise. For example, a recent study in Philadelphia revealed that more than 25 percent of murder victims caused their own deaths by picking a fight with someone who had a weapon. In one case, a teenager, who knew his gun was unloaded, brandished it at police officers, inciting them to shoot him in self defense.

We call these "chronic suicides"—the daredevil who shouts, "Look, no hands!" as he rides his bicycle on a two-lane highway, the twelve-year-old, wearing his Superman cape, who jumps from the roof, the hundreds of thousands of adolescents slowly destroying themselves with drugs and alcohol.

In one case that we discuss in detail in Chapter 6, a teenage boy sneaked out of his Brooklyn home in the middle of the night and rode the subway to a station in a South Bronx slum. He slouched against a column flashing his gold watch, encouraging muggers. He sustained nearly fatal injuries at the hands of four muggers who stole his watch and money.

The Chicago *Tribune* recently reported the case of Nicole Lee, a thirteen-year-old who repeatedly ran away from home. On what was to be her fatal run, she met a pimp who, when she refused to become a prostitute, killed her. "I think maybe she had a premonition that she wasn't going to live to grow up," her mother surmised. "I'm not surprised she stood up to them (the pimp and his girlfriend). Nickie was always flirting with danger. This time she just stepped out too far."[4]

Speculation continues as to whether Mary Tyler Moore's twenty-four-year-old son, who died of a gunshot wound to the head in October 1980, killed himself by accident or on purpose. Although Richard's friends and family claimed his death was an accident, Hollywood Police Lieutenant Dan Cooke suspected suicide. Richard collected guns and knew how to handle them but died, according to Lieutenant Cooke, while "putting the shell in, taking it out and placing the gun at his head." He was reportedly discussing with a friend his latest romance and playing "She loves me, she loves me not," the barrel of the .410 gauge shotgun pointed first at the right side of his head, next at the left. On the third "She loves me," he pulled the trigger and died instantly as the bullet ripped into his face.

Auto fatalities, which, in any given year, account for about 37 percent of all deaths in the 15–24-year-old group, probably represent the biggest block of suicides disguised as accidents. The person killed in a head-on collision, while driving at night in a car with no headlights on the wrong side of an expressway, would probably be pronounced an accident victim—unless there was positive proof of suicide.

Forensic experts speculate that approximately one quarter of these "accidents" are deliberate. Adding these so-called "autocides" to suicides, they argue, easily makes suicide the number one killer.

A girl we saw at the clinic is an example of a hidden statistic of suicide. Her death was officially ruled an accident, although she died in a car crash after speaking repeatedly about wanting to smash her car as she had been smashed around by her father.

Other examples:

A young man in Washington took LSD and tried to walk across a branch of the Potomac River. He drowned.

A suburban Chicago boy was electrocuted in his basement during a flood. He had spoken of fantasies of being electrocuted.

A ninth-grader from St. Louis jumped from the top bleacher during his high school homecoming game. He had recently been depressed after failing to make the football team. His death was officially recorded as an accident.

We think that many so-called "accidental" poisonings are also actually suicide attempts. Each year brings one hundred thousand cases of intentional self-poisonings among children ages five to fourteen. Dr. Matilda McIntire and Dr. Caro Angle compared fifty young poisoning victims with fifty other children of similar age and background. They found that 88 percent of the poisoning victims, compared to only 12 percent of the controls, had a history of behavior problems. These children were also more likely to have had alcoholic, hostile, or rejecting parents.

Suicide Rate: Tripled in Twenty Years

In the end, though, the official suicide statistics, as unreliable as they are, are all we have. And although the absolute numbers may be a shadow of reality, they are still disturbingly high, and the relative numbers—the increases—are downright shocking. Between 1955 and 1975, the rate of teen suicide almost tripled—from 4.1 per 100,000 in 1955 to 11.8 per 100,000 in 1975. Between 1965 and 1975, the suicide rate almost doubled. Between 1974 and 1975—the latest statistics available—the rate rose by a walloping 10 percent.

While the actual rate of suicide among older people is higher than among the young, the rate of *increase* of young suicides far exceeds that of older groups. Teen suicide, as we have seen, increased 300 percent between 1955 and 1975. The rate for the general public rose less than 20 percent. The increase for young people is ten times the growth in the suicide rate for the population as a whole.

Dr. Beatrix Hamburg of the National Institute of Mental Health warns, "Adolescence is the only age group in the country in which

the death rate is rising. . . . Improved health measures have prolonged life for the elderly and increased survival in early childhood, but teenagers are dying in increasing numbers."

Even Little Children Are Killing Themselves

The very young—children between two and ten—are also attempting to destroy themselves in ever increasing numbers. We are
finding with suicide the same sad phenomenon we found with
drugs. First, drugs were popular among college students. It didn't
take long before heavy drug usage slipped into high schools, then
junior highs, now elementary schools.

Time reported that an eight-year-old boy tried to hang himself,
but failed only because he could not tie a strong enough knot. A
nine-year-old girl attempted suicide twice. Her mother saved her
the first time by grabbing the bottle of rubbing alcohol she was
trying to drink. The second time the mother saved her daughter by
grabbing her after she had swung one leg over an eighth-floor
balcony.[5] Dr. Mohammad Shafii, a professor of psychiatry at the
University of Louisville, lamented, "In the clinic we have seen five
or six-year-olds who have attempted suicide by hanging or jumping out of a window."

At the 1982 convention of the American Psychiatric Association, psychiatrist Perihan Rosenthal described her encounters with
six suicidal children who had at least one thing in common—they
were all under five years old. Four-year-old David wrapped himself in a blanket and set it on fire. When asked why, he answered,
"Because David is a bad boy, there will be no more David." Following his parents' divorce, Benji, two and a half, stopped eating
for two weeks, threatened to throw himself in front of cars, and
bit himself until he bled. In therapy he made a boy doll plunge
from a dollhouse roof and the top of a toy truck. "Why is the
little boy hurting himself?" Rosenthal asked. "He is a bad boy.
Nobody loves him," Benji explained.

Suicide hitting innocent children? It is so ghastly a thought that
the National Center for Health Statistics does not even compute
suicide figures for children under ten. There is a belief—lately

shown to be erroneous—that suicide in children under ten is so rare as to be unmeasurable.

Yet when Pittsburgh psychologist Maria Kovacs surveyed 127 elementary school children, 41 percent admitted having thought about suicide. Michael Peck's research suggests that "up to 10 percent of the youngsters in any public school classroom may be considered at some risk for suicide."

Although there are no reliable figures for those under ten, there are figures for 10–14-year-olds. Rates for that group have risen nearly as fast as the rate for 15–24-year-olds. In the decade between 1968 and 1978 the rate increased by 32 percent.

We know now that depression, the most common impetus to suicide, also strikes children. Depression is not, as we might like to think, the exclusive property of the middle-aged and elderly.

The median age of depressed patients has been dropping steadily. Today, more than half the patients in U.S. mental institutions are under twenty-one. At the 1980 meeting of the American Academy of Pediatrics, Dr. Nicholas Putnam of the University of California Medical Center estimated that "one in five children may be suffering from symptoms of depression, outstripping that for the middle-aged and exceeded only by the rate of depression among the elderly."

Among depressed children, suicidal wishes are extremely common. Cynthia R. Pfeffer, professor of psychiatry and pediatrics at Albert Einstein School of Medicine, found that among approximately 100 children referred for outpatient treatment to a New York hospital, 33 percent had threatened or attempted suicide. (Studies in the 1960s showed that no more than 10 percent of children sent to outpatient clinics showed suicidal behavior.) The number leaped to 72 percent for children who were hospitalized. Child psychiatrist Donald McKnew of the National Institute of Mental Health estimates that about half of the depressed children seen at NIMH are suicidal.

Suicides Among College Students: An Epidemic

As mentioned earlier, suicide is the third leading cause of death among young people.‡ For those of college age, it is officially the second leading cause, having risen from fifth place in the early 1970s. In the period between 1968 and 1975, suicide deaths in the 20–24-year-old age group more than doubled.

The high rate among this group is not surprising. For most students, college means living away from home for the first time. As we'll see later, suicidal high school students often plan their suicide attempts so they can be discovered by parents and saved. This option isn't open to the student living in the college dorm.

In 1976 half the deaths on a large midwestern campus were due to suicide—a figure that remains constant nationally. A few years ago, a researcher studying a random sample of 792 college students, of all grade levels, found that 30 percent had entertained suicidal thoughts during an academic year. Freshman year—the first time away from home—is, not surprisingly, the toughest. According to psychiatrist Lee Robbins Gardner of Columbia University's College of Physicians and Surgeons, one study of college freshmen revealed that 70 percent had thought of suicide in one given year. While writing *Too Young to Die,* a book about youth and suicide first published in 1976, Francine Klagsbrun sent questionnaires to a randomly selected group of high school and college students. More than one in ten said they had actually attempted suicide.[6] *

Putting It All into Perspective

To bring these numbers down to size, it's useful to consider youth suicide figures for the Irene Josselyn Clinic's service area—

‡ *Officially,* that is. Remember, it is probably really the number one killer.
* More than half the students reported that they knew people who had attempted suicide. Nearly a third said they had friends or relatives who had actually killed themselves.

ten Chicago suburbs that run along a twenty-mile stretch of lake-front. In this area, one of the wealthiest in the country, more teens take their lives than anywhere else in Illinois. Their rate is three times the national rate. During a seventeen-month period ending in summer 1980, twenty-eight teenagers killed themselves—eighteen died by gunshot, eight by hanging, and two by lying down in front of trains.

When, in July 1979, an extraordinarily talented, intelligent, and attractive nineteen-year-old from Winnetka hanged herself, the area received vast amounts of local and national media coverage and was instantly dubbed "the suicide belt." The girl, as a matter of fact, was the third teen from the area to take her own life in a two-week period. *Time* magazine quoted a Winnetka resident who overheard two youngsters coolly discussing suicide, "just like they were discussing what kind of socks to buy."[7]

The North Shore, of course, is not unique. In the San Francisco Bay area, officials claim that fifteen of every one hundred kids try it, and one third succeed. In 1980, sixteen teens from Ohio's Cuyahoga County killed themselves; twenty from Dallas County, Texas. In the eighteen months since the spring of 1980, officials of Larimer County, Colorado, outside Denver, have reported twelve cases of adolescent suicide. According to County Coroner Pat Allen, "Just last week we had a nineteen-year-old woman who stabbed herself with a knife. We had two college students . . . who hanged themselves within a period of three weeks. . . . We've had people jumping from high buildings, cliffs up in the mountains, we had several gunshot wounds, both male and female."[8]

Hope in All This?

As high as the suicide death rate is, it seems moderate when compared to the attempt rate. For every young person who completes suicide, there may be fifty to one hundred others who attempt it and "fail." As we said at the opening of this chapter, at the very least, every hour fifty-seven American children and teens attempt suicide.† The incidence of suicide attempts has increased by as much as 3,000 percent per year.

The fact that the attempt rate so outstrips the completed rate offers us hope—and the reason for writing this book. Most young people who attempt suicide do not want to die. Suicide is, in fact, the nation's number one *preventable* health problem—preventable because experts believe that, except for a very few, all the people who commit suicide want to live.

They die because they believe they are not loved. And so parents can prevent their children from becoming just another grim statistic. As Dr. E. S. Shneidman of the UCLA School of Medicine put it, "Until the very moment that the bullet or barbiturate finally snuffs out life's last breath, the suicidal person wants desperately to live. He is begging to be saved." Dr. M. S. Weiss of the University of Missouri Medical Center recently completed a study showing that many young people who attempt suicide have a "relatively low psychological intent" to go through with it. They may be trying to force their parents to pay attention to them or they may be trying to punish their parents. They are performing a desperate version of holding their breath until turning blue.

Consider this recent letter to syndicated advice columnist Ann Landers: "I'm 16-years-old and tried to kill myself three weeks ago by jumping in front of a car. I didn't really want to die. I just wanted someone to pay attention to me. God was with me. The car stopped in time and my only injury was a broken shoulder and some cuts and bruises. My attempt at suicide was a cry for help. Nobody would listen when I said I was going crazy. I had to show them. Some 'screwy' people aren't looking for death, Ann. They are looking for love."⁹ ‡

Ambivalence is the most important psychological concept in understanding suicide. Ambivalence—the simultaneous wish to die and the fantasy of rescue, the person who wants to and doesn't

† This number is also much too low, considering that its source is hospital emergency room records. Many suicide attempters can be managed out of the hospital and thus their attempts are not recorded.

‡ This letter was one of four published in the same column and written in response to an earlier published letter from a man who worked in a hospital emergency room and wrote, "Screwy people who attempt suicide are nuts—they louse up the environment. If they want to die—good riddance." Interestingly, all the letter writers were young people, the oldest twenty-six years old.

want to, who stumbles into death while gasping for life, who cuts his throat and cries for help. The ambivalence is so strong that many suicide victims actually have been found dead, still grasping the telephone receiver.*

Nobody commits suicide out of the blue. People, especially young people, give warnings repeatedly, as if to plead, "Please help me. I beg you. Please help me. I don't really want to die." Study after study has shown that approximately 80 percent of people who committed suicide gave repeated warnings. On the North Shore, 100 percent of those twenty-eight "successful" suicides talked openly about killing themselves prior to doing so.

When talk fails, the warning always becomes more dramatic. Four out of five persons who kill themselves have attempted to do so at least once previously. The authors of *Vivienne: The Life and Suicide of an Adolescent Girl* described in detail the months leading to Vivienne's suicide by hanging. The warnings were evident, but nobody—not her parents, her sister, her friends, her teachers—did anything. On her school admission form, she explained that she felt herself somehow destined for death. In a book report she speculated that death would be a kind of haven. Death will be glorious, Vivienne concluded, and she scrawled a message to that effect across the wall of the bathroom, a room in which she made five suicide attempts. After describing in a letter to her favorite teacher her attempt to overdose on pills, she pleaded with him to help her, to please send her some scrap of hope, of happiness, of encouragement, anything that would give her a reason to go on living.[10]

A suicide attempt that turns deadly is the last in a long series of cries for help. "I tried everything but nothing seemed to help," wrote a college student before putting a bullet through his head. "There is nothing I can say that would make you see what is happening to me."

Adolescents are resilient, optimistic. Except for the most severely depressed, they believe that something, someone will turn

---

* Recently in Chicago a young man tried to leap from a footbridge into rush-hour traffic speeding beneath him on Lake Shore Drive, one of the city's major arteries. Minutes before, he had called 911, the police emergency number, and announced, "My name is Tony and I'm going to the pedestrian bridge and jump off and kill myself." Two policemen answered this man's cry for help by rushing to the scene and yanking him to safety.

up. Usually it's their parents they hope will turn up, tune in. They want their mother or father to find them, save them, love them.

When a Chicago radio station, WFYR, devoted a call-in radio program to the subject of teen suicide, Barbara, who had attempted suicide three times, was one of many teens who aired her pain. "I don't want to commit suicide. I want my parents to recognize that I feel so terribly bad and I want them to help me; to make me feel that I'm cared for. . . . I was hoping to be saved by them, that it would shake them up to realize that they should, you know, share their love while they had the chance."[11]

Nine out of ten teenage suicide attempts take place in the home. Seventy percent of teens who attempt suicide do so, like Bobby Bentley, when their parents are home. And they do so between the hours of three in the afternoon and midnight, when they can be seen, stopped, and saved. If they really wanted to die they would not take the chance of being discovered. (Adults choose the hours between midnight and dawn to kill themselves.)

Another hopeful statistic is that in the few months before committing suicide, 75 percent of victims had visited their family doctors. Many also were seeing a psychiatrist—other forms of cries for help which, in this country at this time, most often go unheeded.

For it is one of the most pervasive myths of suicide that once a child decides to commit suicide, there's nothing we can do to prevent it. There is plenty we can do. We can, in almost all cases, save our children's lives.

But not if we cling to the myths that surround suicide, that muddy our understanding, that mar our ability to act. The most common and the most deadly of these myths are the subject of the next chapter.

2

The Deadly Myths

---

1. Nothing could have stopped her once she decided to kill herself.

2. The person who fails at suicide the first time will eventually succeed.

3. People who talk about killing themselves never do.

4. When he talks about killing himself, he's just looking for attention. Ignoring him is the best thing to do.

5. Talking about suicide to a troubled person may give the person morbid ideas.

6. People under a psychiatrist's care rarely commit suicide.

7. Suicides often occur out of the blue.

8. People who kill themselves are insane.

9. Once a person tries to kill himself and fails, the excruciating pain and shame will keep him from trying again.

10. My son was depressed and suicidal. But the depression has lifted. He's so much better and happier. He's finally out of danger.

11. Only a certain type of youngster commits suicide and my child just isn't the type.

12. Suicides are mainly old people with only a few years left to live.

13. Suicide runs in families, so you can't do much to prevent it.

With the exception perhaps of incest, few subjects are so shrouded in myth and misunderstanding as suicide. At the start, then, we shall set out to shatter the most common and most deadly of these myths.

1. NOTHING COULD HAVE STOPPED HER ONCE SHE
   DECIDED TO KILL HERSELF.

On Wednesday afternoon, a gray, chilly day before Thanksgiving, a young woman was buried in Scarsdale, New York. She had attempted suicide four times previously. "Nothing could have stopped her once she decided to kill herself," her mother told a local reporter several weeks later. "We tried everything. Nothing we did made any difference. She was hell bent on killing herself—just hell bent."

It is graceless to pick apart the words of a grieving mother and unconscionably easy to criticize a parent's actions in retrospect. However, the latest research shows that very few people are really "hell bent" on suicide.

"Nothing could have stopped her once she decided to kill herself" is one of the most deadly myths of all. Francine Klagsbrun said it well: "Even the most hopelessly suicidal person has mixed emotions about death, wavering until the very last moment between wanting death and wanting desperately to live." As we said before, the basic drama of suicide is an individual who simultaneously cuts his throat and cries for help.

With help, that person—so torn between wanting life and wanting death—can be pushed toward life. Very few people who attempt suicide really want to die. What they want is not to go on living if living means such pain.

One recent study showed that fewer than half of all attempters subsequently admitted to having wanted to die. Only a little more than a quarter expected to die and, by the next day, almost 90 percent were glad they had survived.

Time and again we are faced with suicide victims who have shown enormous ambivalence about killing themselves. The following suicide note, for example, comes from the files of the Los Angeles County coroner. It was written by a seventeen-year-old boy shortly before he hanged himself: "Dear Mom and Dad. I have to kill myself. Have fun on the camping trip. I wish I could be there, but I feel too much hatred toward you both and Kevin and Brian. All my love, Michael." Or consider this note, written by a ten-year-old: "I hate you Mommie. I'm going to kill myself. Love Johnnie."

We recently heard about a case in which a sixteen-year-old acutely suicidal girl insisted she was going to kill herself on a skiing trip. After much deliberation, her therapist allowed her to go, but insisted that she call her immediately upon returning. The girl called, reporting she had broken her leg and was frantically worried she had taken too much pain medication. "I wouldn't want to OD," she explained.

In *Too Young to Die,* Francine Klagsbrun told of a young women who spent weeks planning every detail of her suicide. At the appointed hour, she jumped from her seventh-floor apartment window. By a twist of fate, a tree broke her fall and she survived. She described, later, how she felt as she jumped. "As I began to fall, I wanted more than anything to be able to turn back, grab hold of the window ledge and pull myself up."[1]

In another recently reported suicide, a boy jumped from a tall building, but an awning broke his fall. Bystanders who saw him jump rushed to his side and heard him plead, "Don't let me die. Don't let me die."[2]

For almost all young people, suicide is a gesture designed not to remove themselves permanently from the picture but rather to accomplish some specific goal, to win attention, or to punish parents. Kathy, thirteen years old, slashed her wrists one week after her father moved out of their Evanston, Illinois home. The cuts were superficial and the act committed in the bathtub around 4 P.M., shortly before she knew her mother would be bathing and dressing to go to a neighbor's wedding. "I didn't really want to die," she explained. "I just hoped and prayed that if Mom and Dad knew how upset and unhappy I was, Dad would move back in. Since that didn't happen, maybe next time I'll do a better job."

Like 90 percent of young suicide attempters, Kathy decided to gamble with death at home so that her mother could stop her and save her. Like 70 percent of suicidal teens, she chose the hours between 3 P.M. and midnight, when her mother would be most likely to find her.

Fifteen-year-old Alan went behind the football stadium one evening after practice and cut his wrists with a hunting knife. He couldn't see a way out of his problems. His girlfriend had broken up with him, he was having trouble with trigonometry, and the coach told him he might not make the team. He tried to talk to his parents, he said, ". . . but they seemed to have stuff of their own on their minds, and I thought I shouldn't bother them." He also suggested to some of his friends, " 'Maybe I should just kill myself,' but I guess they thought I was joking."

Alan didn't really want to die. "I remember thinking about climbing the water tower and jumping, but I guess I knew that would really kill me." As he expected, the coach found him and called an ambulance. ". . . I guess I knew somebody would come along and find me," he said later.[3]

"Nothing could have stopped her once she decided to kill herself." Unfortunately this is a myth that dies hard. Even so informed an authority as syndicated advice columnist Ann Landers recently succumbed to it. Consider this letter and Ann Landers' reply.

Last month my daughter killed herself. Please print this letter, which I found in her pocketbook. If I had read it sooner, I know she would still be with me.

"To whoever finds this letter: Maria hates being a secretary. It is not what she wanted to be when she grew up. The people she works for are cruel. Maria can't think straight anymore. Last night she cried herself to sleep. I can tell Maria is a nervous wreck by the pain in her eyes and the different way she has been acting. Why can't others see it? She has considered suicide but is too weak for that. So instead she will move out of New York and start life over. Maybe new friends won't reject her and maybe she will find peace of mind. Maria is so tired of being hurt. She feels hopeless and afraid. Won't somebody help her? I know I must be a great disappointment to everyone. I can't handle this anymore. I am at work now. It's my first job. Maria will be fired soon and have no one to talk to. I have no friends to share my pain. I can handle being fired, but I can't handle rejection and loneliness. I want so much to be happy. My name is Maria."

Ann Landers advised Maria's mother not to feel guilty, not to believe she might have stopped Maria had she only been a better and more perceptive mother. "The experts now say suicide victims almost always get the idea early in life, and once they view it as the ultimate escape from the pain of living, very little can be done to stop them. Maria was severely ill, as evidenced by the fact that she starts her letter pretending she is someone else. . . . I hope you can accept the fact that no one can save people like Maria. They must want to save themselves."[4]

"Nothing could have stopped her once she decided to kill herself." Not true for another reason. An acute suicidal crisis lasts for a short time—a matter of hours or days, not months or years. The individual is either helped or dies. There are ways of helping a person over the severe crisis—ways we shall discuss in Chapter 11. Helping a person to endure a period of severe crisis can thus be a lifesaving end to what started as a seemingly hopeless situation.

2. THE PERSON WHO FAILS AT SUICIDE THE FIRST TIME WILL EVENTUALLY SUCCEED.

Only one percent of all survivors of suicide attempts kill themselves within one year; only 10 percent within ten years. The crisis, we repeat, is temporary and the overwhelming majority of those who are lucky enough to be helped through it never try suicide again.

Even when overwhelmed by problems and obsessed by the desire to die, suicidal people can be reached. For many potential suicides, in fact, the first try is a turning point. Somehow the suicide attempt can stem the depressive slide, pushing the person not over the edge but into a more productive phase.

The suicide attempt can also shock a previously inattentive family into action. The boy who seemed "just a complainer" or "just your average moody teenager" is now recognized for what he is: a youngster who, for a moment at least, decided he preferred death to life. The family finally may take him seriously and realize that, without help, their son might make that decision again.

3. PEOPLE WHO TALK ABOUT KILLING THEMSELVES NEVER DO.

The third myth has graduated to adage, but unlike most adages, there's nothing harmless about it. It allows parents to ignore suicidal talk and to avoid taking action. "You'd be better off without me," a daughter tells her mother. "I'm no good to anyone," a son assures his father. "People who talk about killing themselves never do," the parents assure themselves, as they chalk up these desperate pleas for help to "just a stage" or to typical teen turmoil.

The simple truth is that most people who commit suicide do talk about it. Eighty percent of adolescent suicides make open threats beforehand. Suicidal gestures such as threats or attempts must be considered danger signals and taken very seriously.

And for those who believe the first attempt is simply harmless adolescent acting out, keep in mind that the majority of people who kill themselves do so on the first attempt.

Undoubtedly some young people are driven to suicide because their parents believe this myth—they ignore warnings or brush them aside. At a certain point a person will kill himself in order to show he is serious—especially when that person is an adolescent to whom proving himself assumes a sometimes exaggerated importance.

Roy, a sophomore in a suburban Philadelphia high school, had threatened suicide frequently without ever actually, as one friend put it, "taking the plunge." He had told a guidance counselor, a history teacher, and Chuck, his best friend, of his plans. Although none had taken him seriously (or broken his confidence to tell his parents), they had listened sympathetically, assuring themselves, as the counselor recalled, "We're safe as long as he continues talking about it. When we should start worrying is when he stops talking—or rather threatening." What stopped Roy's threats was his death—a self-inflicted gunshot wound through the right ear.

Shortly before his death, Roy and Chuck got into an argument in the lunchroom. Roy again threatened suicide, which infuriated Chuck. "Oh, why don't you shut up already?" Chuck exploded. "All you do is talk about it." Roy felt an implied challenge. Two days later, he accepted it. Chuck, who recounted his argument with Roy, said he intended to berate Roy for allowing suicide to monopolize his conversation, not to challenge him.

(Unfortunately, Chuck is almost as literally a casualty of suicide as was Roy. For fifteen-year-old Chuck is now dragging through life feeling responsible for his friend's death. Nearly every suicide leaves in its wake awful guilt and assorted "victims" of the victim. Chuck now desperately needs the help that was denied Roy. See Chapter 13 for a full discussion of "Helping the Survivors.")

4. WHEN HE TALKS ABOUT KILLING HIMSELF, HE'S JUST LOOKING FOR ATTENTION. IGNORING HIM IS THE BEST THING TO DO.

As we've seen, ignoring him is the *worst* thing to do. People who talk about suicide do want attention—in the same way a drowning person wants a lifeguard to rescue him. Each and every one of those twenty-eight adolescents from Chicago's North Shore who committed suicide within a two-year span, talked about suicide just prior to death. (One of the young men became an expert on suicide—discussed it all the time—in class and out. He was planning his own suicide.)

Mark Cada, fifteen, shot himself to death early in the morning on Saturday, January 31, 1981. He climbed into the foothills of the Rockies, in the backyard of his parents' home in Loveland, Colorado, and put a shotgun to his head. Just before, he had stopped in his sister Chris's room, given her a note to give to his girlfriend, and told her she was a great sister. "I thought when he came in my room maybe he was thinking about doing it (committing suicide) but I didn't think he would," Chris explained. When Mark blew his head off she was watching cartoons on television. Their parents were sleeping late.[5]

There is no starker or more terrifying warning of an impending suicide than an attempt—no matter how feeble or unlikely to succeed. "He just wanted attention," is the exasperated comment which often follows. Indeed, that is precisely what he wanted. Without it, his next attempt may prove fatal. A friend of Mark's put it this way: "Attempting suicide is just another way of saying, 'I'm really screwed up and I need something other than just me to get me out.'"[6]

People tend to think of suicide as a solitary act—the very essence of privateness. In reality, most suicides—maybe even all suicides—are dyadic, involving both the suicidal person and what psychiatrists call the "significant other" in the person's life. For a young person, the significant other is almost always a parent. The suicide attempt is a nonverbal message to the parent—an urgent plea for attention, love, help, and understanding. He wants to be taken seriously.

In *Children with Emerald Eyes,* Mira Rothenberg described ten-year-old Anthony, who tried to drown himself. He locked himself in the bathroom and held his head under water until he passed out. Rothenberg asked him why he did it. Anthony lowered his eyes and said it was to make his father sorry—then Daddy would love him.[7] In other words, he wanted his father's attention.

Over and over again, we find children performing the most dreadfully dangerous acts to win attention—the fifteen-year-old girl who threw herself on the commuter railroad tracks, in the path of the train in which her father was riding; the nineteen-year-old girl who raided her mother's medicine cabinet and swallowed the contents of half-filled bottles of Valium and Dilantin (an antiseizure drug); the twelve-year-old boy who jumped from a third-floor balcony to the garden where his parents were hosting a cocktail party.

For a Harvard College course on death and suicide, Dr. Shneidman, then a visiting professor, asked students to write an essay on suicide. One young man reconstructed the day he attempted suicide. It was the first Saturday after the first snowfall. He had a paper to write, his roommates were out, he had a "general feeling of disgust and inadequacy. No drive, no energy, no 'inspiration.'" He described the dorm as "very quiet, deathly quiet" and complained that he had "lots of acquaintances, not so many friends."

"I crave attention," he wrote. He called Betty, an old girlfriend. She wasn't in. "How could I change something?" he asked himself. "Why not die?" he answered. He counted the aspirin he planned to take, but first called another high school girlfriend who "admires me, sort of." She wasn't in either. "There seems to be a conspiracy to isolate me tonight." Then he went searching for his roommates. He couldn't find them. The proctor wasn't in either. He swallowed the aspirin, then called Betty again. Still no answer, but he talked to the operator about death. "Good to hear a voice." He wondered if his parents and friends would be sorry.

He went out for a walk, attracting attention by going coatless, and then staring into a police car until the officers took him to the hospital. "Have I commanded attention?" he wondered. Besides the attention of the doctors, whom, he happily reported, "plagued" him for blood samples all night, Betty called, the proctor called, an assistant dean was alerted. "I don't think I really wanted to die," he concluded. "I did want attention."[8]

When the seventeen-year-old son of Susan White-Bowden, a feature reporter for a Baltimore television station, shot himself to death, Ms. White-Bowden recalled that, several weeks before he died, he had told two friends he was going to kill himself, but they didn't take him seriously. "I guess they thought he was saying that to get sympathy, and he didn't really mean it. . . . I think he was reaching out and saying, 'Stop me.' "[9]

Chris, sixteen, from Omaha, Nebraska, shot himself to death at the beginning of his junior year. When his mother took him back-to-school shopping, he told her, "Don't buy me anything. I won't be needing any clothes." That was certainly a remark that reflected enormous ambivalence about his suicide plan.

The more Vivienne Loomis' cries for help were ignored, the more explicit they became. She wrote a theme for English, read aloud in class, that might have been titled "The Joy of Suicide." In a book report on Elie Wiesel's *The Accident,* she explained that she understands perfectly the person who lives for death; that living in a world where everything is superficial, insipid, and mean makes death seem not only an escape, but a blessed event, a sanctuary. On the high school application form mentioned earlier, Vivienne added that, for her, death is a fact of life rooted deeply in emotion and poetry.

In a letter to her favorite teacher, a young man who had moved across the country, she lamented that crying no longer provided even temporary relief. Crying had become part of her routine, like eating breakfast. When she finished crying, the hopelessness remained, the misery was unrelieved.

In another letter to her teacher, she wrote that concern for her parents was the only thing that kept her from putting down her pen and hanging herself then and there.

A letter from this teacher reached the Loomis house after Vivienne's death. He never mentioned Vivienne's suicide attempt, never even used the word suicide. Instead he wrote of the beautiful view of the mountains from his apartment in San Rafael and of his relationship with Fran, ". . . slowly becoming deeper and better."[10]

These cries for attention must be heeded. For even if the adolescent does not "succeed" in killing himself, he has developed a dangerous way of relating to people and events in his life. While other people deal with their problems in a constructive way, the suicidal adolescent deals with his problems by trying to kill himself. For that reason alone, we must never belittle the seriousness of the attempt. We must certainly not implant in the adolescent the idea that he must kill himself to prove himself to us—to prove how seriously troubled he really was.

5. TALKING ABOUT SUICIDE TO A TROUBLED PERSON MAY GIVE THE PERSON MORBID IDEAS.

Wrong, wrong, wrong. You don't give a suicidal person ideas about suicide. The ideas already exist. Talking about them will help to bring them into the open where they can be dealt with honestly and directly. Talking about suicide will not "put the idea into his head." Most would-be suicides are relieved to discuss what has so obsessed them. Far from being dangerous to talk about suicide, it's dangerous not to talk about it.

Parents should heed psychiatric experience, which shows that the suicidal patient derives enormous comfort from talking about suicide, so long as he knows that the psychiatrist will stick with him through the self-destructive impulses and depressions. (Even the psychotic patient—most suicidal people are not psychotic—benefits from hearing, "Your ideas are crazy, but we can come to understand them.")

If a friend or classmate of your child's commits suicide, it's important for the two of you to discuss it without delay. The death of a friend sanctions suicide, makes it an acceptable way to deal with problems.

A couple of weeks before Chris's suicide (Chris is the sixteen-year-old from Omaha described earlier) he repeatedly tried to talk to his mother about a boy from his school who had recently killed himself. His mother studiously avoided discussing the subject, except to lecture Chris that this boy had inflicted on his family a tragedy from which they would never recover.[11]

In December 1978 in Ridgewood, New Jersey, on the same day that a high school student who hanged himself was buried, a classmate also hanged himself. It was only after this second suicide that administrators directed counselors and teachers to talk to students about what happened, to answer questions and allay fears, to get students talking together about suicide. Only then did the principal make a special plea to parents to talk to their children about suicide.

6. PEOPLE UNDER A PSYCHIATRIST'S CARE RARELY COMMIT SUICIDE.

Jody C. was in his freshman year at an Ivy League college when he killed himself. His parents had known for two years that their son was deeply troubled and, although obviously disappointed in "this neurosis," as Jody's father termed it, they had been generally supportive. Mr. C. had willingly paid the psychiatrist's bills for a year and a half before the suicide. They felt better and calmer since their son had begun seeing Dr. Levine, and they thought that Jody felt better too. When the Dean of Students called to tell them that their son had been found by the campus police hanging in a wooded area behind the student dining hall, they were shocked. "How could he have done this?" his mother gasped. "He was seeing a psychiatrist."

"Our son is seeing a psychiatrist regularly. There's no reason to worry" is another deadly myth. Most people who kill themselves have seen a physician—in many cases a psychiatrist—shortly before they kill themselves.

Studies have shown that fully three quarters of all those who commit suicide have seen a physician within a month or two of the day on which they take their lives (40 percent within the previous week). Among adolescent suicides, two thirds have undergone psychiatric or psychological counseling. One third have been hospitalized.*

Psychiatrists are not a guarantee against suicide. They may, ironically, be too attuned to suicide to help a suicidal patient. So aware are some psychiatrists of the high risk of suicide in certain patients that they choose not to get involved. They don't want to feel guilty or responsible for a suicide that occurs during treatment, so they may change the subject when a patient mentions suicide, or they may evade the issue by prescribing tranquilizers—which not only exacerbate depression, but also often become the suicide weapon.

Psychiatrists themselves have an extremely high suicide rate—the highest in the medical profession, which, in turn, has the highest suicide rate of any professional group. Still, psychiatrists are a better bet than their colleagues in other specialties. Physicians who do not have psychiatric training can be frightfully ignorant about suicide. A poll reported in the *Journal of the AMA* found that 91 percent felt their knowledge of suicide was insufficient. So it is not surprising that if a patient complains of aches and pains that have no apparent physical basis, many doctors will not question him about his mental health.

7. SUICIDES OFTEN OCCUR OUT OF THE BLUE.

In St. Paul, Minnesota, on August 25, 1979, fifteen-year-old Eddie Seidel jumped to his death from a bridge. In his suicide note he explained he was killing himself because his favorite television program, "Battlestar Galactica," had been canceled. One newspaper commentator lamented that the young today are so shallow that they can't even get properly depressed—that they kill themselves "out of the blue" and for reasons utterly trivial.

This boy's suicide was undoubtedly stirred by causes more profound than the cancellation of "Battlestar Galactica." For it is a

---

* Although it's understandable why suicidal people would seek the services of a psychiatrist, it's less understandable why they would see other medical specialists. If they've decided to end their lives, why should they be concerned about any ailment or disease, real or fancied? The answer, again, ambivalence about dying—seeing a doctor may provide another forum for their cry for help.

myth that suicides occur "out of the blue." The myth provides a convenient reprieve for relatives and friends who may have chosen to ignore the hints, the threats, the terminal misery. Suicide is usually a response to a long, deep depression, often caused by some terrible loss—the loss of a parent, the loss of a parent's love or attention, the loss of status, of a positive self-image.

The act of suicide may appear capricious and impulsive. It's not. The person, as we have seen, leaves a long trail of signs. The suicidal act is typically preceded by long and careful deliberation. For example, Vivienne Loomis' closest friend recalled: "Vivienne had thought of jumping in front of a car, but she didn't want anyone to have to feel guilty about killing her. So it wasn't an impulsive thing. She was really planning it."

Vivienne described for her teacher in gruesome detail her suicide rehearsals. Standing in front of her mirror she would try to strangle herself with her own hands. She squeezed until her ears began ringing, her vision blurred and she saw in the mirror what appeared to be a swollen decapitated head. Later that night she took one of her sister's long silk scarves and walked to a public park. She stood in the shade so car headlights couldn't catch her, wrapped the scarf around her neck and pulled as hard as she could. She continued pulling until supplies of blood and air were cut—until her lungs were at the point of bursting. Then she would let go. She tried several more times before giving up and realizing that if she wanted to asphyxiate herself, she'd have to use a noose.[12]

A young woman named Diane called WFYR, Chicago during a program on teen suicide. She had attempted suicide many times, she said. Once she was pronounced DOA (dead on arrival), "but as you can see I'm alive now." She was in a coma for a month after taking four hundred Seconal and Nembutal. It was only because of the persistence of her mother, who made the doctors take the sheet off her face and try harder to revive her, that Diane survived.

"I had planned it for three months. I had it down pat," she told the show's moderator, Bruce DuMont. "Did you leave clues?" DuMont asked her. "Uh-uh. None. I don't think anybody who takes that many Seconal and Nembutal wants to be stopped."[13]

We assume wrongly and dangerously that the person who kills

himself has descended into a mindless fog. He must make choices that require sustained energy, concentration, determination, and courage. As Albert Camus observed, "An act like this is prepared within the silence of the heart, as is a great work of art."

8. PEOPLE WHO KILL THEMSELVES ARE INSANE.

Not true, although constantly heard. Only a small portion of suicides can be classified as insane or psychotic—according to one recent study, less than 10 percent. Most suffer from deep depression; from loneliness, feelings of hopelessness and despair. They are miserably unhappy. They may be neurotic. They may have a character disorder. But they are not insane.

It is obviously quite possible *not* to be mentally ill and still to be very suicidal. In fact, in a study of suicidal patients at two New York hospitals, psychiatrist Ari Kiev found that mildly and moderately disturbed patients posed a greater risk of suicide than psychotic or schizophrenic patients.

It is garden-variety depression—not psychosis or schizophrenia or other exotic mental illnesses—that triggers most suicides. And there is nothing rare about depression. It's estimated that as much as 80 percent of the U.S. population will eventually suffer from varying degrees of depression.

9. ONCE A PERSON TRIES TO KILL HIMSELF AND FAILS, THE EXCRUCIATING PAIN AND SHAME WILL KEEP HIM FROM TRYING AGAIN.

Joey was barely sixteen when he stole the keys to his father's Cadillac, floored it in reverse, and smashed into the oak tree in the front yard of his suburban Minneapolis home. He had left a suicide note hanging from his bedroom bulletin board explaining that he was an outcast at school and ate lunch alone every day. In the journal he left behind, he described a "cold" relationship with his father, a traveling salesman who had lavished many of his weekend hours on his once flawless car.

Joey survived (he was wearing his seatbelt—talk about ambivalence!), but only after months of hospitalization and physical rehabilitation. The orthopedic surgeon assured Joey's parents that the boy's struggle to regain his health took such a total commitment, such courage that he undoubtedly "straightened out." The parents happily believed the surgeon.

And so they believed another dangerous myth. "Once a person tries to kill himself and fails, the excruciating pain and shame will keep him from trying again." As Francine Klagsbrun pointed out, the opposite is true. The first attempt is the hardest. Once the barrier between thought and action is crossed, subsequent attempts are easier, if conditions that brought about the first attempt haven't improved. Remember, of every five people who commit suicide, four have made one or more previous attempts.

Compared with the general population, suicide attempters are sixty-four times more likely to commit suicide eventually. Joey, after he had suffered through a grueling and painful rehabilitation, found little change in his home or school life. Eight months after his first try, he chose a less spectacular, but in his case more deadly, form of suicide—carbon monoxide poisoning. His mother found him, early one Sunday morning, dead behind the wheel of her husband's brand-new Cadillac.

In *The Savage God: A Study of Suicide,* A. Alvarez observed that a person "who has been to the brink" is three times more likely to go there again than someone who has not. "Suicide is like diving off a high board: the first time is the worst."[14]

As Vivienne Loomis practiced the act of strangulation, as she became familiar with its sensations, it seemed to lose its horror. On Monday night, July 9, she wrote matter-of-factly in her journal that she had spent the past half hour in the back bathroom practicing strangling herself. She was practicing, she explained, because she knew she would need that skill very soon.[15]

"I suppose it's like tennis; you don't get it right at the first attempt," observed one suicidal patient. "With practice, though, you improve and finally succeed."

10. MY SON WAS DEPRESSED AND SUICIDAL. BUT
    THE DEPRESSION HAS LIFTED. HE'S SO MUCH
    BETTER AND HAPPIER. HE'S FINALLY OUT OF
    DANGER.

Ethan, a student at an elite San Francisco private school, was
hospitalized for severe depression and threats of suicide. The
depression was conspicuous. He had lost interest in school,
friends, even in his hobby, bicycle racing. After about a month in
the hospital and intensive psychotherapy, the depression began to
lift. He instructed his best friend to buy him the latest bicycling
magazines, his mother to bring him his school work. Two weeks
later he was discharged from the hospital. Two weeks after that he
was dead. In Big Sur on a bicycle tour, he drove his bike off a
cliff.

His mother was dumbfounded. "But he seemed to be getting so
much better. He seemed so happy."

Ethan's case is not unusual. Clinical studies have shown that
half the people who were in a suicidal crisis and subsequently
committed suicide did so within ninety days, when they appeared
well on the way to recovery.

Paradoxically, depression can be most dangerous when it appears to be lifting. Like Ethan, its victims may become more communicative, and start resuming former activities. Family and
friends relax, believing the crisis has passed. It hasn't. Depression
often saps people of the energy and sense of purpose needed to
act. While in the depths of depression, the person may wish to die
and may actually plan to end his life, but he lacks the will power
to do it. As the most severe symptoms lift, the ability to put morbid thought into action returns, and suicide plans made earlier can
now be executed.

What causes the depression to lift? Depressions, even without
treatment, tend to be self-limiting. They may return, but they are
periodic. They do not linger indefinitely. Also, the decision the
person has made to kill himself may loosen the depression, filling
him with profound relief. With death in sight, a calm settles in—a
sense of peace. He's now determined to enjoy his final days. The
calm, of course, is ominous—the calm before a storm.

A young woman who had seriously contemplated suicide wrote a letter to Chicago *Tribune* columnist Bob Greene. She described how she constantly composed suicide notes in her head because the thought of her parents' (and her psychiatrist's) grief and guilt cheered her, made her feel, in fact, positively triumphant. "I was becoming so relaxed and so confident about my suicide, it was really becoming the most comforting thing in my life."

Similarly with Mark Cada: "He sat two chairs over from me in math," his friend said, his voice brimming with grief and shock, "and he was really starting to talk to everybody. I thought everything was okay and that the kid was really looking up and everything."[16]

When a seventeen-year-old suburban Chicago boy named Jack Stillson killed himself—the third suicide from his high school in five weeks—his friends, relatives, teachers, and employer had the same response: "But things seemed to be going better for Jack than ever before." In a eulogy, Wheeling High School principal Thomas Shirley told Jack's classmates, "For reasons completely unexplainable and unknown to us, Jack chose to end his life despite the many indications that things were going better for him and life was on an upswing."

Similarly, a Dayton, Ohio teenager, Dallas Egbert, killed himself at a point when friends felt he had overcome his depression and was no longer actively suicidal. He had just moved into his own apartment, a move he had desperately wanted. A psychologist who talked to him a few days before his death recalled, "Dallas had just left home; he was in his apartment, and he seemed happy. In that period he was not the typical suicidal individual."

Finally, Frances Kryzwicki, twenty-five, a newspaper reporter who jumped to her death from the Chesapeake Bay Bridge in the summer of 1980, also exhibited the "calm before the storm." A friend with whom she played cards on the night of her death recalled, "She seemed very peaceful and calm." Although Frances had made an earlier suicide attempt, her friend felt "that was all behind her"—especially on that night when she seemed so "happy and confident and ready to get on with her life. She certainly had stopped complaining."[17]

The patient who attempts suicide and seems to bounce back to life and happiness very quickly, may, paradoxically, be the patient in most danger. For the patient who ceases to complain may simply have given up.

Psychiatrist Ari Kiev interviewed patients who were hospitalized after a suicide attempt. He found that the patients who complained most were also most likely to have improved during the course of the year and not to have made a second attempt. The patients who complained least were most likely to have died during that year from another attempt.

The hospitalized patient presents a special problem. The confinement stymies suicide plans, and so patients may fake recovery in order to be rewarded by immediate discharge. Also, if, immediately following a suicide attempt, the patient really does seem less depressed, friends and relatives might take this as evidence that he got what he wanted out of the attempt—sympathy.

"Sure he's feeling fine," they say. "Everybody's fawning over him." This sort of attitude on the part of relatives accounts for the dangerous rapidity with which many hospitals discharge seriously suicidal patients. Many doctors, unfortunately, treat "failed" suicides as only temporary risks.

In one study, 55 percent of the patients who were hospitalized after a suicide attempt attempted suicide again in the hospital or after their release. Hospitalization does not provide insurance against suicide. Researchers have shown repeatedly that few populations have suicide rates as high as those found in mental hospitals. They estimate that suicide is at least five times more common among those in mental hospitals than among the general population.

11. ONLY A CERTAIN TYPE OF YOUNGSTER COMMITS SUICIDE AND MY CHILD JUST ISN'T THE TYPE.

When Alexandra, a nineteen-year-old from a lakefront suburb of Chicago, hanged herself, the people who knew her best were aghast. "She just wasn't the type," they repeated in shock and bewilderment. She was beautiful, with long, thick, chestnut-colored hair, from a very wealthy and loving family. She was a good student, a natural leader, involved in many community activities. She was well-read, well-mannered, well-connected, compassionate, and confident—every high school girl's dream of the person she'd like to be.

"She just wasn't the suicidal type" is, unfortunately, the saddest and most common epitaph heard by those of us who deal with suicide. That there is a certain type who commits suicide—the spoiled brat, the tattooed delinquent, the moody loner, the ghetto dweller —is another myth. Suicide strikes people of all social classes, races, religions, all personality types, all levels of intelligence. Researchers recently found that although nonsuicidal students had a higher grade-point average than suicidal students, only 8 percent of the suicidal students were failing. Thus neither the stereotype of the brilliant but neurotic student as the likely suicide nor the failing student is accurate.

"Suicide could never happen to us" is a variation on the same sad theme. Suicide happens to typical people in typical families.

Staff members at the Irene Josselyn Clinic looked into the circumstances of twenty-eight teen suicides and many more attempts that occurred on the North Shore over the last two years. They were unable to identify a typical suicide profile. Many of the children were high achievers and socially adept, not the sort you usually associate with suicide.

You usually associate with suicide the outcast, the social misfit, the painfully shy adolescent. But anyone who reads a newspaper has seen stories galore of suicides who don't fit the mold. A seventeen-year-old hanged himself from a tree limb in the yard of his home in Chappaqua, New York, a wealthy Westchester County community. The boy had a girlfriend, was popular at school, had high grades, and recently had been named a commended student under the National Merit Scholarship program. A fifteen-year-old sophomore at Barrington High School outside Chicago hanged himself in the garage of the family home. He was on the varsity wrestling squad and the sophomore football team. His English teacher described him as "outgoing, not a loner at all. He was the average all-American kid. He didn't seem depressed."

In Columbia, South Carolina, the twin sons of a well-to-do gynecologist, both popular and both sports enthusiasts, were found dead in a bedroom of their parents' home. Each had been shot once through the head. About the first of the two boys who killed themselves in Ridgewood, New Jersey, a friend said, "He loved to make people laugh. Nobody thought he had any problems. He was very popular and well liked. He just wasn't the type." The other boy was the exact opposite. He was shy, unpopular, a loner, and he left a note in which he said he worried about what others thought of him. The school psychologist had already labeled him a "boy with suicidal tendencies."

Tom Kane, whose suicide was the subject of an article in *Baltimore Magazine,* was handsome, extremely popular, outgoing, a champion lacrosse player. He liked to sing, was active in dramatics, and had a solid B average. "He enjoyed himself immensely," his father summed up. The president of the college Tom attended told Tom's father that, "If he had made a list of people most likely to do this, Tom would have been very close to the bottom."

Another boy whose suicide was analyzed in the article, John Woytowitz, had discussed his problems with several of his teachers. The teachers failed to sense how deeply disturbed he was because he simply didn't seem suicidal. He seemed so stable, so willing and expert at helping others. "Whenever anyone had a problem," his mother recalled, "they would go to him. He was the counselor."[18]

Alexandra's mother wrote about her shortly after her death, ". . . she did not fit the stereotypical model of the depressed girl who throws herself into the Chicago River on Christmas Eve because she thinks nobody loves her. She was not involved with drugs, alcohol, or other anti-social experiments: her vices were Marlboro Lights and an occasional Chablis. She never sought thrills from drag racing or motorcycles; she 'got her kicks' from tutoring black children suffering from racially related learning problems. She had never been violent; she espoused the youthful ideals of international peace and a world court. She was not recognizably depressed, she never closed herself inside her room and shut the door against the world except to go to sleep at night."

Finally, a young woman who wrote a letter to Chicago *Tribune* columnist Bob Greene about her desire to kill herself explained, "If you told the people that I know that I am close to a mental breakdown they'd be surprised. 'She's always been so quiet. She never let on.' . . . I keep that damned smile on my face because it's undignified to show that you're falling apart."[19]

12. SUICIDES ARE MAINLY OLD PEOPLE WITH ONLY A FEW YEARS LEFT TO LIVE.

This too is a prevalent myth. In fact, people over fifty are less likely to take their own lives today than they were ten years ago, and people under fifty are more likely.

As we saw in Chapter 1, while the actual rate of suicide among older people is higher than among the young, the rate of *increase* among young suicides far exceeds that of older groups. Today the increase for young people is ten times the growth in the suicide rate for the population as a whole.

The above statistics apply to completed suicides. Younger people are far more likely than older people to *attempt* suicide. Sixty to seventy percent of attempts are made by people under forty-five, with the highest rates in the twenty-to-twenty-five group. While the average age of the attempter is decreasing, suicide attempts are so rare among the aged that they are statistically insignificant. Older people do not generally cry for help. They simply do it and end it.

13. SUICIDE RUNS IN FAMILIES, SO YOU CAN'T DO MUCH TO PREVENT IT.

This is another myth that keeps parents from paying enough attention to distressed teens. The implication is that because there is no history of suicide in your family, those threats your child is making are probably "just talk." While there is conclusive evidence that one suicide in a family may lead to others, there is no conclusive evidence that the tendency toward suicide is in the genes. Most experts believe that suicidal tendencies cannot be inherited.

There are, however, sociological and psychological traits predisposing children of certain families to suicide. Statistically, a person is nine times more likely to commit suicide if he comes from a family with a prior suicide. The occurrence of a suicide provides a model for other family members. If they should get depressed, they're more likely to imitate the model.

In one study of adolescents who had killed themselves, researchers discovered that almost all had mothers who were themselves depressed and preoccupied with suicide. Alvarez, who devoted part of *The Savage God* to his own suicide attempt, recalled that when he was a child both his parents put their heads in the gas oven. "It seemed to me then a rather splendid gesture, though shrouded in mystery, a little area of veiled intensity, revealed only by . . . unexplained, swiftly suppressed outbursts. It was something hidden, attractive and not for the children, like sex. . . . Maybe that is why, when I grew up and things went particularly badly, I used to say to myself, over and over, 'I wish I were dead.'"[20]

If, before the child is thirteen, he lives through a suicide of a close relative, especially a parent, he may suffer from what psychiatrist Robert Jay Lifton calls "survivor guilt." "What did I do to make my mother kill herself?" he wonders. Or, "Why did my father die while I stayed alive?" He may feel he has no right to continue living or he may yearn to join the parent in death.

In studying fifty attempted suicides, two New York psychiatrists found what they called a "death trend." In 95 percent of these cases there had been "the death or loss under dramatic and often tragic circumstances of individuals closely related to the patient." In 75 percent of the cases, the deaths had taken place before the patient had completed adolescence.

These studies and statistics aside, the fact remains, many of the suicides we've studied come from families in which, over the generations, there has been absolutely no hint of suicide.

We know now the gigantic proportions of the problem of suicide. We know that parents can make all the difference in whether or not a child kills himself. But how do we catch him before he does it? What signs—distress signals—should we look for? The answer to that important question is the subject of the next chapter.

3
Distress Signals

---

1. Acting out: aggressive, hostile behavior
2. Alcohol and drug abuse
3. Passive behavior
4. Changes in eating habits
5. Changes in sleeping habits
6. Fear of separation
7. Abrupt changes in personality
8. Sudden mood swings
9. Impulsiveness
10. Slackening interest in school work and decline in grades
11. Inability to concentrate
12. Loss or lack of friends
13. Loss of an important person or thing in the child's life
14. Hopelessness
15. Obsession with death: a death wish
16. Evidence that the child is making a will

In September 1978, Rick M., a seventeen-year-old freshman, arrived at the University of Missouri. He was variously described as "perfectly normal," "an all-American kid," "a typical teenager." So sure were his parents of their son's ability to cope with a new situation that, after helping him settle into his dorm room, they immediately left on vacation.

Rick promptly asked his new roommates' advice about an easy way to commit suicide. "Throw yourself in front of a train or get yourself a gun," they joked. Four days later, Rick took the first suggestion. After leaving a note in his biology notebook explaining that he was "having a hard time adjusting" and just wanted to "rest in peace," he put his head on the railroad tracks moments before the arrival of a freight train. Questioned later, neither his family nor his roommates said they suspected Rick was capable of suicide. "He seemed a little down, but that's all," said one roommate.

When Alexandra committed suicide, the epitaphs from friends and relatives began to sound like a Greek chorus.

"Nobody had any idea there was something wrong," said one of Alexandra's many friends. "She was the queen of everybody . . . the one everybody followed."

"She had everything going for her and no sign anything was wrong," lamented her brother.

So concerned was she with others' problems that she never mentioned her own. She held weekly "rap sessions" in her parents' home to give her friends a chance to talk about what was bothering them. "She could always help people," said one friend. "She did everything for everybody else."

She really didn't seem to have problems. In a letter home from college she wrote, "I'm so excited to discover the new wonders coming my way. How lucky I feel to leave one magic land of beauty and civility only to enter another." After that first year at college she returned home to a summer job as a waitress, to a boy she cared for, and to her growing interests in poetry writing and photography.

"She gave no hint that she was unhappy," another friend insisted—even in the last weeks of her life. She was, a reporter for the Chicago *Sun-Times* wrote, "everybody's model of a well-adjusted teenager. She was beautiful, she was accomplished, she cared. She glowed, and those around her basked."[1]

But soon the first wrinkles in this apparently flawless personality surfaced. Few of Alexandra's friends reached out to help her, one girl observed. Alexandra seemed so perfect that no one ever imagined she could possibly have any problems. "I think she was lonely. She was close to her family but she wanted someone she could really talk to—somebody special to love."

Closer examination reveals other problems in Alexandra's life. She was unhappy at the small New England college she attended

and despaired of ever being able to transfer elsewhere (an acceptance letter from the college she wanted to attend arrived the day
after her death). She worried about being able to form meaningful
relationships, about the limits of her talent, creativity, and energy.
She was, in fact, seeing a therapist.

So there were signs, admittedly unclear, of Alexandra's distress.
The goal of this chapter is to describe the signs that suicidal teens
are likely to exhibit; the signs that should make us take action.

We have opened the chapter with the cases of Rick and Alexandra because, as any relative of a child who has committed suicide knows, the signs are not nearly so clear as suicide-prevention
books would have us believe. Often the signs, relatives agree, are
apparent only after the tragedy. In retrospect, it is easy to find the
signs, said Rob Loomis, the older brother of Vivienne, who
hanged herself at age fourteen. He explained that every member
of the Loomis family was struggling with his or her own problems;
that there was nothing, until Vivienne's first suicide attempt, that
hinted at the gravity of her problem.[2]

During a nationally syndicated television show on teen suicide,
the father of Dan, sixteen, who came close to killing himself in his
high school washroom, explained, "People say, 'Well, how can
these things happen to your children and you not notice them?'
Well, all I can say is you can sit in a house and the sun goes down
and you never see it go down and the next thing you know it's
dark."[3]

But still, as murky as these signs often are, they are there, they
are detectable. When NBC News broadcast a segment on teen suicide, the reporter interviewed the mother of a boy who committed
suicide at age fifteen. She said she regretted that she hadn't known
which supposedly "typical" behavior was, in fact, typically suicidal. She regretted that she hadn't watched her son more closely.
". . . my thought now is to go back to a very much more . . . su-
pervised time, and . . . pay a lot more attention to what's happening in terms of . . . all the traditional things, who their friends
are, what time they come in, how they're doing in school . . . do
they show any erratic behavior . . . very withdrawn, hiding out in
their rooms . . . getting into fights with anyone—everything that
looks like extreme behavior."[4]

Iris Bolton is the director of LINKS, a youth counseling agency in Atlanta. She is also the mother of a twenty-year-old who committed suicide. Her involvement with LINKS came after her son's death. At the time, "I knew nothing about the signs. I did not know what to look for. Would that I had. I had no training in that area. I was a typical mother . . ."

Her son did show signs that he was preparing to die—some of the signs that we discuss in this chapter. He bought ice cream for the entire family the night before he died, as if he were hosting his own farewell party. Just before he killed himself, Mrs. Bolton recalled, "He looked bad." On his way out of the house, his mother asked, "Are you okay?" He answered, "Oh, no worse than any other day." "Well," Mrs. Bolton lamented, "that's a key clue. I could have known."[5]

The emotional stress that prompts suicide has been building for a long time. The suicide decision, although it may appear capricious and impulsive, is usually not. It is premeditated.

Few people come right out and say, "I've got X, Y, and Z problems and I want to die." They'll drop sometimes quite subtle hints and they'll undergo one or more specific behavior changes— usually observable changes.

A friend of Alexandra's made, perhaps, the most penetrating comment on spotting signs of trouble. "We didn't see any signs of trouble with her. The problem is, you don't see things when you don't look for them."

We shall discuss these signs of trouble—these distress signals—in three categories:

I. General distress signals: behavior that has become almost a fixture, a backdrop, in the child's personality—aggressiveness, hostility, drug and alcohol abuse, passivity, eating and sleeping too little (or too much), terrible fear of leaving home (numbers 1–6 in the list at the opening of this chapter). The danger here is that parents get so used to these traits they are no longer alarmed by them. They become an accepted instead of an aberrant feature of the child's personality. In themselves, alcohol abuse, or extreme passivity, or separation anxiety would damage a child's self-esteem and depress him, but they would probably not trigger suicide. They are the soil in which grow the other problems that do lead directly to suicide.

II. Specific behavior changes: behavior that ushers in the suicidal preoccupation; behavior that is sudden and, for that child, abnormal—wild mood swings, failure in school, impulsiveness, feelings of haplessness, loss of friends (numbers 7–12).

III. Final precipitants to suicide: those events that push the child over the brink (numbers 13–16). The child may be able to live with his drug habit, his constant need to be aggressive or to withdraw. He may be able to survive failure in school and lack of friends, but then some one awful event—for example, the death of a parent—makes him believe that life is no longer worth living; that suicide is his only choice. He may, at that point, write a will or become so obsessed with death that it monopolizes his conversation.

The first six distress signals set the stage for trouble. The next six indicate a loss of control, of balance. The last four signal impending doom. As the child passes through this 6-6-4 pattern, this prelude to suicide, he suffers a constant slide in self-esteem. During the first phase, he tries to cover up his loss of self-esteem. During the second, he can no longer hide his pain. During the last, he is so totally and relentlessly plagued by a sense of hopelessness that he cares only about ending his life.

Consider the case of Roberta who, at least in retrospect, clearly passed through all three phases on her slide into suicide. She killed herself during her sophomore year at a North Shore high school.

Roberta's parents were both lawyers and spent long days at the office and many days of the month out of town. Roberta seemed to adjust, assuming an increasing amount of responsibility at home and doing extremely well in school. She wanted to be as successful a lawyer as her parents. She had highly specific goals. "She was so determined," her friend Marsha recalled. "She had the most definite goals of any freshman I knew. When I needed help in working harder, I looked to her as an example."

By the time she reached high school, traits she had had since the elementary grades became more noticeable—and obnoxious. She was extremely aggressive in the classroom. She was determined to get the highest grades and the most attention. As a release from the mostly self-imposed academic pressures (her parents were rather apathetic about her scholastic achievements) and the family-imposed domestic pressures, she began using marijuana and alcohol.

She was obviously losing weight, but when friends expressed concern, she said she had inherited colitis from her father and found it difficult to eat. She looked too as if she found it difficult to sleep. She began depending on her mother's sleeping pills. They worked so well that she often missed her early classes (her parents regularly caught the seven-ten into the city and so weren't home to get her out of bed).

By mid-freshman year, Roberta's problems had become more disturbing. She had entered Phase II. Her grades began to fall. And, according to Marsha, Roberta turned very moody. "It wasn't that she was up and down but more like rowdy one moment and passive the next." She was also impulsive. She once sneaked out of the hospital, following minor surgery, to attend a concert. Another time, after she broke her leg, she removed the cast herself.

Toward the end of her freshman year, Roberta entered the final phase. Her friends found her difficult to be around because she "dwelled on death all the time." Roberta, who was once the life of the party, seemed not to care what her friends thought. Marsha recalled a textbook Roberta had lent her in which Roberta "had written in those boxes on the inside cover, 'Condition issued: New. Condition returned: Dead.'"

Finally, Roberta seemed to simply withdraw. Even her best friend Marsha saw increasingly little of her. Just after the start of sophomore year, Roberta came to school and vomited in one of her classes—and later in the morning in two other classes. Strangely, she resisted going home, displaying that ambivalence we've mentioned earlier—perhaps realizing that if she went home to an empty house she would commit suicide.

She stayed home for the next three days. Early in the morning on the fourth day, she killed herself. No one had thought to call. She had used up her welcome.[6]

I. General Distress Signals

1. ACTING OUT: AGGRESSIVE, HOSTILE BEHAVIOR

Martin T. was a tenth-grader when his wild behavior finally got him expelled from school. Earlier in the year, his father had been fired from his job as sales manager for a Worcester, Massachusetts, corporation. Rumor around town had it that he drank too much. He soon found another job with a company headquartered in San Diego. The family was to join him out West after the close of the school year.

The events that ultimately resulted in Martin's expulsion included threatening a teacher with a knife, terrorizing smaller children at the adjacent elementary school, stealing a teacher's car and narrowly missing a pedestrian.

His mother blamed the absence of her husband for Martin's uncontrollable behavior, pointing out that his father was "the only one who could keep Marty in line." She didn't mention, however, that Martin, the youngest of five sons, had been in almost constant trouble since early elementary school. Also, the boy was estranged from his father whose consuming interest was sports, an area in which Martin showed little ability. (Martin was five feet four and weighed 150 pounds—"full of baby fat," as his father put it.)

Mrs. T. had assured the principal of the school to which Martin was to transfer that her son would be "back to normal" once the family settled into their new home. She was wrong. Martin, who had gotten involved with a group of older boys, all dishonorably discharged from the Navy, was arrested for holding up a gas station. While out on bond, he caused an auto accident that was fatal for the young woman driving the other car. A court-appointed psychiatrist argued that the head-on collision was really a suicide attempt. Martin made his first *obvious* suicide attempt six months later.

There are, basically, two broad patterns of behavior that suicidal children exhibit. One pattern is akin to that exhibited by a suicidal adult—gloominess, noncommunication, withdrawal. The other is aggressive behavior, like Martin's, taking the form of disobedience, sassiness, defiance, and rebelliousness. In a study conducted by Dr. Richard Seiden of the University of California at Berkeley, 60 percent of those who attempted suicide had tried all of the techniques in one or both categories. Less than 18 percent of the control group of those who had not attempted suicide had tried any of them.

In 1974, another researcher, D. Shaffer, gathered detailed information about the previous personality patterns of thirty children under the age of fifteen who had committed suicide. From interviews with relatives and teachers and from medical records, Shaffer found that the children consistently fell into one of two groups. Some were described as having a "chip on their shoulder," as being impulsive, erratic, and showing poor self-control. The others tended to be quiet, uncommunicative, perfectionist, and self-critical.

Let's be more specific. How exactly would children who fit the aggressive pattern act? They might commit petty crimes such as shoplifting. They might joyride. They might abuse alcohol and drugs. They might run away from home, become sexually promiscuous, get into fights with members of their own family and, occasionally, engage in serious violence—all behavior that generates excitement and covers up or "masks" their painful, depressive feelings. (See "Masked Depression" section of Chapter 10.)

Lynn S., from Chicago's North Shore, was attractive, popular, and talented, active in improvisational theater. Her mother, an increasingly bitter housewife, believed she had sacrificed career success to raise children. The marriage was in trouble, but husband and wife said they stayed together "for the children."

Lynn was running away regularly, becoming sexually promiscuous, and failing almost all her courses when her mother kicked her out of the house.

A social worker attached to the community's drop-in center, where Lynn spent a great deal of time, corralled Lynn and her parents into family therapy. "What therapy did for the mother," the social worker recalled, was "convince her that she really didn't like her kid at all"—a fact about which Lynn didn't need much convincing. She was soon taking drugs, slicing up her arms, and also using them to snuff out cigarettes. "It's hard when your mother doesn't love you," she explained to the social worker.

During therapy, Lynn's mother described her daughter as "manic." From the time she was a kindergartner, Mrs. S. recalled, "Lynn was always running around, with a concentration span of about two minutes. It was like she was always running away from something."

Indeed she was. Potentially suicidal children often seem unable to sit still because they are running away from their problems. In a study of thirty-nine disturbed children, psychiatrist Cynthia Pfeffer found that the 33 percent of the subjects who were suicidal showed significantly more motor activity during the six months preceding their evaluation. Again, such hyperactivity may indicate what psychiatrists call masked depression. Frantic behavior and extreme risk taking keep the young person's mind off his problems.

For example, little children won't say, "I feel depressed, lost my appetite, want to kill myself." But little children with those feelings might do something like kick the neighbor and get Mommy to punish them.

In his book *The Age of Sensation,* based on interviews with Columbia University students during the 1970s, psychiatrist Herbert Hendin explained that the language of amphetamines—speed, flying—does more than describe the high this drug produces. "It also suggests how much these students seek a life in which they are moving too quickly to think about what they are doing or how they feel."[7] They may slow down just long enough to kill themselves.

2. ALCOHOL AND DRUG ABUSE

Parents should consider any child who abuses drugs or alcohol to be a suicide risk. Red lights should start flashing, for substance abuse is a key warning sign—second only to depression as a spur to suicide. Nearly half the adolescents who commit suicide are drunk or high shortly before their death. The figure is an astonishing 85 percent for adolescents who attempt suicide but survive.

Psychiatrist Frank Crumley's study of middle-class adolescents in treatment with him following a suicide attempt showed that of the twenty-four patients, 60 percent were chronic, not casual, users of drugs or alcohol. They had a "notable history of substance abuse, either marijuana, other drugs or alcohol."

Drug and alcohol abuse are indications of underlying feelings of hopelessness, anxiety, or depression. It often follows that when those escape hatches fail to relieve anxieties, the troubled youngster decides on the "final fix." In other words, the young person can abuse drugs or alcohol for years, but when something terrible happens—so terrible that neither drugs nor alcohol can numb the pain—he may panic and try suicide.

"Teenage Suicide: Don't Try It"—the nationally syndicated television show mentioned earlier—included extensive interviews with a boy named Tom, eighteen, whose father had beaten him since childhood. Tom reacted to this and other family problems by getting hooked very early on drugs and alcohol. "When I was in sixth grade—that was the first time I ever smoked pot. And I was real young when I drank my first beer . . . six or something—and from then on it was all downhill. Life didn't seem precious. It's kinda worth living but I ain't got much." When he reached his teens and his problems became more severe, and the drugs and alcohol less a novelty, Tom tried to kill himself, first by overdosing and next by slitting his wrists.[8]

We must not forget that alcohol and drugs are often the direct means of death. A mix of scotch and barbiturates, for example, can be deadly, as many grieving parents know. And so can the mix of drugs or alcohol and a depressed person.

Dallas Egbert, considered by his teachers to be a genius, entered Michigan State University at age fifteen. He had no friends, and, after he joined the Lesbian-Gay Council—he wanted desperately to be part of a group—one of his roommates moved out. Dallas was shattered and upped his intake of drugs and alcohol. The coroner's report showed that on the night before Dallas killed himself he had taken cocaine and several other drugs. Because he was already subject to fits of depression, the cocaine would have deepened that depression and might have led to the suicide.

Alcohol not only exacerbates depression but also affects judgment. A large amount drunk before committing suicide tempers the fear of death. A person might commit suicide impulsively or accidentally in a foggy state of mind. In addition, alcohol deepens aggression. When this aggression is turned against oneself, suicide is too often the result.

Even if the thought of suicide never crosses the mind of a drug or alcohol abuser, he is killing himself as surely as the teenager who slashes his wrists. The difference is that he is doing it more slowly. Youngsters who abuse drugs and alcohol suffer almost unbearable despondency. They hate themselves and their lives and feel useless and worthless in much the same way that suicide attempters do. Rather than kill themselves directly and quickly, they choose to kill themselves slowly. They are what Karl Menninger called "chronic suicides"—people who might find the idea of taking their lives to be utterly repugnant. They will do everything to destroy themselves except admit that destroying themselves is what they're doing. They justify their actions by, as Menninger wrote, "claiming that they are only making life more bearable for themselves."

3. PASSIVE BEHAVIOR

It was Hamlet who said, "Or that the Everlasting had not fix'd/ His canon 'gainst self-slaughter! O God! God!/How weary, stale, flat and unprofitable,/Seem to me all the uses of this world!" It was Kurt Vonnegut who wrote, "How nice—to feel nothing, and still get full credit for being alive."

Although separated by nearly four centuries, both Shakespeare and Vonnegut were referring to that dragged-down feeling that suicidal people would undoubtedly recognize. As opposed to those who can't sit still, many suicidal young people can't get moving, feel it's too much trouble and there's nothing much worth doing anyway.

In the words of Jan, a suicide attempter, "It's like being wrapped in Saran Wrap, trying to get through but never making it past the plastic." Timothy described it this way: "I am in prison, caught in a net from which I cannot escape. . . . I get more and more tangled and every day is a useless struggle. It is undignified to live on like this."

Two of the most widely read novels of the 1970s deal with teen suicide—*The Bell Jar,* by Sylvia Plath, and *Ordinary People,* by Judith Guest. First published in England in January 1963, just a few weeks before Plath killed herself, *The Bell Jar* is based closely on the events of her twentieth year—a year that culminated in an unsuccessful suicide attempt.

Plath described her protagonist, who resembles herself in nearly every particular, preparing to return home after a summer in Manhattan as a student editor on a woman's magazine. "It was becoming more and more difficult for me to decide to do anything in those last days. And when I eventually *did* decide to do something, such as packing a suitcase, I only dragged all my grubby, expensive clothes out of the bureau and the closet and spread them on the chairs and the bed and the floor and then sat and stared at them, utterly perplexed. They seemed to have a separate, mulish identity of their own that refused to be washed and folded and stowed."[9]

Ordinary People is pure fiction, about the suicide attempt of Conrad Jarrett. But the character rings true, as many young people who have themselves attempted suicide have confirmed. After his return home from a mental hospital, Conrad seemed unable to get going. "He rolls onto his stomach, pulling the pillow tight around his head, blocking out the sharp arrows of sun that pierce through the window. Morning is not a good time for him. Too many details crowd his mind. Brush his teeth first? Wash his face? What pants should he wear? What shirt? The small seed of despair cracks open and sends experimental tendrils upward to the fragile skin of calm holding him together."[10]

Besides the obvious clue of the young person who just sits for hours at a stretch in his room, young suicide attempters may provide a verbal clue by describing themselves as feeling numb: "I felt so numb," explained one young attempter, "that I had this urge to cut myself to see if I'd bleed." Another youngster described himself as feeling as if he were watching himself on television. "I felt the whole thing was out of my hands, that I could no more change what happened to me than I could change what happened to Kojak last week."

Jay's Journal is the daily diary of a boy who committed suicide. Just before his death, Jay wrote, "Dear World, I don't want to get my hair cut. I don't want to tend kids. . . . I don't want to do my biology assignment or English or history or anything. I don't want to be sad or lonely or depressed anymore, and I don't want to eat, drink, eliminate, breathe, talk, sleep, move, feel or live anymore. . . . I'm not free, I feel ill, and I'm sad and I'm lonely."[11]

In a recent Chicago *Tribune Magazine* article a mother described the events that preceded her daughter Susan's suicide attempt. "One time . . . we went to a shopping center to do some errands. Susan said she was afraid she couldn't find the TurnStyle. I said, 'What's the matter with you? Are you seven years old?' I yelled at her. But hers was the behavior of a person shortly before a breakdown . . . meaning that a person can't cope with daily life. . . . There were 17 years of accumulated fears and questions and anxieties and disappointments and hurts. Have you ever seen something shoveled into a bag until it can't hold any more? That's what happened to Susan. It paralyzed her."[12]

Shortly before his death by suicide, Dallas Egbert wrote a poem entitled "Final Destination." The last several lines read:

> Whenever I decide there's
> a place I'd like to be,
> Soon as I can find there's
> a goal to be achieved,
> Come the time I'm shown that
> there's something left for me,
> then I'll go,
> But until then
> I think I'd rather sleep.

Unlike the person who is hostile and acts out, the passive youngster is afraid to let go, to get angry with people because he fears he might explode and clobber someone. Beneath his lifeless and compliant manner lies enormous rage—rage that seems best extinguished by thinking about suicide.

Two days after writing the following poem, its teenage author committed suicide:

> I still suck my thumb and I hate
> death;
> I am afraid what will happen if I lose control.
> Somewhere in my head aggressive
> thoughts killed my father . . .

So I suck my thumb.
I am a nice little boy,
Passive.
I wouldn't hurt anyone.[13]

4. CHANGES IN EATING HABITS

In retrospect, most parents of children who attempted or committed suicide recall that their children's eating habits changed dramatically—but that they (the parents) didn't think much about it. One mother recalled that, in an effort to cheer up her eleven-year-old daughter, she prepared all the girl's favorite foods. The girl either nibbled at them listlessly or refused them totally. The mother of another girl recalled that her daughter, then seventeen, who had been obese in her early childhood but had, through enormous self-discipline, become very thin, started eating voraciously. "It was certainly behavior that was totally out of character."

The mother of a sixteen-year-old boy said her son, who had a big, healthy appetite, just "seemed to lose interest in food. He picked and picked until my husband would lose patience and tell him if he wasn't hungry he could be excused. The night before he died, I heard him go downstairs at around 2:00 A.M. and I figured he was going to raid the refrigerator." As it turned out, he was going to clean and oil a hunting rifle. That was the weapon he used to kill himself.

Most suicidal children will show changes in eating habits like those described above—changes that will be one of many early signs of trouble. A minority of children—almost always girls—will show extreme eating disorders that usually last several years and come to monopolize their lives. Parents should consider these disorders—namely anorexia nervosa and bulimia—urgent distress signals. These children are, like alcoholics or drug addicts, killing themselves slowly, rather than instantly with a bullet through the heart or a noose around the neck.

Anorexia Nervosa: a malady that strikes mostly teenage girls—an estimated 500,000 in the United States alone. Most of these girls are deliberately, or at least unconsciously, suicidal. They are, after all, starving themselves to death. As one anorectic put it, "I hate food for what it does to me, which is to say sustains me."

(Fifteen percent of those with serious cases of anorexia nervosa die.)

Anorectics, like alcoholics, suffer from a profound sense of inadequacy and self-hatred. "I didn't think I was worth anything," another anorectic said. "I had no friends, no one to talk to. I was really depressed. I wanted to kill myself. I had thought of taking a knife or pills, but I couldn't. That was suicide and I knew suicide was a sin. So I just stopped eating. I went down from 120 pounds to 80 pounds." On a recent Phil Donahue show, an anorectic explained, "When I got out of high school, all I knew was that I hated myself, and I felt I hadn't accomplished anything. And all I wanted to do was get away by myself and think. And the first thing I did when I went away was lost weight. . . ."[14]

The anorectic believes that her ability to lose weight is her sole claim to fame. As Aimee Liu explained in her book *Solitaire,* a description of her own bout with anorexia, "I'm becoming famous around school for my display of self-discipline. My audience stands in awe of me, and I love it. Here's my chance to surpass Kimmy, my way of earning social stature. In this one respect, I'm the best, but if I let it go, all is lost, and so I cling to my diet tenaciously." Aimee, a highly intelligent, beautifully exotic girl, dark, part oriental, despaired of ever fitting into her WASPy high school crowd, full of lovely blondes like Kimmy, or of competing with her intimidatingly accomplished parents.[15]

Unfortunately, many physicians are ignorant of the causes and dangers of anorexia. They will sometimes assure parents that there is nothing wrong with their daughter, that she is just "going through a phase." A woman wrote to syndicated advice columnist Abigail Van Buren. Her niece was five feet five inches tall, weighed seventy-five pounds, was pale, listless, and ate literally nothing. The girl's parents were doing nothing about her condition because two doctors assured them there was nothing wrong. "You're lucky," one doctor said. "I have a daughter her age and she's too fat!"[16]

Binge and Purge: Physician David Herzog was on a college lecture tour when he first began to hear of bulimia. Bulimia is a grotesque cycle of gorging on high-calorie snacks—some bulimics consume as many as 16 pounds of food at one sitting—and then purging by inducing vomiting or gobbling laxatives—some bulimics take as many as 300 laxatives per week.

When students told Herzog that they heard women vomiting in the bathroom all the time, he got interested in the affliction and now directs the Eating Disorders Clinic at Massachusetts General Hospital. College authorities say the practice is epidemic on some campuses. As many as 25 percent of college-aged women exhibit bulimic behavior. Eighty percent of Herzog's patients at the clinic are bulimic.

Like anorexia nervosa, bulimia is a disorder with emotional, not physical, roots. Like victims of anorexia, bulimics are 95–98 percent female. Almost all are single, white, ambitious, educated, and middle or upper class. Although children as young as eight gorge and purge in secret, generally bulimics are college-aged—eighteen is the average age at onset.

Bulimics are difficult to detect because although they can suffer serious, even fatal side effects—ranging from tooth decay from repeated exposure of the dental enamel to the acid in vomit, to ulcers, hernias, dehydration, stomach rupture and even disturbance of the blood's chemical balance, which can cause heart attacks—they appear to be of normal size and weight. They gorge and purge in secret. Theirs is a solitary, lonely pursuit—engaged in by terribly depressed, potentially suicidal, young women.

Like an addiction to alcohol, this obsession with food comes to dominate the person's life. Many of those afflicted, such as Jan, a senior at one of the University of California campuses, have no time for anything but bingeing, purging, and studying. She reported: "I have no social life at all and no friends. How could I? My daily routine is disgusting and smelly. I'm doing it (bingeing and purging) sometimes as many as ten times a day. I spend fifty dollars a day on junk food. I don't have much left for clothes or movies or anything. I don't think I can or want to be cured. I see suicide in my future."

Jan began bingeing and purging when she was nineteen and a sophomore at the university. "I was too heavy, my grades were just so-so, and I felt my parents were disappointed in me. Clearly I wasn't going anywhere. I pigged out because I was so nervous, unhappy and angry, but then I purged because I couldn't bear my parents' disappointment and anger when I went home for a week-end."

The experts believe that there is a significant relationship between bulimia and depression. Dr. Craig Johnson, director of the Eating Disorders Project at Michael Reese Medical Center in Chicago, found that 60 percent of the women he surveyed reported feeling depressed nearly all the time. Twenty percent had made at least one suicide attempt or gesture.

In a letter to the editor of *Newsweek*, a nineteen-year-old former bulimic wrote, ". . . I will always remember how it feels to hunger and never find enough food to fill the mysterious emptiness."[17]

5. CHANGES IN SLEEPING HABITS

Unable to sleep at night, Steve frequently dozed in class. At home he seemed barely able to keep his bloodshot eyes open during dinner.

Sleep disturbances can take various forms. The young person may have trouble falling asleep or staying asleep, awakening at the smallest noise that wouldn't disturb the normal sleeper. He may snap awake in the early morning around four o'clock, the hour that Ingmar Bergman called "the hour of the wolf." Because of his fitful sleeping, he probably suffers from a total loss of stage four or Delta-wave sleep. The latest research indicates that a minimum amount of Delta, which is the deepest and most restful stage of slumber, is necessary for physical and mental health.

On the other hand, like the person who wildly increases his intake of food, he may sleep too much, in some cases practically around the clock. After Mark Cada shot himself to death, his parents tried to recall what signals Mark had given of his plan to kill himself. "During the last week," Mark's father said, "there were some signals that indicated that things had changed with Mark. They weren't strong enough signals to really alert us to a problem but . . . he seemed to be sleeping more. He'd go to bed early . . . and then he'd get up and go off to school before we really had a chance to talk to him."[18]

John Woytowitz went to the opposite extreme. According to his father, in the weeks before the twenty-one-year-old college student killed himself, "He stayed up all night and played the guitar a lot in his room."[19]

The troubled young person who can't sleep soon appears exhausted, run down, and, often, hypochondriacal. Norm B., for example, was once a high school letterman. He not only dropped out of athletics, but also nagged his mother to chauffeur him to and from school. He was too tired to walk, he insisted, and, besides, he felt as though he was coming down with something. He went to bed early every night, but, in the hours before dawn, his parents could hear him rummaging in the medicine cabinet and pacing the floors.

6. FEAR OF SEPARATION

Going to kindergarten, going away to college, breaking up with a girlfriend, moving to a new neighborhood are difficult for anyone. But for the troubled or depressed young person they can be debilitating.

Barry C., eighteen, had shown what his mother described as a "morbid" fear of separation since age eleven months—when he screamed hysterically at the arrival of anyone at the home, fearing always that the person was a baby-sitter. (Barry's was not an abnormal reaction for a child who is attached to his mother. However, this fear of separation usually eases as the infant reaches the toddler stage.)

When Barry was three, his father died and Mrs. C. found a job. She was able to leave Barry with her mother-in-law, who lavished love and attention on the boy, but Barry still protested vehemently every morning when his mother dropped him at his grandmother's. After several weeks he apparently realized his protests were getting him nowhere and gave up. "I certainly felt, at this point," Mrs. C. recalled fourteen years later, "that things were never the same between Barry and me. He missed his father terribly and I think he thought of me as sort of dying too."

At age four, Barry's grandmother—worried that he spent too much time around an "old lady"—enrolled him in nursery school, patiently and lovingly orienting him to the new routine. But Barry was miserable and showed it by throwing toys, hitting other children and having earsplitting temper tantrums, which terrified his teacher (she insisted he turned "deep blue" each time). After three weeks of this, the director of the school advised Barry's mother to keep him home and to slowly introduce him to other children.

Kindergarten was a similar disaster except that the principal of the public school couldn't ask Barry to leave. The boy was very bright—taught to read at age three by his grandmother—and adjusted somewhat to the academic side of school, but never to the social.

Instead of trying to befriend his classmates, he tried to befriend his teachers—male or female of any age; they were the people who seemed to really matter to him. The boy's advances frightened most of them and they made studied attempts to avoid him.

By age fifteen, Barry had given up on teachers and seemed fixated by older girls—seniors—in his high school. During most of his sophomore year he dated Mary, age seventeen. For Barry, this relationship was extremely intense. When he wasn't with Mary, he was calling or writing her. He was reduced to tears once when he saw her talking to another boy in the schoolyard. When she broke up with him at the end of the year (to resume a relationship with an old boyfriend who was home from college), Barry was reduced to temper tantrums, not unlike the ones he had suffered in nursery school.

By the time he was a senior in high school, Barry had become a regular and heavy drug user. He had also been in trouble with the police on several occasions, once for driving under the influence of drugs and twice for shoplifting expensive items from the sterling silver section of a department store. He made his first suicide attempt shortly before high school graduation.

Margo T.'s story is remarkably similar to Barry's. Margo, the daughter of a widowed working mother, lived in Marin County, California. As a preschooler she refused to stay in a day-care center, eventually working herself into such fits of rage that her mother had to hire a woman to stay home with her. In the second grade, Margo developed what was later diagnosed as a school phobia. The school psychologist said that Margo was terrified by any separation from her mother. He suggested Margo's mother accompany her to school and remain there until the little girl calmed down.

In high school Margo had few friends, but at age fifteen started going steady with an older boy who had dropped out of school. He was a boy whom other girls in her class would have shunned, but Margo craved his attention, the way she had once craved her mother's. When he broke off the romance, she was devastated. "I felt like I lost part of myself," she said. "I didn't think I could live without him."

She got scant sympathy from her mother, who said the breakup was the best thing that ever happened to her daughter and that eventually Margo would realize this. Margo never did. She became increasingly withdrawn and, several years later, on her first attempt, killed herself.

In her book *Unfinished Business,* a study of women and depression, Maggie Scarf traced the case of Debra Thierry, nineteen years old when Scarf interviewed her. Debra was an adopted child, "acquired" as she put it. "I am not the daughter my mother wanted," she insisted, describing herself as a "defective purchase." She thought of herself as "litter . . . like drifting newspaper . . . something that's floating around, underfoot, being kicked aside."

When she was thirteen, her parents sent her to horseback riding camp, against her hysterical pleas. She begged to come home but they insisted she finish what she started. Desperate, she faked illness, and was sent home. And so she learned that she could manipulate her parents, that she could assuage this awful fear she had of separation.

She was also afraid to go to school and at bedtime began wrapping a towel tightly around her leg so that, by the next morning, it was so badly swollen she had to miss school. The doctors were puzzled but eventually diagnosed her as having lupus arthritis, a fatal disease. She was triumphant. As a fatally ill child she was getting all the tenderness she felt her parents had so suddenly withdrawn by insisting she go to camp. Later the doctors came up with a new diagnosis—a brain eruption, an aneurysm. They said there was little hope for her survival but scheduled brain surgery. "They were getting ready to operate and I sure wasn't going through with that!" Debra recalled.[20]

In the hospital she wrote a letter of confession to her parents, who had nearly bankrupted themselves to pay her hospital expenses. Then, shortly before her fifteenth birthday, she took an overdose of sleeping pills, the first of several unsuccessful suicide attempts.

II. Specific Behavior Changes

7. ABRUPT CHANGES IN PERSONALITY

When Ted's parents got divorced, family, friends, and teachers all remarked on the sudden and seemingly total change in his personality. Before the divorce, the fourteen-year-old had been a studious, quiet, almost withdrawn boy—a boy who all agreed was very difficult to get to know. Now he was gregarious—obnoxiously so—and in school he was the class clown.

Ted's mother, who worried incessantly about the effect of the divorce on her only child, was pleased with the change. "I suppose I didn't realize just how much tension there was in our home. Once Ted's father moved out, he could finally laugh again. I thought that was just great."

She changed her mind, however, when the school counselor called to report that Ted was constantly disrupting the class with cruel wisecracks and jokes. The class clown is a personality type often seen in depressed children. It is another mask for depression. Ted was finally treated for just that after a bungled suicide attempt.

Sudden changes in personality are frequently a sign that the child has moved into the second stage—he has become actively preoccupied with suicide. Consider these other, very general, descriptions of cases we have seen: Nancy, a gregarious and easygoing child, suddenly turned withdrawn and sullen. Toni, once the class "doer" and arranger, the chairman of umpteen committees, abruptly dropped all extracurricular activities. She hurried home after school, always alone, mumbled a greeting to her mother en route to her room, where she closed the door until forced to come down for dinner. Ryan, a hostile child, turned overly solicitous and ingratiating toward his teachers and classmates. Anne, normally quiet and shy, became loud and obnoxious.

The reasons why a child undergoes these sudden personality changes differ in every case. Nancy was depressed and, as she put it, "tired of putting on an act for everybody." She knew in the back of her mind, she said, that she was going to kill herself, so she no longer cared what others thought of her. She was free to act sullen and, frequently, just plain rude. Toni, also depressed, said she felt so sad, so worthless, she could no longer bear to make small talk and "small plans." She was, she said, "simply exhausted." All she wanted to do, she explained, was "pull the covers over my head and stay in bed."

Ryan explained his personality transformation as "a last-ditch effort to change—and not a very convincing or successful one." He tried suicide, he said, when he realized he was no happier in his new personality than he was in his old.

8. SUDDEN MOOD SWINGS

Gary's friends were alarmed by the nineteen-year-old college freshman's unpredictable moods. One minute he'd be rounding up players for a game of touch football. A half hour later he'd slip away from the game to sit alone, slouched over the steering wheel of his car.

Moodiness, it is often said, comes with the territory of adolescence. To some extent that's true, but roller-coaster moodiness—especially persistent ups and downs—is not normal. Parents should take such behavior as a warning that their child is unhappy, unstable, and increasingly sapped of energy and structure. If these mood swings continue, the risk of suicide increases each time the child plunges into despair.

Two pages after he described himself as being in the depths of despair, Jay rhapsodized in his journal:

> Golly gee I'm glad I'm me
> There's no one else I'd rather be.
> I smile on every bird and tree.
> Life is a ball. I'm in love with me!

A couple of pages later, he was back in the pits. "I pretend I've got lots of confidence and I'm a big jock . . . but deep inside I'm a frightened, insecure, can't-make-it failure."[21]

9. IMPULSIVENESS

The case of the youngster who received a failing grade on a physics final at 3 P.M. and at 4 P.M. was found hanging from a tree behind his dormitory is familiar to any child psychiatrist. "The vast majority of young people who commit suicide," said Reginald Lourie, the author of a study on the subject, "have trouble controlling their impulses."

The adolescent, characteristically geared toward action, over-reacts without giving himself a chance to think things through. An adolescent may be less depressed than an adult but commit suicide over some seemingly trivial event out of an inability to delay self-destructive action.

Fortunately, before an adolescent kills himself, he will usually show this impulsiveness in less fatal ways. He might get a D on a physics exam and tell the professor, on the spot, that he is dropping the course—immediately. He might have a minor dispute with a roommate and move out, before making alternative arrangements. He might, in the middle of the night, start driving across the country to see his cousin in California.

10. SLACKENING INTEREST IN SCHOOL WORK AND DECLINE IN GRADES

Lisa, an honors student, suddenly started reading Gothic novels during history lectures. There were other signs as well—signs her parents noticed but didn't think meant much until a year later when their daughter barely survived a suicide attempt. "We were nagging her about taking the tests for the National Merit Scholarship competition," Lisa's father recalled. "If anyone was going to win from Lisa's school, the faculty thought it would be her. She kept saying, 'Don't worry, it's taken care of,' and we figured she meant it. Lisa, after all, had made us nothing but proud about her grades."

As the deadline approached, a school counselor called Lisa's mother to ask why Lisa hadn't taken the National Merit exam. The counselor, suspecting something was "terribly wrong" with Lisa, set up a family conference and asked the school psychologist to sit in. Lisa explained, convincingly, that she simply didn't feel like taking the test this term but would take it next. "I have too much work in my regular courses. I just don't have time for it."

The psychologist advised Lisa's parents to "lay off." More pressure, he said, is "exactly what she doesn't need." When the quarter ended and Lisa's report card showed a drop in her grades from all A's to all B's, her father decided that while this was a big decline for a girl who had previously gotten nothing but A's, "it was ludicrous to start cross-examining her as to why she was getting all B's. I mean, a lot of kids do a lot, lot worse than that."

But not perfectionists like Lisa. Feeling suddenly terribly depressed and not understanding why, she had, in her words, "become a total catatonic, a dropout."

She later said that, because her parents considered her to be "Miss Perfection," she felt she would be disappointing them by telling them how sad she felt. "My parents are too perfect to understand depression," she explained. "Whenever my mother heard of someone in the neighborhood who was suffering from depression, she'd say, 'We're too busy to be depressed in this house.'"

Because school is the major activity in a child's life, it is also one of the best barometers of his mental health. If a child's grades fall precipitously (and in Lisa's case a decline from all A's to all B's was precipitous), chances are something is wrong. Get that child talking about what's bothering him. When a child swerves from a long-established pattern, something usually is.

Like Lisa, Roger showed an uncharacteristic apathy about grades. For if there was one outstanding feature of Roger's personality, it was his competitiveness.

Roger decided to drop out of the grades race near the end of his senior year. Although he was doing well on exams, assignments that required out-of-the-classroom concentration were getting turned in late if at all. His parents and teachers chalked up Roger's "peculiar" behavior to "senior blahs."

He considered not going to college the following fall—he had been admitted to one of the top, and most competitive, schools in the country—but said later that he didn't know how to break the news to his parents. "The only thing they knew about me was what a good student I was. It was my whole identify. It would have been like my older brother, who's very good-looking and popular, telling my parents he was gay. *They* would have killed themselves."

Roger was majoring in pre-med and signed up for advanced-placement math and science courses. As he fell more and more hopelessly behind, he also became lonelier and lonelier. He was the only student from his high school at the university. He was used to being held in awe. Here he was just another student who couldn't make the grade. So shattered was his self-confidence that this once outgoing, friendly boy became painfully shy. He made his first suicide attempt toward the end of his freshman year when he was put on academic probation and dropped from the pre-med major.

11. INABILITY TO CONCENTRATE

Stacy read and reread the chapter on which she was to be tested the next day. She retained nearly nothing and failed the test. Reading even the lightest magazine article had become a terrible chore. Her mother suggested she relax by watching television. An hour later she found her daughter sitting in front of the set as if in a daze. Asked what program she had just watched, Stacy was unable to say.

12. LOSS OF OR LACK OF FRIENDS

Both types of presuicidal youngsters—the very aggressive and the very withdrawn—have one thing in common. They tend to be loners.

Some children, as they move closer to suicide, drop their friends or make themselves so obnoxious that their friends drop them. In any case, a very important warning sign to parents should be a loss of friends in their child's life.

Consider Toni, the girl described earlier in this chapter as once the class "doer" and arranger who suddenly dropped all her extra-curricular activities and retreated to her room—alone. Toni had once been perhaps the most popular, and certainly the most socia-ble, girl in her class. But as she began snubbing or avoiding her friends, they started doing the same right back. (It's a rare teen-ager who will stick with a friend who acts strange or hostile.)

Nancy, earlier described as the once gregarious child who suddenly turned withdrawn, also dropped her friends—but more gradually than Toni. At first, she told the friends whom she cared about least that she was busy. Her more important friends eventually got the same treatment but usually coupled with the angry outburst, "Leave me alone already."

As she slowly alienated herself from her friends, Nancy seemed to forget that she was the one who was doing the alienating. "Nobody cares about me," she complained to her puzzled mother. "My friends are all dropping me." Her depression was now mixed with a profound and unaccustomed loneliness.

Many teenagers who end up suicidal have never had friends to lose. As children, they survived this friendless existence by developing consuming interests in hobbies such as stamp collecting—hobbies that could be pursued alone. But once they reach adolescence, and especially as the first sexual urges start stirring, they really want friends—but are utterly unable to make and keep them. Their role as class loner or queer has already been set in concrete and their classmates refuse to let them swerve from it.

Classmates and teachers offered conflicting descriptions of computer whiz Dallas Egbert. But what recurred in all their remarks was an image of loneliness. Over and over they said, "He was a loner." Donald Sheer, Dallas' seventh-grade science teacher remembered, "He was almost a caricature of a whiz kid, a little kid with big glasses carrying a big briefcase and computers. Changing classes he was always walking by himself." "People were pretty cruel to him," one classmate recalled. While Dallas was onstage during a talent show, some students began taunting him and one yelled, "Tell them how queer you are."

Dallas' brilliance, coupled with his immaturity, isolated him from his peers. College life was in many ways even tougher because Dallas was so much younger than everyone. When he sought acceptance from a small group of homosexuals, he further alienated himself from his roommates. "Alienation is a good word for it," said Dr. Lawrence Reed, a psychologist who treated him. "He was completely alienated—from his parents, from his peers, from everyone."

In rehashing the events leading to Dallas' death, his father lamented, "I should have picked up on it (how unpopular Dallas was). I just didn't see how he could be so brilliant and not be good at coping with social situations."[22]

Marsha was in the psychiatric wing of a Fort Lauderdale hospital after trying to drown herself outside her parents' ocean-front condominium. Her junior high school classmates and teachers wrote her a group letter to cheer her during her hospital stay. "Of all the kids in our class," one girl wrote, "you are the last one who I would have ever thought was so sad. You're shy, but so are lots of kids. You always had your homework done and you never got in trouble like me. I always thought you were lucky and maybe too smart to talk to kids like me."

Marsha's homeroom teacher offered a different characterization. "She was aloof, she seemed to have no friends, she was more than quiet—she was isolated. I always had the feeling that she wanted attention but she didn't know how to ask for it."

"Now I hope you'll notice me," was the first sentence of Marsha's suicide note. Like many suicidal children, Marsha craved attention, but she was so good, so polite, so seemingly well-adjusted that her behavior didn't demand it. "I didn't need a lot of people around me," she continued, "just one very close friend—you Mom or you Dad, or one very close girlfriend. I thought I'd find one in junior high school but I finally admitted to myself that wasn't going to happen. I have no one, and I'm not trying to be dramatic. I really have no one."

In a study of youngsters in the New Jersey school system who committed suicide, Dr. James Jan Teusch of the New Jersey Department of Education found that these children were not involved in any activities outside the classroom, were socially isolated, had no close friends. The crucial difference between those who attempted and those who completed suicide was the presence of some one person they felt close to—a confidant who could share their innermost thoughts and who accepted them just as they were. Similarly, one quarter of the youngsters in a study of teenage suicide attempters by Dr. Joseph D. Teicher, director of adolescent psychiatric services at the University of Southern California, felt there was no one to whom they could talk.

The year before she committed suicide, Vivienne Loomis wrote in her journal about her longing for a friend, about how lonely she felt because she didn't have a really close friend.[23]

Chicago *Tribune* syndicated columnist Bob Greene published a long letter he received from a suicidal nineteen-year-old sophomore at Northern Illinois University: "I feel like a total nonentity. . . . At college, I have a room on a coed floor. . . . I'm an outsider, a lone wolf who's noticed and tolerated by the rest of the floor, but is not really a part of things. I feel like I'm living inside a glass booth, cut off from everyone even as I sit next to them. I'm one of those awkward, self-conscious people who sits a little off to the side of the group, wearing a paper-mache smile that's beginning to crack. . . . There are nights when people are laughing and talking out in the halls while I sit inside my room, door closed, biting my knuckle to keep from crying because I so desperately want to be part of the group."[24]

During the Christmas holidays, 1980, a student at a Seven Sisters college killed herself. According to a librarian with whom she occasionally talked, she had no one who really cared about her. The girl's parents were divorced. Her father had remarried and she felt he wouldn't want her to come home for Christmas. "I would interfere with his new family," she explained. She was estranged from her mother.

About a week before Christmas vacation, she told the librarian, with great excitement, that she was going to spend the holidays with close friends in New Haven. In reality, she had no friends in New Haven or anywhere else. She checked into a psychiatric hospital where, one week later, she killed herself.

III. Final Precipitants to Suicide

13. LOSS OF AN IMPORTANT PERSON OR THING IN THE CHILD'S LIFE

For the child who is already suffering—from aggressive or impulsive behavior that he can't seem to control, from a dependency on drugs, from a lack of friends, from a terrible dread of going away to college—a parent's death or divorce may be more than he can bear. Loss of an important person in a young person's life is a significant danger sign. If a child who has some of the problems discussed in the chapter suffers such a loss, he may choose suicide as the final solution.

The loss need not be of a parent. It might be of a boyfriend, even a pet, or something more intangible like an ideal or self-esteem.

A discussion of the reasons why young people commit suicide fills chapters 4–8. Loss is a key reason and Chapter 8 is a detailed look at the kinds of losses that can push a teenager into suicide. But for now we offer brief descriptions of cases we've seen in the last couple of years in which loss was the final warning signal before a suicide attempt.

Judy had a poor and frequently hostile relationship with her mother. But she adored her father. He was a traveling salesman and during school vacations she almost always joined him on the road. He was, she said, "her best friend." Her mother, who was jealous of the closeness between her husband and her only child, frequently pointed out that Judy's father was her "only friend"—a cruel but true statement. Snubbed by her classmates at an early age, Judy claimed not to want to have anything to do with those "silly children." Her father had a heart attack while driving on an interstate highway and died when his car went off the road. Judy made her first suicide attempt on the day of his funeral.

When Wally was a freshman in high school, his parents, whose marriage had been shaky for years, got divorced. Wally was obviously having a lot of trouble adjusting. He was getting into frequent and sometimes violent clashes in school. Once an average student, he was now failing almost every course, and his father, fed up, enrolled Wally in an out-of-state military academy. Wally was thoroughly miserable there and uncharacteristically withdrawn.

He made his first suicide attempt following a visit from his father, who informed Wally that he was remarrying and moving into his new wife's home. The new wife had three sons of her own, one of whom was Wally's age and all of whom lived at home and attended the local public high school. "You don't need me anymore," Wally wrote in his suicide note. "You have a new family and I can bet you won't be sending your new sons away."

Throughout elementary and high school, Melissa's teachers had told her that she was the most diligent and finest student they had ever taught. She got all A's consistently, was very ambitious and very rigid when it came to her plans for the future. She intended to go to Harvard College, then to Harvard Law School and, after a stint clerking for a Supreme Court justice, she would become Massachusetts' first and youngest woman governor or senator. She applied to Harvard College and to a state college "as a safety net." She was positive she'd get into Harvard and when she didn't (perhaps because she seemed too narrow, having no extra-curricular activities and no interests outside studying)—and real-ized it was too late to apply to other prestigious schools—she at-tempted suicide.

14. HOPELESSNESS

The 3 H's of suicide are shorthand for haplessness, help-lessness, and hopelessness. By the time the child reaches the third H, hopelessness, he may be on the verge of suicide.

Generally speaking, people with suicidal tendencies have a hap-less quality about them—one thing after another seems to go awry. The person overreacts and begins to feel helpless. He doesn't see how he can ever get up the energy and initiative to get back on track. The risk of suicide becomes very high when the feeling of helplessness turns into one of hopelessness, feeling trapped by un-bearable, unending suffering. Those who work with suicidal ado-lescents consider hopelessness the strongest indicator of suicidal intent—stronger even than depression. That hopeless feeling means the youngster has stopped seeking solutions to his problems and regards death as the only escape.

In his study of teenage suicide attempters, Dr. Teicher reported that half of the young people felt there was never any solution to their problems. Even suicide attempts, some said, failed to solve their problems. So they made certain the next attempt would be the last.

The youngster who is stymied by hopelessness obviously has no expectations for the future—is, in fact, convinced that there will be no future. A woman who works with teens in a community drop-in center described it this way, "When a kid is going through a bad time, I ask him how he feels about the future. If he says that he knows that he's going through a bad time now but that things will get better, I relax a little. If he tells me he's without hope, I'm always on the lookout for suicide."

In a hospital outside Minneapolis, a social worker interviewed a potentially suicidal girl. "You're sixteen now," she said to the girl. "When you're eighteen, what do you think you'll be doing?" "Nothin'," the girl replied, shrugging, and mumbled, "won't be here, I hope." The social worker recommended to the staff psychiatrist that the girl be admitted. "A child who is not fantasizing about the future, who has no dream, may have already decided that there will be no future," she explained.

Vivienne Loomis wrote a poem the year before her death in which she lamented the fact that she simply had nothing to look forward to.[25]

A suburban Chicago girl, who wrote a long essay about her suicidal intentions, fantasized about the future. But her fantasized future was so bleak that, as she said, "I'd have to be crazy to want to live for that." She wrote: "I see myself half a century from now with no toes, bent mildly over a wooden cane on some wooden bench in a park looking like warped wood myself, all bent out of shape in the sun, so tired, barely able to move, strung together loosely by pain and drive, old rotting bones and rough browning skin which always smelled like medicine. And I would just sit there, forever watching the goddamn world move nowhere in front of me with only stacks of dirty dishes and roaches to look forward to at home."

This sense of having nothing to look forward to is a key element in a young person's decision to try suicide. The girl whose despairing essay we just quoted explained that her brother used to sneak up behind her and beat her up, so, "I am always afraid of what I can't see behind me. . . . I am more afraid though of what I *can* see in front of me, my dark, hopeless future." Later, she wrote, "I have already, at age 20, run completely out of things I want to do on this earth."

As Sylvia Plath put it in *The Bell Jar*, ". . . I buried my head under the darkness of the pillow and pretended it was night. I couldn't see the point of getting up. I had nothing to look forward to."[26]

After Mark Cada killed himself in a Denver suburb, ABC-TV interviewed several of his friends. One boy, himself suicidal, warned parents of "the one thing they should watch out for—the 'I don't give a damn attitude.' Like you just really don't care about anything."[27]

Hopelessness manifests itself in various ways. The youngster may become apathetic—lose interest in living. What made Karen's mother contact the school psychologist was her daughter's sudden loss of interest in getting her driver's license—an event she had talked about ever since her fourteenth birthday. When she turned sixteen and her mother offered lessons and to take her for the test, Karen said, "Not now, maybe later."

Hopeless youngsters seem unable to get pleasure from food, sleep, hobbies, friends, accomplishments. Ed Kane, whose twenty-four-year-old son, Mike, killed himself in 1980 during his freshman year at the University of Maryland Law School, said Mike "had that inner fire to achieve. He would work like hell to get what he had, but he didn't get satisfaction from the things he did. That's a lifelong characteristic. He never seemed to enjoy his wins."[28] *

Sylvia Plath described a similar feeling in *The Bell Jar*. Having, over enormous competition, been chosen by a Manhattan fashion magazine as a student editor, "I was supposed to be having the time of my life. I was supposed to be the envy of thousands of other college girls just like me all over America who wanted nothing more than to be tripping about in those same size-seven patent leather shoes I'd bought in Bloomingdale's one lunch hour. . . . I just bumped from my hotel to work and to parties to my hotel and back to work like a numb trolleybus. . . . I couldn't get myself to react. I felt very still and very empty."

By the time a youngster has sunk to the level of hopelessness, he has usually lost interest in his appearance and in the opposite sex. "I was still wearing Betsy's white blouse and dirndl skirt," wrote Plath. "They drooped a bit now, as I hadn't washed them in my three weeks at home. . . . I hadn't washed my hair for three weeks, either. I hadn't slept for seven nights. . . . The reason I hadn't washed my clothes or my hair was because it seemed so silly. . . . It seemed silly to wash one day when I would only have to wash again the next. It made me tired just to think of it. I

* Ed Kane lost two sons to suicide. Tom, twenty-one, killed himself in 1978.

wanted to do everything once and for all and be through with it."[29]

Typically, the one activity that appeals to a hopeless young person is self-deprecation. The parents of Chris from Omaha, Nebraska, talked about the perverse pleasure their son took in putting himself down. He had, according to his mother, an "incredibly" wide range of interests and talents. "He knew everything there was to know about butterflies and he painted."

"So, he was very talented," Chris's father added, "but he wouldn't acknowledge it." He believed he was a "nothing." Also, although he was perpetually complaining to his mother that he was ugly, he was, in fact, very popular with girls and nice-looking.[30]

Vivienne's favorite teacher described her as a person who "didn't think she was worth much." Eight months before she killed herself Vivienne wrote in her journal of her utter worthlessness. She wondered why she should even bother to kill herself, because it is impossible to kill a nothing. She reasoned that the person who ends his life must have had something to end. He now feels miserable because he once felt happy. Vivienne explained that she feels nothing, and so what does it matter if she lives or dies.[31]

"Why was I born?" asked one young woman in a note left behind. "What's the use of living anyway? Everything I do turns out wrong. I might as well be dead."

15. OBSESSION WITH DEATH: A DEATH WISH

Arnie's conversation was studded with statements such as, "Sometimes I would just like to take a gun and blow my head off . . . but I'm only joking." Or, "Oh, I don't care. I won't be around anyway to find out what happens." Or, "You won't have to worry about me much longer." Or, "I would like to sleep forever and never get up."

Psychiatrist Herbert Hendin said that the students he interviewed "were drawn to death as a way of life." Indeed, the only love affair in a suicidal child's life may be his love affair with death. John Woytowitz, who hanged himself at age twenty-one, retreated to his room for hours at a time to listen to his favorite songs, "Suicide Is Painless" (the theme song from *M*A*S*H*) and "Vincent," which tells the story of Vincent Van Gogh's alienation and suicide.

Josh was a seventeen-year-old from Atlanta who so identified with James Dean that he left his suicide note to the dead movie actor. There were some similarities in their lives. Dean's mother died when he was nine and he seemed, as a result, preoccupied with suicide. (He died, at age twenty-four, in a car accident that many suspected was really a suicide attempt.) Josh's mother died when he was twelve, and he was, without a doubt, preoccupied with suicide.

His bedroom was filled with Dean memorabilia—posters from *East of Eden, Rebel Without a Cause, Giant*—in all of which Dean played a lonely, suicidal young man. On Josh's nightstand, the police found an article from the New York *Times* describing the twenty-fifth anniversary of Dean's death. The reporter recalled one of Dean's favorite tricks—making a hangman's noose which he then tied tightly around his own neck. He left the noose permanently hanging in his living room.

Josh died in his bedroom from a homemade noose tied to his ceiling fan. "After a while James Dean was all Josh talked about," said his sister Katie, then married, with a new baby, and living in Florida. "Nobody could stand being around him. He was just so obsessed, just real excited by it. It was like he felt he had to commit suicide to be worthy of James Dean. And he drove like a maniac. If he hadn't hung himself I've no doubt he would have died on the road, just like James Dean."

Poets Sylvia Plath and Anne Sexton, both of whom killed themselves, had a romance with death. In her poem "Lady Lazarus," Plath almost boasted of her recent suicide attempt. She concluded the poem with,

> Dying
> Is an art, like everything else.
> I do it exceptionally well.
> I do it so it feels like hell.
> I do it so it feels real.
> I guess you could say I've a call.[32]

Anne Sexton, who killed herself in 1974, wrote a poem titled "Wanting to Die" (1966), in which she described her desire to die as "the almost unnameable lust."

I know very well the grass blades you
mention,
the furniture you have placed under the sun.
But suicides have a special language.
Like carpenters they want to know which tools.
They never ask why build.[33]

Suicidal adolescents are often big risk takers because life for them has such little value. They seem to have a death wish. These are the children who stroll across an expressway, who jump out of the kitchen window instead of using the stairs, who speed around corners during an ice storm.

Newspaperman James Wechsler recalled the first suicidal gesture he noticed in his son. The boy almost walked into a car as he crossed the street. The death wish remained potent. He had repeated auto accidents, he drove his motor bike into a bus, he pushed his hand through a window, he almost strangled on the strings of his guitar.[34]

In Chapter 5 we shall discuss why some young people feel they need to punish themselves, but for now let's just state the obvious. Be on the lookout for an abnormal preoccupation with death. Be on the lookout for cuts, for the child who is always falling, always burning himself, always bruised. He may be trying to send his parents a message, like one young woman who appeared at breakfast every morning with cut arms. Her parents ignored the gashes and the growing depression until one day she severed an artery.

16. EVIDENCE THAT THE CHILD IS MAKING A WILL

Like an adult on the verge of suicide, the youngster who is preparing to die will try to get his affairs in order. He may give his little brother his cherished stamp collection. He may give a classmate his biology notes. He is, in effect, making his will.

Mark Cada did something his friends considered very strange. He gave his class ring—a ring he had just gotten—to a girl. "When you're a sophomore and you get your class ring," one friend explained, "it's a big deal. And most people really hang onto 'em."

Mark gave the same girl a crystal necklace. She was baffled. She didn't realize that Mark figured that, once dead, it would be too late to show her how he felt. "He said it was supposed to be for

Christmas, but, you know, Christmas had already passed. And I was wondering, you know, why would he do something like that."[35]

Conclusion

Most young people, at some stage of their adolescence, will exhibit one or more of these danger signs. They may be part of normal growth—unless they persist for more than a month or unless the child exhibits several danger signs simultaneously.

The next and crucial question is what causes the distress signals described in this chapter? What causes a child to become, for example, a drug user, a loner, and, finally, a suicide. "Why Do They Do It?" is the subject of the next section.

We'll begin, however, with an exploration of what death means to a child, what a child expects to get from death. We must remember that, while most adults see death as an ending, something to be avoided at all costs, many children see death as a beginning, as their last hope for happiness.

PART II

Why Do They Do It?

4

A Child's View
of Death

It looked like a "made-in-Hollywood" scene. But it wasn't. It was real and it was horrifying. A young reporter on the evening news gazed directly into the camera and, instead of reading the news, announced: "In keeping with Channel 40's policy of having the news first, you are going to see another first—an attempted suicide." Then she shot herself in the head.

In another American city, a teenaged girl called a local television station to warn that at 8:10 P.M. at a particular commuter station a man—she gave her father's name—would push a girl in a yellow dress in front of a train. As the 8:10 train pulled into the station, she jumped, surviving but losing both legs.

On August 26, 1980, the story of the suicide of Dallas Egbert, the genius from Dayton, Ohio, who died alone in his apartment after shooting himself in the head, made headlines. On that same day, another young boy's suicide received much less notice. Brett Soingnet climbed to the balcony of a New Orleans church and killed himself as thirteen hundred people bowed their heads in prayer around him.

Most people do not choose such a public forum for their suicide, but suicide, no matter what the setting, is, in one sense, a very public act. It is seldom committed in a vacuum. It is almost always intended to send a message to another person. Suicide is a last, desperate attempt to communicate. Because the person invariably has failed repeatedly to communicate with words, he is now down to his last card—communicating with his death.

Most adults find the thought of taking their lives totally repugnant, out of the question. Many youngsters do not. Why the
difference? A view of death that is unique to the young. Even
religious adults understand that if they were to hang themselves
this afternoon, they would be out of the picture, gone, finished.
Young people often have a vaguely formulated notion that they
would be around to observe what happened after their deaths, to
gloat over their parents' grief.

Perhaps because their lives have just begun and they have not
yet experienced the physical and mental deterioration that pre-
pares adults for death, they cannot really conceive of finality. To
them, death does not necessarily mean "The End"—especially not
these days, when deaths of siblings are rare and three-generational
families are even rarer. Most children have never seen a person
die or experienced the attendant grief.

An adult who is deeply disappointed and momentarily contem-
plates suicide would probably also think, "What happens if I
shoot myself and instead of ending up dead, I end up a vegetable?
What happens if I jump out the window and instead of dying, I'm
simply paralyzed?" Children don't generally dwell on the consequences. In a perverse twist on the optimism that we like to think
the young come by naturally, they just assume their suicide will
come out right (i.e., result in their deaths and cause awful anguish
to their parents. The parents, realizing what they lost, will be
transformed into paragons of affection. The young person, of
course, sees himself as coming back to reap the rewards.).

The task of maturation is one of moving from the pleasure principle to the reality principle. Adolescents are at a point midway,
where fantasy still overtakes reality. Thus they can think of killing
themselves and still being able to return. It is the presence of both
poor reality testing and the desperate need to communicate that
makes suicide palatable to the adolescent—and that creates such a
good opportunity for intervention. (As we show in Chapter 11,
asking the child, "What if you end up a vegetable?" is one good
way of pulling him back to reality.)

A child's view of death is a curious thing and in this chapter we
shall, by using cases of actual suicides or suicide attempts, show
the most widespread notions—fantasies really—to which young
people cling.

Revenge

Whereas an adult who feels unloved might confront a spouse with his fears, suspicions, and anger, a young person might make his point by killing himself. L. Bender and P. Schilder studied suicide in eighteen children under thirteen and found hardly any case in which spite was not the motivator.[1] According to psychiatrist Donald McKnew, a leader in childhood depression and suicide research, "I would say that in all cases of desired or attempted suicides, mother and father were intended to be spectators. The message is, 'I'm not very happy.' The other message is, 'It's your fault.' "

In a now classic study, psychologists Shneidman and Norman L. Farberow asked a carefully selected group of people to compose suicide notes as though they were about to kill themselves. They then compared the contents of these notes with real suicide notes taken from the files of the Los Angeles County Coroner. One of their key findings was that the genuine notes included more angry feelings and more wishes for revenge than the fake notes. One genuine note contained the statement: "I hope this is what you wanted."[2]

In Woodbury, New Jersey, the daughter of a prominent radiologist left the family room and went to the garage, where she doused herself with gasoline. Upon returning to the family, she said, "Look what I have done!" as she ignited herself and proceeded to go up in flames before her parents' eyes.

In November 1980, twenty-one-year-old Tobias Wasinger of Zion, a Chicago suburb, called his girlfriend, who had recently broken up with him. He pleaded with her to come back. She declined. Five minutes later, he called again. After she said she wouldn't talk to him, he told her to look out the window because he was going to kill himself. Several moments later, he drove past the young woman's house at high speed, hopping the curb, speeding forty feet on the parkway, and dying instantly after hitting a tree.

In Tom Sawyer, Mark Twain showed a clear understanding of

this childhood fantasy. Frustrated by his aunt, Tom found comfort in the fantasy of drowning himself in the Mississippi. He savored the vision of the pitiful spectacle he'd make when, curls all wet, his body was brought to his aunt. He imagined her saying, " 'Oh, if I had only loved him more. How differently I would have treated him if we had only known.' " The vision brought tears of self-pity to his eyes.

A child's view of death includes, almost always, the belief that after death he or she will remain behind, hovering invisibly over the scene, relishing, even gloating over the parents' grief. During an ABC "Nightline" program on teen suicide, a girl named Jennifer, who had made a serious suicide attempt, said she found comfort in "how it would hurt the people around me and how it would cause problems for them." Winnie, seventeen, who tried to kill herself twice, said that before her first attempt, "I had a long argument with my parents and everything. It was kind of to get back at 'em."[3]

Another ABC program, "Discovery," focused on Mark Cada's suicide. One of Mark's friends, who had also contemplated suicide, explained, "I think about really getting back at 'em. It's like you have nothing you can really hit 'em below the belt with so go for it all."[4]

Chris from Omaha was typical in that he argued with his parents just before his suicide. After several minutes of raised voices, Chris's father decided that the conversation wasn't going anywhere. "I'll discuss it with you in the morning when I get up," he said, walking out and slamming the door. Chris ran out of the house to a vacant house in the neighborhood, where he shot himself.*

Chris knew his father would search for him and he knew the vacant house was the first place he'd look. "And to my nightmare," Chris's father recalled, "I saw him through the basement window and it was all over as far as I was concerned. I guess the best way

---

* We are not suggesting that parents should never argue with their children. Arguing is one form of communication. (*Not* arguing, stifling anger, pretending that everything is okay can be most damaging of all.) But parents should, after an argument, assure their children that they love them—especially those children who have a low self-image, who interpret parental anger as more proof that they are thoroughly unlovable.

to describe it is to be struck by lightning . . . and to just become numb."[5]

Undoubtedly, this is precisely the response Chris had hoped for. But, of course, he had a bullet in his head and couldn't relish it.

Some young people are lucky enough to realize this *before* they kill themselves. A young woman, for example, wrote a letter to a Chicago *Tribune* columnist describing her desire to get even with her parents by killing herself. "It relaxed me to think about it. I would be very angry at my parents and then I would think about my suicide and I would think that when I was dead they'd feel pretty sorry." She changed her mind in time. "I realized that no one would think any more kindly of me. If they thought anything, it would be that I was a kind of nothing."

The Romance of Suicide

"You know dying is cool. . . . It's more like, you know, dramatic . . ." said suicide attempter Gina, sixteen, on ABC's "Nightline."[6] Mark Cada's death, said his girlfriend, ". . . was a fantasy. He climbed up on the mountain, just as the sun was coming up. Really romantic setting."[7]

Recently, a young couple, who fancied themselves a latter-day Romeo and Juliet, hiked deep into the Great Smoky Mountains. The two eighteen-year-olds had decided that all adults were artificial and evil, so they agreed, near a blossoming creek, to end their lives. He died. She lived to tell their story.

All these children shared a hope—that they'd find in death the romance, the adulation, that eluded them in life. They imagined themselves the talk of the school and they were seduced by the prospect of, at long last, being the center of attention.

They lived in a culture that encourages such fantasies; that, if movies and television are any reflection of its values, seems to hold life cheap and respect most those who take most chances with it.

Unfortunately, the notion of the romantic suicide is not a passing fad. It is certainly not a twentieth-century phenomenon. As A.

Alvarez noted in *The Savage God,* it is a tradition written deeply into Western literature.

And the most tragic, dramatic, and appealing variety has always been the suicide of the young and beautiful, of those who have yet to fulfill their enormous potential. We have already mentioned *Romeo and Juliet.* Two centuries later, in 1774, Johann Wolfgang von Goethe, then twenty-four, published *The Sorrows of Young Werther,* about a young artist of "excessive sensitivity" who killed himself after being torn apart by uncontrollable passions.

Goethe created a veritable epidemic of romantic suicides throughout Europe. Suicide became fashionable. Men who wanted to appear to be suffering for their art, for their genius, began to dress like Werther in blue tailcoats and yellow waistcoats, to speak like Werther, to plan to destroy themselves like Werther, and thus prove to the world that they were just as sensitive as Werther. Suicide clubs proliferated.

The Romantic era of the nineteenth century had as its dogma the belief that true feeling cannot survive into middle age. The poets whom the Romantics most idolized, the ones they considered "genuine," were Keats, who died at age twenty-five, Shelley, who died at twenty-nine, and Byron, who was pushing it when he died at thirty-six.

The protagonist of a popular satirical novel of the period (1844) said something with which many teens today would undoubtedly agree: "A suicide establishes a man. Alive one is nothing; dead one becomes a hero. . . . All suicides are successful; the papers take them up; people feel for them. I must decidedly make my preparations."[8]

Today's suicide has his own literary models. A Harvard College student who wrote an essay about his own suicide attempt modeled himself after a character in a Herman Hesse novel. In his essay, "My Suicide Attempt and the Encouragement of Herman Hesse," he wrote, "The works of Hesse relate closely to my own attempted suicide. . . . My attempt may now be regarded . . . as analogous to Hans' experiencing the 'exquisite torment' of love."[9]

The twentieth century has produced no shortage of suicides for the young to idealize as models, heroes, geniuses whose creativity and vision were too pure for this decadent world. Virginia Woolf, Hart Crane, Randall Jarrell, Mark Rothko, Ernest Hemingway,

John Berryman, Sylvia Plath, Anne Sexton are among those who died by their own hands.

In the 1960s, we added a new twist to the suicide as hero—dying for a cause, which is even nobler, not to mention more socially acceptable, than dying for, say, unrequited love. In 1969, Joan Fox and Craig Badiali, both seventeen, asphyxiated themselves. In the twenty-four suicide notes they left behind, the New Jersey teenagers, both active in high school politics, said they killed themselves to protest the Vietnam War. Their suicide pact generated an enormous amount of publicity, including a book, *Craig and Joan*.

The media depicted Craig and Joan as both tragic and heroic. On the one hand, their deaths were a terrible waste, but on the other, "How courageous!" Craig and Joan seemed to have, for the moment, made their point—that killing themselves to protest the war was somehow more meaningful and heroic than writing a letter to a congressman or carrying a placard in a demonstration.[10] It was a message that surely was not lost on other young people who felt depressed and ineffectual.

Peter Walker, a Canadian youth who committed suicide, had read *Craig and Joan*. In his "trial suicide letter," written before his "trial suicide," he wrote, "So I guess I am like Joan and Craig and dying for peace and love." Peter apparently saw Craig and Joan as superior, heroic, soaring above the masses in sensitivity, commitment, character. If they were too good, too pure, too sensitive for this polluted, warmongering world, then, by God, maybe he was too. Peter eventually blew half his face away with a shotgun.[11]

A Harvard College student taking a course on "Death and Suicide" showed just how pervasive is the myth of the romantic suicide. He placed the following ad in a Boston "underground" paper. "M 21 Studt gives self 3 wks before popping pills for suicide. If you know good reasons why I shouldn't please write Box D-673." He got 169 responses. He soon realized that "quite a few of the responses take it for granted that because I can visualize the possiblity of my suicide, I must be extraordinarily sensitive and an interesting person to know." One student wrote him, "Some of the people I admire tremendously have attempted suicide. I guess they are such complex and interesting persons I find a lot in them to like."[12]

"Intimations of Immortality"

Young people who commit suicide often lack a sense of their own mortality. To them, death is still a somewhat vague notion. Suicide may even become a means of testing these feelings of immortality.

Young people of all eras have felt this way, but for the television generation, the sense is heightened. Most youngsters' experience with death is limited to what they've seen on the screen. Their favorite star dies in one series and is reborn in the next. He faces death fourteen times in the course of a two-hour movie and survives each effortlessly.

Two requests that Peter Walker made in his suicide note showed a lack of understanding of the finality of death. First, he asked that his ashes be scattered in the wind or in the soil where he will "sprout each year and live forever."

Second, he planned every last detail of his funeral, including the musical accompaniment. His suicide note was full of specific instructions to his family. For example, he requested that the Beatles' "A Day in the Life," about a man who killed himself by blowing his brains out, be played during the funeral.

Peter believed he'd be around to attend his own funeral, like Tom Sawyer. Like adolescents generally, he was morbidly concerned with appearances. He planned his funeral with the care he'd have planned a party that was to make or break his social reputation. The point is that Peter, who was a highly intelligent young man with an IQ well above average, apparently thought that the next school day he'd be accepting congratulations for that terrific funeral.

The Shneidman and Farberow study mentioned earlier of real versus fake suicide notes revealed another striking difference. The genuine notes gave more concrete instructions, sometimes listing things to do, as if the writer were going to be around to make certain his wishes were scrupulously followed.

Unfortunately, for many young people, it takes a serious suicide attempt to make them realize that they're not immortal. "Only when I had made the attempt," wrote one college student, "did I sense that one cannot die and do it again; that, irrespective of any notions of immortality, I could not command the attentions of others in the state of my own non-being . . ."[13]

When the very young make a suicide gesture, the problem is magnified. For they have an even more tenuous sense of reality and mortality. They often see death as a sort of magical, mystical place. One eight-year-old boy who jumped out the window thought that, as soon as he cleared the frame, he'd be sucked upward to rejoin his dead father in heaven.

"Suicide Is Painless"

Dr. Pfeffer studied fifty-eight disturbed children in an attempt to figure out which factors separate suicidal children from those with other serious psychological problems. "Most important," she wrote, "would-be suicides were more preoccupied with death, considering it a pleasant and temporary state."

When suicidal young people are asked how they think of death, they will often say that they see it as a long, peaceful sleep that will somehow make things better. Vivienne Loomis thought of death as ethereal, as a sanctuary. Death was going to be the one graceful, lovely thing in her life.[14]

Suicidal adolescents often believe, in the words of the popular theme from M*A*S*H, that "suicide is painless." Edwin Shneidman describes the case of Beatrice Kern, who tried to immolate herself but survived with hideously painful burns. She recalled thinking as she doused herself with gasoline and prepared to strike the first match, "It was going to be good, it was going to be something that was going to fulfill me. . . . Well, then what I proceeded to do is I got the matches out, and even then no thoughts went through my head at all of the pain that it was going to entail, the misery, the hurt, any of that. It amazes me now that I really didn't think these thoughts. I guess I don't know why I didn't think the burns would really hurt . . ."[15]

Jennifer, the girl interviewed on ABC's "Nightline," explained that before her serious attempt she just "diddled around with suicide." She simply took pills and went to sleep. There was nothing painful about it. "I never had to get my stomach pumped, or anything." Death to her meant being "laid to rest, and everything's going to be okay for me."[16]

Timmy and Sue had broken up five days before he killed himself. Sitting in his car, he recorded a suicide note. "It's hard being brought up. They go all through life without no love. It gets so lonely, and lonely could be so painful. . . . Baby, please make my death worth something. I love you very much. If there's a chance for me and you in another world, baby, don't be late. Bye." Thirty minutes later, Timmy was dead, overcome by carbon monoxide poisoning.[17]

Timmy wasn't sure, but he wanted to believe that there was probably a better world waiting for him. It's a belief we hear more and more frequently from youngsters who are desperately unhappy in this world. At the New York State Psychiatric Institute, which overlooks the Hudson River in the vicinity of the George Washington Bridge, a researcher encountered three patients with the same fantasy: "I will escape from this place, run out on the bridge, jump and drown, and later come out alive and new on the other side."

Dr. William Worden of the Harvard Medical School is doing research on suicide at the Suicide Prevention Clinic of the Massachusetts General Hospital. He speculated that an increase in the belief in reincarnation may be partly responsible for the recent jump in suicide rates. One college freshman, who had attempted suicide twice, told him, "I'm kind of looking forward to death, just to try something new. It's another place to go. I'm really curious to find out what's on the other side."

Sixteen-year-old Jason Perrine and fifteen-year-old Dawn Swisher were obsessed with the possibility of reincarnation. Friends reported that after the pair read Richard Bach's *Illusions,* a book with a theme of reincarnation, they began leading lunchroom discussions of suicide and rebirth.

Then the two started planning their suicides. The plan was to steal a red Italian sports car and die in a flaming crash at their old junior high school, after which they would move to a "higher plane of existence." A year later, to the day, the plan called for two friends to kill themselves in the same way, except in a green sports car. Dawn and Jason crashed into the North Mercer (Washington) Junior High at 5 A.M. Jason was killed instantly. Dawn, who apparently had last-second doubts about reincarnation, just barely survived, after diving under the dashboard.

Will, a boy from a St. Louis suburb, died after jumping from the roof of his town's municipal building. His suicide note was full of references to *The Little Prince* and its author, Saint-Exupéry. Saint-Exupéry was forty-four when he disappeared in his plane in 1944, in the midst of World War II. Not a trace of pilot or plane was ever found. Saint-Exupéry was a crack aviator who had flown heroic missions against the Germans. Thus a series of flying accidents that resulted from extreme carelessness seemed especially incongruous for this aviation pioneer. In retrospect, it appears that he had been trying to kill himself for years and that his last crash was probably suicide. (He had written a will the night before.)

A year before his death, he wrote *The Little Prince,* the story of a pilot whose plane crashes in a desert. He meets a beautiful little boy who introduces himself as the ruler of planet Asteroid B-612. The pilot overhears the boy making an appointment with a poisonous yellow snake and tries in vain to dissuade him from keeping this apparently deadly rendezvous. The boy admits that the snake will bite him but he explains that he will only look dead, that he will have shed his heavy body in order to free his soul to soar to new heights.[18]

A sixteen-year-old girl from a Chicago suburb left a suicide note with the kind of emphasis that has become increasingly common. She explained that she was about to kill "just the bad part of myself." She implied that the good part would somehow survive and make a "new beginning." She believed that after her suicide, the good part would return as an infant who could live life over again. In a poem she left behind she talked about returning to the womb where "finally I will be protected, wrapped in water and warmth."

The "Now" Generation

Adults find it difficult to understand how a social or academic failure in high school can push a young person over the edge to death. "I know high school isn't great," an understanding mother will say, "but it's only three more years, and I got through it. You will too."

Impatience, impulsiveness come with the territory of adolescence. The adolescent has a "right now" orientation. He cannot comprehend the fact that three years is a short time in the scheme of a whole life.

Anne Tucker, Vivienne Loomis' best friend, understood this impatience much better than most young people. Her teenage sister had also committed suicide. "I think when you are fourteen life isn't so precious. It wasn't as if we had some kind of perspective on what the rest of our lives would be like. Everything was very much *then* and very much involved with what we were dealing with then. . . . Now I think about things—what I am going to do after I get out of school. We weren't thinking about that at all. We were thinking about right now—not next year in high school even. . . . Time seemed so long to us—to get through a week, even a day!"[19]

On June 26, 1982, Ellen Chow, fifteen, and Edmund DeBock, sixteen, climbed to the roof of a YMCA in a Chicago neighborhood. Holding hands, they leaped to their deaths. Just before, they told friends, with whom they shared two six-packs of beer, that they were looking for "a better world." Eddie asked, "What's it like up in heaven? Let's try it."

The couple, who talked incessantly of suicide for nine months before, were unhappy with this world for one main reason. They wanted to marry so they could be together all the time, but they couldn't because they were too young. Waiting until their eighteenth birthdays was apparently more than they could bear.

Suicide Is Not Painless—or Glamorous

Some high schools today are offering courses on death, with time devoted to suicide. Unfortunately, few high schools offer such courses and those that do often limit discussion to "Famous People Who Have Committed Suicide"—which encourages rather than discourages suicide. Students would benefit much more from learning some of the following:

• A thriving business in Chicago called "Cosmic Cleaning Service" specializes in "suicide cleanups." Bill Sheridan, a Chicago fireman, described one job—"an apartment where a man shot himself. We had to plaster over a hole in the wall and repaint it. Then we had to dye the rugs. . . . If you lose a loved one and he has to be cleaned off the wall, it's not a nice thing."[20]

• Psychiatrist Victor M. Victoroff, of the Huron Road Hospital in Cleveland, takes a slide show to area schools. Included in the show are graphic views of young people brought to the emergency room following a suicide attempt. The slides show in sickening detail a mouth and tongue burnt by swallowing household cleaners; a girl with a tube up her nose through which the contents of her stomach is being drained; a closeup of a misaimed gunshot wound that, instead of killing the boy, blew away part of his face; the protruding black tongue of a boy who strangled himself. "I want the kids to know," Victoroff explained, "it's not this dreamy scene where they're laid out looking like Snow White while everybody sobs about how wonderful they were."[21]

• Years ago, according to a story that appears time and again in the literature of suicide, the mayor of a town was confronted with an epidemic of suicide among the local young women. He was determined to demythologize suicide. He stopped the epidemic by proclaiming

Why Do They Do It?

that the nude body of any young woman who killed herself would be exhibited in the public square.

• A. Alvarez wrote after his own suicide attempt, "We all expect something of death, even if it's only damnation. But all I got was oblivion. . . . I thought death would be . . . a synoptic vision of life, crisis by crisis, all suddenly explained, justified, redeemed, a Last Judgement. . . . Instead all I got was a hole in the head, a round zero, nothing. I'd been swindled . . . death is simply an end, a dead end, no more, no less . . ."[22]

• The opening of a recent television program on teen suicide contained a poignant line. "This is what happened in Omaha, Nebraska, when three teenagers committed suicide within three months. One of them lived in this house. His name was Chris. He was sixteen years old. All that remains of him are his parents' memories."[23]

5

Children as
Status Symbols

Within a four-week period, four classmates at New Trier West High School, on Chicago's North Shore, killed themselves. What possible reason could teens, successfully competing at one of the best schools in the country, have for snuffing out their potentially successful lives?

"To some extent," said Chicago psychiatrist Harold Visotsky, "the epidemic of adolescent suicides can be traced back to Viet Nam. Young people became disillusioned with the magic of government and this extended to all institutions, including the family."[1]

In *Too Young to Die,* Francine Klagsbrun postulated that one reason for the dramatic increase in teen suicide is life in the "shadow of nuclear war." Children grow up with the "ominous knowledge that the world can be annihilated within seconds. They learn that resources have become limited, the environment despoiled. Wars, government scandals and disillusionment with the country's leaders have made Americans cynical of government."[2]

Dr. Norman Bernstein, a professor of child psychology at the University of Illinois, attributed the rising teen suicide rate, in part, to "a loss of belief in the future, not just because of the bomb but because of the economy."

What really causes a person to destroy a life that is just beginning? Certainly not Vietnam or Watergate or oil slicks or the bomb or the recession. The causes are internal, not external. Young people can handle societal problems; what they can't handle are their personal problems, feeling hopeless, neglected, utterly alone. Most of all, they can't handle feeling that their parents' love is conditional—and that they must perform, beat out the competition, if they hope to win that love.

Harvard University psychologist Tom Cottle put it beautifully when he called the sort of love too many parents offer "contingency love, love on the bonus plan." In essence, parents are telling their children, "I really think it is important for you to achieve, and when you do, I'll think about loving you."

A lot has been written lately about how quickly children grow up and away from their parents; about the substitution of peers for parents as the dominant figures in a child's life. Don't believe it. Parents remain far and away the most important people in a child's life. They also remain the most important factors in a young person's decision to commit suicide.

Children as Status Symbols

Parents should not be made into the all-purpose whipping boys. Sometimes they have the best intentions—*and* a suicidal child. But too often those intentions are best for the parents, not the child.

A disproportionate share of suicidal children seem to come from two very different sorts of families. Some have parents who totally neglect them, sometimes abuse or abandon them. (These are typically children from terribly deprived and disrupted backgrounds.) Others have middle-class parents who appear determined to be loving and concerned, but in reality are just determined; determined to mold their children into academic or athletic or social successes—in other words, into status symbols. These parents give their children an enormous number of material things and lessons in every conceivable skill and sport. But they do not give them love—the assurance that they will love them no matter what, in failure as well as in success.

The child from a home in which love is a prize that must be won, like a scholarship or a hockey game, reaches adolescence carrying a big and terrifying burden. "If I'm not what my mother wants me to be—a top student—does that mean she won't be able to love me?" asked one twelve-year-old boy whose parents had just been informed he had been rejected from Chicago's most prestigious private high school.

We are not disputing the necessity of guiding children, or of imbuing in them the importance of academic and even material success. These are extremely important goals, especially in times of shrinking resources and opportunities. But there is a big difference between helping a child make decisions and making those decisions for him; between helping him realize his potential and his dreams and forcing him to realize his parents' unfulfilled potential and dreams.

There are today simply too many children who realize, at increasingly earlier ages, that only by being a perfect projection of their parents' fantasies will they win love.

Not surprisingly, several of the suicidal young people we interviewed described a similar dream in which they were marionettes hanging from a string controlled by their parents. "I see myself dancing on a stage," one young woman said, "only I have nothing to say about what steps I'm doing. My mother is up above me holding that wooden thing with the strings attached. I don't even want to dance."

Several adolescents who suffered under unrealistic parental expectations told us they felt like actors, playing a role for Mom and Dad while keeping their real selves hidden. Michael, from an affluent Chicago suburb, gave up his dream of becoming an auto mechanic for his parents' dream of a college education and a "suitable" profession. (Neither parent had a college education, although the father had become enormously wealthy as a building contractor and real estate developer.) "I really want to be a mechanic," Michael admitted, "but of course I can't do it for a living."

The mother of one North Shore girl discouraged and later prohibited her daughter's dates with a boy from the wrong side of the commuter tracks, who was apprenticing to become an electrician. The boy did not fit the mother's image of her daughter. She never considered her daughter's image of herself and, several years later, after becoming engaged to a college classmate, the daughter killed herself. A North Shore boy whose father insisted he "follow in the old man's footsteps" met the same fate. The boy's suicide note read, "I had no choice." And indeed he didn't. His father allowed him none.

The affluent suburbs which, as we've shown, produce more than their share of suicides, also produce more than their share of parents whose main concern is not how happy their children feel about themselves but how those children reflect on their parents. Strangely, many of these parents exhibit the Great Expectations Phenomenon—something one would expect in lower-middle-class immigrant families. There is an expectation—a demand, really—that the kids be more accomplished than their parents. If the child suffers setbacks, he may feel that he has failed not only himself but also his parents.

One of Mark Cada's friends, who himself had considered suicide, described the terrible pressures he and Mark felt. "They (parents) expect so much from you and sometimes you can't put out that much. You can't live up to their expectations and they get mad at you and you think, 'Well, what am I gonna do because if they're going to get mad at me for putting out my best then it's not even worth being here?'"

He called "parental pressure" his biggest problem. How does he deal with it? "I just go through really heavy depression and then I break into their liquor cabinet and have a few drinks."[3]

In a study of the backgrounds of suicides who attended fifty-two California colleges, Michael Peck traced the students' problems back to early adolescence. Sensing parental pressure to succeed the children became anxious, discouraged, and, eventually, ineffectual. Feeling they had failed to live up to their parents' expectations, they became discouraged, then humiliated, and then hopeless.

"Liberated" Mothers

A new fact of life in the 1980s may have helped push the youth suicide rate to its current record heights. Back in the days when a woman's job—except in unusual circumstances—was to

raise children, mothers seemed to make fewer unrealistic demands. But today an increasing number of women feel, perhaps
unconsciously, that they sacrificed their own talents and careers to
full-time motherhood. These women are more likely to demand
that their children prove worthy of the sacrifice.

This feeling of opportunities missed is especially prevalent
among women whose children are now in their middle or late
teens. These women had children in the days when the feminist
movement was still nascent. Like their mothers before them, most
quit jobs to devote themselves to children, with nary a thought or
protest. But as their children grew, so did the belief that by being
full-time housewives and mothers they might be denying themselves.

Already middle-aged, many of these women feel their chance in
life is lost. So they push their ambitions on their children, and
God help the children if they don't share their mothers' goals.

The mother of Carrie T., a suicidal girl we interviewed, was an
only child from a wealthy family. When she married, her husband
joined and eventually headed her father's business, a prosperous
picture-frame-manufacturing company. Under her husband's direction the company languished, several times almost to the point
of bankruptcy.

Mrs. T. felt that she could have done a much better job, and
would have, if she hadn't had a child to care for. Carrie, she concluded, would not make the same "mistake." Before Carrie graduated from elementary school, Mrs. T. was pushing a career in law
—because so many of the battles her husband lost were fought in
the courtroom. After law school, Mrs. T. decided, Carrie would
take over the company from her father and revive it.

At age thirteen, Carrie was an average student. Her mother's
plans were just too big and ambitious for her. She buckled under
the pressure and expectations. When it became obvious the girl
might not get into college, much less law school, Mrs. T. seemed
to just give up on her—to treat her like a losing investment. Because Carrie was obviously not destined to rescue the failing company, Mrs. T. treated her as if she weren't destined for much of
anything.

Not all mothers insist their daughters join the Fortune 500.
Some still covet the traditional wins. But what parents with tradi-

tional and untraditional goals have in common is this insistence that their children compensate for their own shortcomings and missed opportunities.

Marilyn was a sixteen-year-old junior at a North Shore high school at the time we interviewed her. Her older brothers were handsome and smart; one a student at Harvard College, the other studying at Oxford University in England. Marilyn's academic and social life was much less impressive than her brothers'. And her mother wouldn't let her forget it.

"My mother has always thought my two older brothers are perfect," she explained. "I mean, to her, they're a combination of Robert Redford and Albert Einstein. It wouldn't have been so bad if she hadn't been so disappointed in me. She'd be playing bridge, and a neighbor would be bragging about her daughter's going to the country-club dance with Dr. So-and-so's son. My mom would come home and be disgusted with me because I haven't had a real date in my whole life. Then when grades came out, she was really furious because—as she put it—I wasn't 'Harvard material.'

"I decided to kill myself when girls started getting asked to the junior prom. I couldn't bear the thought of spending prom night with my scowling mother. Instead, I spent it with her in the emergency room, with tubes sticking out of my nose. I was thinking, 'Boy, you can't do anything right. You're even a flop at killing yourself.'"

During family therapy, Marilyn's mother admitted that as a girl she had been unpopular. "I was always the last one chosen at dances. I just wasn't pretty and gay." Parents with poor self-images see their own personality traits in their children and find them distressing. Out of a distaste for herself, Marilyn's mother was trying to pressure her daughter into a mold she couldn't fit. She was telegraphing to Marilyn her own feelings of inadequacy.

In *The Age of Sensation,* Herbert Hendin described the case of Alan, a boy who had nightmares in which he was forced to eat an apple as big as a house or drink champagne from a glass as big as a house. He lay awake at night wondering what it would be like to be hungry. When he described his dream to his mother, she snapped, "I don't want a crazy child. If you're going to be crazy, you're not my son." In the years to come, Alan's mother continued to refuse to acknowledge any feelings that didn't match her idea of what he ought to feel.

In college, Alan decided he wanted to major in music, for which he had a long-standing love. His mother, who knew nothing about music, told him he had no talent for it and, if he persisted in this foolishness, she would cut off his support.

Another of the students Hendin interviewed was Amy, a college revolutionary. Whenever her parents disapproved of Amy's actions they insisted that it was not really Amy who occupied a building or got arrested. They insisted she was led by others and if she thought about it or was "really herself," she would see things their way. Amy told Hendin of an incident from her early adolescence when she bought a bedspread for her room. Her mother considered it in bad taste and insisted that if Amy thought about it she would see that she also didn't really like it.[4]

Sigmund Freud wrote that suicide is an act of hostility; that the child who kills himself is really committing symbolic patricide or matricide. Yet anyone who has worked with suicidal children knows that sometimes suicide is not an act of revenge or aggression at all. Rather, the child has come to believe that success is so important he can't live without it; that he doesn't deserve to live without it; that without success his parents really don't want him to live. Rather than suicide being an act of revenge or aggression, it is an act of obedience—the last act of homage, the child's final attempt to do what is expected of him.

Get Good Grades, or Else!

Phil Donahue interviewed a girl named Michelle who, in high school, had been a star—in athletics and academics. "My father was proud of me," she said. "Everyone was proud of me. And in one year (in college) I went from a 3.7–8 average down to a 1.9–8. I was put on academic probation. I was trying in school but I was running into something totally different from our high school setting—huge audience classes with 300 people. You can't even see your professor. . . . That particular time my father had laid down the law. He said, 'This is it. This is your last quarter. If you do not get it then you're out'. . . . I think it was wrong of him to put those kind of pressures on me. I succeeded for him when I was in high school. And he loved me and he was proud of me. But why just because I tried and I couldn't handle what they were putting at me, why should he act . . . like he didn't love me anymore . . . that I just failed him." She attempted suicide.[5]

Jamie suffered from pressures similar to Michelle's. He learned early that he could please his parents only by getting top grades. He basked in their love and praise when he did well and shivered from their icy withdrawal when he did average work. During his first year at Princeton, faced with competition from the top students in the country, he panicked.

Home for Christmas, he broached the idea of transferring to the local state university. His parents' cold anger and disappointment made him drop the subject. In late January he was found dead in his dorm room. "I knew I would fail you," read the note at his side.

Many suicides can be laid at the door of parents who consider scholastic achievement the only yardstick by which a youngster's worth and future success can be measured—and that means straight A's. Children get the message very quickly. In a survey of Northfield Township youth—the Township covers part of Chicago's North Shore—86 percent of the children expected to get A's. Obviously a much lower percentage was going to attain such perfection. (Ninety-two percent of the students surveyed ranked good grades as more important than being popular.)

As is the case in other affluent communities, very few North Shore parents see their children as academically average. They give them a lot materially and they expect to be paid back—usually with good grades. When the children can't keep their end of the bargain, they feel like failures.

As one young woman who attempted suicide said, "There was tremendous grade pressure on the North Shore because the only thing money can't buy is intelligence. Therefore, that became a status symbol."

Tena Rosenblum of Jewish Family and Community Services in Highland Park, a North Shore suburb, complained, "I counsel pregnant women who ask the names of the best nursery schools, so their unborn child will have a head start in kindergarten, in order to do well in grade school, which should help them in high school so they can get to the best colleges. Granted, some kids flourish in that kind of atmosphere, but we can't forget that some very adequate, very average kids can't live up to those kinds of expectations, and they become more and more depressed and eventually give up."

Ed Kane of Baltimore, who lost two sons to suicide, warned, "We're taking people and putting a mental thumbscrew on them at an early age, pressuring them, testing them in school every time they turn around." He remembered Mike "in sixth grade, worrying about whether he'd get into law school."[6] Susan Bevis, a social worker on the North Shore, lamented, "I have ninth-grade kids absolutely freaked out if they get a low grade in English because they won't be able to go to medical school."

It's difficult for parents who went to college in another era to recognize the pressures put on young people today. The competition to get into the good colleges that open the doors to the top law or medical or business schools can be, literally, killing.

Some children combat grade pressure by copping out, by failing big and hoping they will then be left alone. But others have too little self-confidence to grab even this pathetic option. One boy left his parents this suicide note: "You've hounded me about grades to the point where I can't even study. You keep telling me that I'll never make it. So I'm doomed to failure—and you've made me feel that failure is the worst thing that can happen. My midyears last week were a nightmare. I can't shake this terrible depression that has come over me. The only thing left for me is the bottle of sleeping pills."

On June 14, 1979, a UPI dispatch from Ann Arbor, Michigan, reported the suicide of seventeen-year-old Agnes Vass, a senior who learned she would not graduate with her class. She put a .22 caliber rifle to her heart and killed herself. School Superintendent Howard Harris said Agnes tried to tell her parents over the weekend that she was going to fail the required English course, but she couldn't. Police reported she left a handwritten suicide note at home, saying how upset she was over her grades; how sorry she was that she had failed her parents.

Today it can cost as much as $10,000 a year to send a child to college. That's an enormous price, even in inflated dollars, and this fact is not lost on the youngster, who feels he must justify the expense. Mickey compiled a list of the reasons he should not kill himself, chief among which was the hefty investment his parents had already made in his education. Rethinking it, he realized he was already a "losing investment," that his parents would only be "throwing good money after bad." He decided to go ahead and kill himself.

Too Much Pressure, Too Little Praise

It is tough on a child when parents make too many demands for early achievement. It is terrible when they don't couple those demands with praise and support.

Parents today might be called the "Yes, but . . ." generation. They foster skills by finding fault, by mixing praise and criticism. "That's nice," a parent responds to an above-average report card, "but why not at least one more A?"

Some parents seem to believe it necessary for children to grow up feeling utterly incapable, as if there were something innately and irreversibly wrong with them; something that makes them less successful than their peers. This was precisely the problem A. S. Neill found with many of the so-called "problem children" brought to him at Summerhill. They had been praised much too seldom. "To every child," Neill said, "adult approval means love; whereas disapproval means hate."

After Bill and Jean Casey's seventeen-year-old son Shaun killed himself, Jean candidly and publicly said (on "The Phil Donahue Show") that she realized they had put too much pressure on him. "We said if you want to be in medical school you have to earn A's. You know, uh, a C average isn't good enough, especially since you are not in a minority or something, you know, you are really going to have to be great to stand that competition."

Listening to his wife, Bill Casey agreed. "We leaned on him too much. We expected too much of him. If I had it to do over again with Shaun . . . I would spend more time hugging him than nagging him about his grades . . ."[7]

"I'm a Fraud."

Some children, pushed by parents to succeed, seem to thrive under the pressure. But because they're fulfilling someone else's desires instead of their own, often their sense of self—their personalities—are very fragile. The smallest setback can send them reeling.

Deep down, many believe they don't really have what it takes to succeed. They believe that they achieved only through extraordinarily hard work. They believe that if they let up, even a bit—to make friends, to play basketball, to develop a hobby—they will fail. They consider themselves frauds and fear that, one day, everyone else will reach the same awful conclusion.

Molly, one of the young women we interviewed, was a Phi Beta Kappa graduate in Russian history of a Big Ten university. She planned to write and teach and was enrolled in the graduate program at the same university.

Molly was a loner. Her friends, none of whom were close, were members of the department. She occasionally had dinner with one or another of them, but none were romantic interests. Getting involved with a man, Molly said, would be "counterproductive" at this point in her career. Usually she had dinner alone, studying as she gobbled frozen dinners and guzzled the innumerable cups of coffee that kept her studying at a fevered pitch.

Molly was the pride and joy of her family—the firstborn and the one in whom her parents, especially her father, placed all their hopes and unfulfilled ambitions. "I wanted her to have what I didn't have—not to have to work so hard, to have people respect her," said her father, who was night manager of a grocery store in Worcester, Massachusetts, where Molly grew up. (Her brother, Joseph, was in the management trainee program for the same chain.) "Joe is satisfied following in my footsteps," her father added. "Molly would never have been."

Actually, it was difficult to say what would have satisfied Molly, because she never really developed any of her own interests. There wasn't time. She had too much studying to do. Molly was

CARL A. RUDISILL LIBRARY
LENOIR RHYNE COLLEGE

very bright, but because her parents had so much invested in her
academic success, she never felt free to experiment, to test the
limits and nature of her intellect. She was convinced that she was
an academic fraud—that if she didn't make a superhuman effort
for every test and paper, she'd be exposed as a colossal fraud.

She was convinced that the very next paper or exam would
show her to be "as average in intellect as my family." She had
worked herself into a state of such fear and insecurity that she
believed that if she took off a single Saturday evening to see a
movie or a Sunday afternoon to read a novel, her grades would
slide and "I'd have to go home and become a checkout girl."

The sole source of pleasure in Molly's life were those relentlessly perfect grades. But as she reached graduate school she was
now competing for jobs, not just grades. She was beginning to be
pushed out of the hothouse atmosphere of academia into "the real
world," where grades did not always accurately measure performance, where politics and vindictiveness sometimes entered into a
professor's evaluation.

During her second quarter at graduate school Molly got her first
C on a paper. She dealt surprisingly well with that shock, but
when she got a D on the midterm in the same course, she felt as if
her life and goals were slipping through her hands. Instead of
being angry with the young assistant professor who, one classmate
said, "seemed jealous of Molly and was probably worried about
having to compete with her for a teaching spot somewhere down
the line"—they were both specialists on the Bolshevik Revolution—
Molly secretly admired the professor, "for being the only one
smart enough to see what a phony I am."

Her confidence was shattered. More low grades followed. A
prestigious teaching assistantship she'd been expecting went to another young woman—a competitor—in the department. Molly decided to kill herself.

Her parents were surprised and delighted to hear from her on a
Thursday night. She said she wanted to come home for the weekend. As usual, the household activities were planned around
Molly's studying. But, to her parents' surprise, she spent much of
the weekend watching television and sleeping. She barely spoke to
her parents or brother.

At dawn Sunday morning, her father heard a shot that sounded as if it came from directly outside his bedroom window. He rushed outside to find his daughter dead in the backyard, his old hunting rifle lying next to her.

Molly was unable or unwilling to describe her terrible fear of failure. She left no suicide note. Sylvia Plath, a straight-A college student, left what amounted to an extended suicide note in her autobiographical novel *The Bell Jar,* published a few weeks before her death. ". . . all my life I'd told myself studying and reading and writing and working like mad was what I wanted to do, and it actually seemed to be true. I did everything well enough and got all A's, and by the time I made it to college nobody could stop me."

During her stay in New York as a college intern on a fashion magazine (another prize she'd won against enormous competition), she met an interpreter for the United Nations. "For the first time in my life, sitting there in the sound-proof heart of the UN building between Constantin who could play tennis as well as simultaneously interpret and the Russian girl who knew so many idioms, I felt dreadfully inadequate. The trouble was, I had been inadequate all along. I simply hadn't thought about it. The one thing I was good at was winning scholarships and prizes, and that era was coming to an end. I felt like a racehorse in a world without racetracks or a champion college footballer suddenly confronted by Wall Street and a business suit, his days of glory shrunk to a little gold cup on his mantel with a date engraved on it like the date on a tombstone."

Back at the magazine, she was having problems with Jay Cee, the fiction editor. "I felt very low. I had been unmasked only that morning by Jay Cee herself, and I felt now that all the uncomfortable suspicions I had about myself were coming true, and I couldn't hide the truth much longer. After 19 years of running after good marks and prizes and grants . . . I was letting up, slowing down, dropping clean out of the race."[8]

Mike Kane, the young man from Baltimore who killed himself during his first year of law school, was another student always on the hunt for good grades. He was an excellent student, in the top quarter of his class, yet he saw himself as a failure, and worse. When he killed himself, he left a warning note to his roommates in the door of their apartment. "Don't enter. Call the police. By the time you read this, I'm gone. I'm crud."

Although he had evidence of his competence (i.e., good grades), he had convinced himself that everyone saw through him. He told his father that a professor he had listed on his résumé as a reference didn't like him. After the suicide, the professor told Ed Kane that Mike had been one of the most stimulating people in the class, and that he had a bright future. The Friday before he died, Mike had an interview with a Baltimore law firm. He was convinced that the interview had been a disaster. Actually, the lawyer who interviewed him had been so impressed that, because summer jobs in his firm were already filled, he placed Mike with another firm. So glowing was the lawyer's recommendation that the firm hired Mike sight unseen. The letter notifying him arrived the day after he died.[9]

Japan: Intense Competition, "An Orgy of Suicides"

American parents should take heed of Japan, where it has become a cultural tradition for a family's prestige to hinge on a child's academic performance. The headline over a recent editorial in a Tokyo newspaper bemoaned "An Orgy of Child Suicides." News stories referred to "the annual slaughter of innocents" as children plunge off skyscrapers, hang and gas themselves, and leap in front of speeding trains.*

Career and grade competition is even fiercer in Japan than it is in the United States. In Japan, if a student fails to get on the academic ladder at a certain point, he never will. Children in Japan do not get a second or third chance. They must take a written exam to enter a "good" kindergarten. The good kindergarten is a prerequisite for a good primary school which is a prerequisite for a good high school which is a prerequisite for a good university.

* Although the suicide rate for young people remains higher in Japan than in the United States, the suicide rate for young males in the United States has surpassed Japan's rate. In 1964, there were 6.3 suicides per 100,000 males ages 15–24 in the United States. The rate in Japan was 19.2. In 1977—the last full year for which data are available—the Japanese rate was unchanged but the U.S. rate had skyrocketed to 21.8.

Not surprisingly, the suicide rate rises every February when students write entrance exams. For failure to get through "examination hell," as it is called, means shame for the student *and* his family, and sharply reduced chances for success in life. Parents do not take chances. Eighty percent of Japanese children attend neighborhood cram schools for an average of three hours after regular school hours, including Saturday and Sunday.

West Germany, where the educational competition and tension is similar to Japan's, also has a high youth suicide rate. (For those under eighteen, the rate is 50 percent higher than it is in the United States.) The country has a punishing system of preselection for higher education, which means that the student who doesn't do well from the start will have no academic future.

According to Professor Walter Leibrecht, an educator in Ingersheim in southern Germany, "Because many families have but one child, the status of the entire family depends on whether that child passes the entrance exam for prep school. It's incomprehensible that a decision should be made for ten-year-olds that will affect them all their lives."

Matt P.'s father was not so much interested in academic success as he was in athletic success. He wanted his son to be fit and trim and coordinated. The fact that twelve-year-old Matt had wide hips, a soft, round build, and no talent for athletics was a profound embarrassment to Mr. P.

Matt was referred to the clinic when his junior high school classmates started calling him a "fag," making him extremely anxious. Looking at his flabby build and feeling his father's distaste for him, Matt began to believe that he was homosexual.

Mr. P. traveled regularly, sometimes in Europe for weeks at a time. Matt's mother had deserted the family when Matt was seven and his brother five, after a psychotic episode requiring hospitalization. Mrs. P. was a shadowy figure living miles away. Matt rarely saw or spoke to her.

Communication between father and son was not much better. At Matt's first visit to the therapist he expressed surprise that she listened to him and challenged and clarified what he was trying to put into words. This first real communication of his life so boosted his self-image that the classroom teasing stopped.

However, when Matt reached physiological adolescence he seemed unable to discuss his sexual concerns with a female therapist and she recommended a transfer to a male. Matt decided to drop out of counseling altogether and to try to make a go of it on his own.

Ten months later he was back, plagued by suicidal urges. "Nobody gives a damn. Nobody's ever home and when he is Father just says, 'Don't bother me with your trivia; I fly to Switzerland tomorrow.'" Although therapy was reinstituted, with family sessions whenever Mr. P. was in town, Matt's suicidal urges grew stronger.

The therapist encouraged Matt to talk to his father whenever he was around. "Dad gave me a whole fifteen minutes last night," Matt reported one day, "and then I realized he was thinking only about what the neighbors would think cause I never played any sports."

Matt said that his father had all but given up on him as someone to be proud of. "Dad told me that I would never follow in his footsteps cause I'm not smart enough. Dad never sees anything that I do as okay." (Matt also told the therapist that his mother, when she was around, had insisted that he be just like her intellectual brother.)

Although Mr. P. was warned repeatedly, it became clear that he was not getting the message that his son was feeling increasingly discouraged and hopeless. The day before he was to leave for Germany, Matt came to the clinic, having taken an overdose of tranquilizers, cached by his mother years ago but still potent enough to make Matt drowsy. He spent three hours at the clinic awaiting hospitalization. He was monitored regularly, and each time he repeated, "I'm checking out. I never mattered for me, only for what my parents wanted. I guess Dad did that to Mother too and that's why she's crazy."

During Matt's hospitalization, a grandmotherly lady was hired as a homemaker, adding structure and warmth to the home. Matt resumed outpatient therapy. His father has not changed, but Matt, now that he has somebody to talk to, has noted his own successes —especially his skill as a debater—and come to understand that he will never fulfill his father's fantasies for him, but is, nonetheless, a perfectly acceptable young man.

Matt and every child mentioned in this chapter had something in common, besides being, in their parents' eyes, symbols of failure instead of status. What they had in common was an inability to talk to their parents. An old hunting rifle fired for the first time in decades, a clothesline noose clumsily knotted, a bottle of pills pilfered from the family medicine cabinet, and, occasionally, a suicide note, were the only ways these children could tell their parents just how unhappy they were; just how frantic they felt at the prospect of failing.

Blocked communication—a constant in the tragedy of suicide—is the subject of the next chapter.

6

Blocked Communication

The child who can talk about his pain—and his plans—to someone who is really listening can usually work out or, at least, work on his problems. The child who can't talk is the child who may commit suicide. Blocked communication is a factor—often *the* factor—in every case of suicide.

In one recent study, 90 percent of suicidal teens said they could not talk to their parents. "The most common factor in the continuing chaos and unhappiness in the young person's life," the researchers concluded, "is the lack of parental appreciation or understanding."

After studying a large group of suicidal children, Dr. Michael Goldstein of UCLA reported that one of the two factors that augured worst for them was poor or disordered parental communication. (The other is an "overly critical, overly involved or actively hostile parenting style.") Morris Paulson, a clinical psychologist who looked for common denominators among "seriously self-destructive" youngsters reported, "Every one of them had a home that wasn't providing the understanding and caring that the child needed."

In our experience, after a child attempts or commits suicide parents will usually admit that there were communication problems in the home. But the typical reaction when we present parents of troubled, but not yet suicidal, children with the results of the studies quoted above is, in the words of one father, "That's ridiculous. We understand him all too well. That may be the problem. Besides, all teenagers think their parents don't understand them."

We have found, on the contrary, that teenagers seem to want to give their parents the benefit of the doubt. "I can talk to my parents," they'll say, while admitting that they'd rather discuss personal problems with friends. But in a crunch, in a crisis, and especially in cases in which children do not have any close friends, they do feel free to go to their parents. The availability of this release valve sometimes saves their lives. For what separates a child who solves his problems from one who sees suicide as the only solution is that the latter simply can't imagine opening up to his parents. Talking to his parents, he has learned from painful experience, is simply not an option.

It never ceases to amaze and sadden those of us who work with troubled children just how callous parents can be to a child's efforts to unburden himself. Charlotte Ross, director of crisis intervention in San Mateo County, California, regularly visits schools to talk to students and thus to pick up where their parents left off or, more likely, never started. "What happens if you tell someone you've got problems you can't handle and you need help?" she asked one boy. "It depends on who it is," he answered. "Like if I was to tell, like, my father, he probably would call me a sissy or something because I can't handle my problems."[1]

It doesn't take very long for a young person to give up on his parents as sources of comfort and advice. A friend of Mark Cada's who had contemplated suicide said it had been "years" since he had talked to his parents. "I don't tell them I'm upset or anything. I just sort of like shut myself in my room, stick on the headphones and I isolate the rest of the world."[2]

Dan attempted suicide in the washroom of his Omaha high school. "Even to this day I feel as though I cannot talk out problems with my parents. Somehow or other I kind of feel as though they're spacing me off. That's one of the reasons why people try it (suicide)." He claimed that a typical conversation with his father consisted of his father demanding, "Get me this! Get me that! Why don't you bring me this?! Why don't you bring me that?! Jump! Jump! Jump! Jump!"[3]

So blocked is communication in some families that violence is the sole form of expression left. In July 1978, an eighteen-year-old named Harvey, whose family lived in one of the North Shore suburbs of Chicago, hanged himself. Harvey, a heavy drug user who twice tried to kill himself by overdosing, had just graduated from high school. He was described by a youth worker as a "very needy but don't-get-close child."

After his parents threw Harvey out of the house, communication practically stopped. Every week, his mother would put money and sometimes a note in the mailbox which he was to pick up between 5 and 5:30 P.M., when no one was home. The plan's purpose was to keep other members of the family from being upset by the sight of Harvey.

Because he didn't have an available family, he was dependent on his friends to take care of him. He maintained his relationship with them by providing them with drugs. He could devise no similar plan to keep his family close.

Communication in this family had disintegrated to the level of those occasional notes from his mother and fist fights with his father and brother—shocking but not that unusual. Michael Peck and Robert Litman found that about 40 percent of the suicidal youngsters they studied reported having been in physical fights with members of their own families. These children and their parents were doing more punching than talking.

In cases in which family communication is blocked to the point of imperviousness, sometimes a therapist can pick up where the family failed. As we saw in the case of Matt, described in Chapter 5, the therapist can become the only person in the child's life who is listening to him and responding. But the problem with substituting a therapist for a family member is that, even today, the therapeutic relationship is not nearly so permanent as the family tie. Consider the case of a North Shore girl named Sarah.

At fourteen, Sarah was a high school senior. She had always been out of step with her classmates, but everyone knew she was a genius. She herself explained that her head seemed twice as big as it should, her brains were too big for her body. When she doodled, she often drew a tiny body and an enormous head filled with cells shooting off. She sometimes bemoaned her capacity to keep eight ideas in her head at once, thinking about each of them simultaneously.

In the spring of her senior year she became withdrawn. She lost interest in planning for college. Her previous pattern of helping her less adept classmates stopped, and her father, a surgeon, decided to refer her for psychiatric help.

When she was first seen by a male psychiatrist, she was totally mute, in spite of supportive and gentle questions. At the end of the session, the doctor suggested that a woman psychiatrist might be more helpful. At that point, for the first time, Sarah looked at his face and formed a yes between her lips.

Sarah was still mute when I saw her. I sensed, however, that Sarah could be reached but that hospitalization was necessary. With great embarrassment, her socialite mother accompanied Sarah to the hospital. Her father was performing surgery and was delayed.

During the course of the next two months, Sarah had daily psychotherapy. Slowly she began to share her sense of embarrassment that all she had going for her was her brain. She described a family with no communication. The only time her two brothers spoke to her was when they wanted her encyclopedic answers. Mother was too busy with fashions; Father was always visiting other surgical theaters or lecturing in Europe. Her best friend was the maid, a Norwegian from a farm. "She doesn't say much but at least she looks at me when I talk."

During her hospitalization, I urged her to try to initiate conversation with her parents. I urged her parents to get to know their children by asking questions about their idiosyncratic interests. It was clear, however, that each family member had given up trying to talk to the others.

Sarah was given day passes to share the family dinner. Each time she came back more depressed. "Nobody cares about anyone else in our family," was her only comment. She continued to thrive in the hospital where small group discussions among patients permitted her an active interchange. Her therapy was productive and she was finally able to say to me, "It is good to have a place when I can talk about me as I am and as I want to be."

Father was scheduled to make a trip to England for a lecture series and several honors. It seemed important for Sarah to be in a protective environment while both parents were away. Arrangements were made for Sarah's transfer to a treatment institution away from the city.

The day before her departure, out on a dinner pass, she went to the nearby river and drowned herself. Apparently she could not tolerate the loss of her therapist and the environment that had become her only talking home. Staff members were stunned. She had seemed much improved. Her ongoing care had been so carefully planned. A brilliant mind had never been honed to its capacity and the gentle girl child within that brain had only just been born.

In most families, communication problems are not nearly so extreme as they were in Harvey's and Sarah's but they can be just as damaging.

In the case of Mark Cada, his mother recalled that although Mark talked to her and her husband when he was younger, the older he got and the more upset he got over his academic, athletic, and social failures, the less he talked. The Cadas mistakenly decided to leave him alone.

Mark became the target on the school bus for punches, ridicule, and tossed food. He couldn't talk to his parents about this unbearable humiliation. He released his anger, first on inanimate objects, later with fatal results, on himself.

"Mark would come home from the bus," his mother recalled, "and if I didn't spot him coming up the cliff I'd hear him. He'd just come in and slam one door after the other. . . . That one day about the nutmeg (some boys had rubbed nutmeg in his eyes) he was just . . . I thought he was gonna punch a hole in the wall."

He'd scream at his mother, "I'm not gonna talk about it" and retreat to his room and his music. He became increasingly introverted. "If we tried to lead him into a conversation or ask him, 'Mark, you know it seems like society's so much harder than it was when we were growing up. I don't know how you can stand it,' he said, 'Well, it's even worse than you think it is.'" And that's all he'd say. His parents decided, again, not to force the issue.

Mark desperately needed professional help, but neither his parents nor his teachers recognized how deep was his despair. (The year before, the Cadas had sought counseling for their son only to be told by a psychologist that as far as he could see, Mark didn't have any "particular problem.")

Mark was crying for help but he couldn't put his plea into words. "In the last couple of weeks before this happened [before the suicide]," his mother recalled, "he'd kind of sit by us and act like he wanted to tell us something and we'd try to get it out of him." But when asked what was on his mind, Mark said, "Nothing." Shortly before he killed himself, he'd sit beside his parents for as long as two hours at a stretch trying to tell them something —most likely of his intention to commit suicide.[4] (In Chapter 10 we'll discuss what exactly the Cadas might have said to Mark in a crisis such as this.)

Chris's mother realized too late that her son had been trying to tell her how hopelessly suicidal he felt. "Three weeks before Chris shot himself," she recalled, "a boy at school he knew in the same class took his life the same way, with a shotgun. . . . Chris came home and told us about this, and he brought it up two or three times. Then one morning, I suppose it was only a week before he shot himself, one morning at the breakfast table he said to me, 'Oh, that girl [the dead boy's sister] is back in my class. She was a year younger than her brother.' And I said, 'Oh, really,' and I thought it was kind of funny that he just out of the blue brought that up and so I pursued the subject."

She did not, however, pursue the subject in a way that encouraged Chris to talk. "That is so terrible," she lectured, "what that boy did. And I said that family will never get over that, never, they'll be living with that the rest of their lives and wondering about it. And I said, 'That is so terrible. If these young people could just know what they are putting their families through when they do this.' And he just sat there, listening to me say this—didn't get much reaction. He just looked at me."

"Why couldn't I have . . . said something?" Chris's father asked. "But I didn't have the tools to figure that out. If I did, maybe he'd be here yet today."[5]

"It's Just a Phase."

Responding to a child's complaint that he's miserable or that he hates school or hates himself with, "It's just a phase" is not responding at all.

Parents of a suicidal young person frequently simply can't

admit that their child is seriously disturbed, that his problems go
beyond typical teen turmoil. They assure themselves: "He'll grow
out of it." Or: "It's best for kids to work out their problems themselves. That's all part of becoming an adult." Or: "The last thing
we want to do is baby her. If we do that now, she'll never grow
up."

Such a response is understandable. Often a teen's problems
seem trivial, especially in comparison with an adult's. Adults
make light of the breakup of a young romance. They know from
experience that there will be more romances down the line. They
forget that the teenager has little experience and knows nothing of
the kind. An adult may listen impatiently to a child's distress over
a failing grade on a chemistry exam. "Big deal," Dad explodes,
thinking about the poor evaluation he has just gotten from his supervisor and the promotion he now knows will go to someone
else. The son, we must remember, unlike the father, has no experience in dealing with major problems. To him, failing an exam is a
major problem.

Parental denial of a child's problems is also understandable because many parents see a child's success in life—or lack thereof—
as a direct reflection on their competence. "My parents like to see
me as having no problems," one girl told us. "I mean they need to
see me as having no problems. We can't even discuss the possibility of my being unhappy." "She needed me to be perfect, because if I was, then people would know that *she* was," another
young woman explained.

Many parents are too quick to dismiss their children's emotional complaints—for one simple reason. They do not think of
them as illness. They would nurse, even baby, their children if
they had a strep throat or the chicken pox. But if those children
felt depressed or fearful, many parents believe it's best to ignore
them—not to reinforce such feelings.

Vanderbilt professor John Killinger created a useful analogy: if
a father accidentally slammed the car trunk on his son's finger,
he would not consider his child's injury to be a figment of his
imagination, something he would outgrow, "just a phase." He
would not deny it happened or worry about what the neighbors
thought of him as a parent if they found out he had to take his
child to the emergency room.

When parents refuse to respond to emotional injuries, some children, if they are desperate for attention, will self-inflict physical injuries. Wrist cutting is one potentially lethal way young people turn emotional injuries into physical ones; a bloody display of emotional scars. (Incredibly enough, sometimes not even this works. One student we interviewed, from a suburb of Philadelphia, was enormously angry that for four mornings running she had appeared at breakfast wearing a short-sleeved T-shirt and neither of her parents had noticed the fresh scars. When this last, pathetic attempt at communicating went unheeded, she tried, but failed, to cut the artery—her first serious suicide attempt.)

Donna was one of many suicidal teens who called Chicago radio station WFYR during a program on teen suicide. Like most of the callers, Donna said she found it easier to talk to the panel of strangers (which included a psychiatrist, a social worker, and a Catholic priest) than to talk to her parents.

She explained that she had tried to kill herself the week before by slitting her wrists, that she was having terrible problems at work and with her boyfriend. "My world seemed to be shattering around me and my parents thought I was just going through a stage and I would learn to handle it and that I worry too much. . . . They were very nice to me but they didn't go out of their way to suggest I get help or anything."[6]

Some parents hound their children with the cliché, "These are the best years of your life." If they thought about it, they'd realize how counterproductive such a comment is and, in any case, they might recall the pain of their own adolescence.

Other parents remember their adolescence as simply awful but figure, "I got through it. He will too." In discussing how relentlessly his son Mark had been "picked on" by other teenagers on the school bus, Frank Cada recalled, "When I was a child I rode a school bus also and I used to get picked on by the . . . they'd kind of use me for a punching bag. I just suffered through it. When I got older, then there wasn't that many kids bigger than me and it stopped. I went through a period in my life where I basically had the same kinds of problems and I was hoping that Mark would basically outlive those kinds of problems and they'd be part of his past."

Frank Cada "outlived" his problems to become a successful

computer engineer. But Frank, unlike his son, had been a good
student and so he could see beyond the school bus. Mark couldn't.
For him, life promised to be a never-ending, humiliating school
bus ride.[7]

Chris also had a parent who believed her son could survive his
adolescent misery just as she had survived hers. "Chris was really
very much like I was," his mother said. "I can remember a few
years I was kind of unhappy with everything and unhappy with
myself and unhappy with the way I looked and I didn't think I
had enough 'in' friends and I was kind of a loner for a while. I'd
shut myself up in my room and read. He really just kind of reminded me of me. That was another reason I wasn't alarmed by
the way he was. I just thought it was something that he came by
genetically."[8]

Young people sometimes behave in the most bizarre, even menacing, manner and their parents still refuse to acknowledge that
anything serious is wrong, that their child is trying to tell them
something. Louis Wekstein, a professor of psychiatry at Tufts
University School of Medicine, told of a twenty-three-year-old
college student who attempted suicide twice, the most recent time
by overdosing.

As a child and adolescent he was a loner and violently cruel to
other children. Parents and son had never learned to communicate. Instead the boy would blow up at the slightest provoca-
tion. When he got angry at his mother, he "discussed" it with her
by going on a rampage and wrecking whatever household items
were in his path. Prior to his most recent suicide attempt, he was
so menacing toward her that she called the police. In the face of
all this, his father insisted the suicide attempt was an accident;
that his son's behavior resulted from a drug kick for which the father blamed peer pressure at college. The father needed to believe
his son was a typical teen of the times.[9]

The mother of Jay, whose diary was published as *Jay's Journal,*
wrote after her son's suicide, "We were very sorry that we didn't
know that Jay was so deeply troubled and depressed. We knew he
was unhappy about a few things and tried to help him all we could
but Jay really masked his real feelings to the point that he fooled
all of us." She proceeded to reduce his problems to a "squabble"
with his girlfriend. Anyone who reads *Jay's Journal* would realize

that Jay's girlfriend was the least of several pressing, serious problems. Jay's parents could probably have saved their son if Jay had been talking to them instead of, or in addition to, his journal.[10]

Remember, teens who need help don't "grow out of it." They become adults who need help—if they live that long.

"Growing Up Dead"

The lethal trait that many suicidal people share is an inability to express anger or pain. They internalize these normal emotions where they fester, until they infect their entire lives.

At the clinic, we frequently see suicidal young people who could be described as "the perfect child." These children are enormously unhappy but never show their anger. Their sole goal is to win their parents' approval and love. They know that angry, demanding children do not elicit smiles and hugs from Mom and Dad. They sense that their parents are most comfortable with a lifeless child who causes no trouble. They try pathetically hard to become that child.

These children are, as Herbert Hendin so aptly described them, "growing up dead"—trained by parents who take no pleasure in their children to stifle their emotions, their demands, their personalities. By nature they are such obedient children that they learn the lesson all too well. Children like these feel as if they're already dead, so the prospect of suicide loses its horror. Because their parents took no pleasure in them, they take no pleasure in themselves either.

Almost everyone knows of—or perhaps even grew up in—a family in which parents—usually fathers—trained their children—usually sons—not to show emotion. This is a variation of the "growing up dead" theme, and it can sometimes have deadly results.

When seventeen-year-old John O'Donnell White, Jr., shot himself to death with his father's gun, his mother discussed the relationship between father and son.

"When Jode was a little kid, a little baby," Mrs. White-Bowden recalled, "I used to hug him and kiss him and my husband used to say, 'Don't baby him. Don't make a sissy out of him. Don't do that.'" Jode grew up to be a man's man, who liked to play soccer, lacrosse, ski, and ride motorcycles. He planned to attend engineering school at the University of Maryland and to get himself certified as an expert motorcycle racer.

The other side of Jode was a very sensitive one. His mother recalled that he used to cry while watching "Lassie" on television. His father discouraged that. "No son of mine is a crybaby." John, Sr. (who shot himself through the head a couple of years before his son did), taught Jode not to show emotion. When he was eight years old, his mother recalled, he severed the top part of his finger in a neighbor's door. "He didn't flinch, he didn't shed a single tear on the way to the hospital or while waiting in the emergency room."

Jode and his father used to wrestle and occasionally hug. That became Jode's sole source of physical contact. John, Sr.'s discouragement of his wife's displays of affection for her son resulted in a physically cold relationship.

Jode had learned his lesson all too well. He was unable to express his feelings about his Dad's suicide. He couldn't open up to the minister or to a close friend of the family's who picked him up from school regularly following his Dad's death. "He beat him (the minister) at chess," his mother recalled. "He'd talk about motorcross, about school, lacrosse, soccer. But he could *never* talk about his father."

Jode desperately sought warmth, affection, and comfort from a fifteen-year-old girl he dated, but she was not interested in the sort of intense involvement Jode needed. One day his mother arrived home to find her son frantic. "Mom, I love her so much. Sometimes she responds to me. Sometimes she doesn't and she won't tell me why. I gotta go talk to her."

Although his suicide note said, "I love her too much," his mother believes that the girl was incidental; that Jode's emotions had been stopped up for so long that he was literally choking on them; that the reasons for his suicide have much more to do with his stifled relationship with his parents than with this teenage girl.[11]

Smothering Overprotection

Families in which parents are extremely overprotective are also families in which there frequently are communication problems. Overprotective parents tend to talk *at* their children rather than *to* them. They treat their children like infants. They might as well be cooing and gurgling at their teenagers for all the substance and give-and-take of their conversation. Parents like these often don't listen to their children or respond meaningfully because they are too preoccupied with telling them what to do and how to do it.

Because it is of paramount importance to parents such as these that everything be done exactly right, they do everything for their children—rather than struggling to teach them and putting up with mistakes and frustrations. The children grow up self-indulgent, lacking confidence, and feeling useless. Their overprotective parents have instilled in them a feeling of "I can't cope." When trouble arises, they are not prepared to face it. They certainly can't talk about it. Frequently, suicide turns up as an answer.

Children from families such as these are often terrified to go off on their own and they fear, to a debilitating extent, that something might happen to their parents, on whom they have become so unnaturally dependent.

Jessica, age eight, had a "school phobia." She was so upset every school morning that she faked illness by forcing herself to cough until she had irritated her throat or by inserting a feather in her nose to induce sneezing. Her parents sought the advice of a psychiatrist when she began choosing dangerous methods of avoiding school, such as slashing her leg.

In the family therapy that followed Jessica's private sessions, her mother, a free-lance management consultant, admitted that she had mixed feelings about raising her only child. "My husband is unwilling to contribute much to the child care. I do almost everything. My career is going to pot. I just don't have the time to devote to it that I used to." Before Jessica's birth, she shared an office with two colleagues. Now she worked at home in order "to be available to the baby." She used to have dinner with colleagues or clients and then return to the office for a couple more hours of work. "My husband (also a management consultant) still does that all the time. It's frustrating, but I feel it's most important to spend time with Jessica."

Paradoxically, a mother who unconsciously resents her child may become, like Jessica's mother, overprotective. Feeling over-burdened, but hiding such feelings, even from herself, she over-compensates and, as the child grows older, becomes smotheringly overprotective. The mother who resents her child can't help but transmit that message, making the child feel that Mother's contin-ued love and protection are not securely hers; making her feel that, when she goes off to school, she runs the risk of her mother's escaping.

As we shall see later in this chapter, some children grow up feeling that they are totally responsible for their parents' mental well-being. A mother who cannot tolerate the thought of her child's independence transmits this message and transmits it clearly. Only by remaining dependent, the child comes to believe, can his parent survive.

Deathly Fear of Punishment

Some children have such fear of talking to their parents that they would rather kill themselves than tell their parents about a failure. Robert was a fifteen-year-old freshman at a Brooklyn, New York, high school when he made his first suicide attempt. He sneaked out of his family's apartment at 11 P.M. and went for a ride on the subway, eventually, at 1 A.M., ending up in a station in the South Bronx. He slouched against a pillar flashing the gold watch his parents had given him for elementary school graduation.

At 3:30 A.M. his parents got a call from a policeman who was with their son at a Bronx hospital. Doctors needed immediate per-mission to operate. Robert had been mugged. He was alive, but barely. The beating had resulted in severe internal injuries and a knife wound in the stomach.

We opened this section with the statement that Robert had at-tempted suicide. He had, in an indirect way. He came out of surgery mumbling, "Why am I still alive?" Robert had chosen "getting the shit knocked out of me," as his means of suicide. He had deliberately provoked a fight with some young gang members. First he refused to hand over his watch, then he began hurling at his attackers racial slurs and insults about their manhood. One of the thugs finally concluded, "This motherfucker wants to be dead. Let's go," he hissed as they left Robert slumped in a heap.

Robert was accustomed to severe beatings. So stifled and twisted was communication in his family that violence was practically the only remaining interchange between father and son. As a child, Robert had been punished regularly and sometimes brutally by a father who had a violent temper, exacerbated by a high-pressure sales job. He had come to believe that he could do nothing right and that he was "rotten at the core." He also discovered that his father was easiest to live with, almost mellow, after he had vented his aggressions on his son.

By age thirteen the boy was increasingly self-destructive. No matter how many times his father beat him, he never got used to it. In fact, it terrified him more each time. He had learned to anticipate his father's beatings by punishing himself. On Friday he found out he had failed a science course. His parents, he knew, would be notified on Monday. He decided to self-administer the final punishment.

When Parents Act Like Children, What's a Child to Do?

When ABC-TV's "Nightline" ran a program on teen suicide, reporter George Strait interviewed a seventeen-year-old girl named Winnie who had attempted suicide twice.

STRAIT: Are you able to talk to your mother?
WINNIE: Sometimes.
STRAIT: Does it help?
WINNIE: Not really.
STRAIT: Does she understand?
WINNIE: She doesn't know where her own head's at, so she can't really help me.[12]

Another young woman, who had attempted suicide and felt she was on the mend, said of her parents, "They know they're failures. They are children themselves."

During a call-in show on Chicago radio station WFYR, host Bruce DuMont asked Barbara, an eighteen-year-old who had attempted suicide several times, "When you told your mother you were suicidal, how did she react?" "My mother is a real shaky person herself," Barbara responded. "She doesn't get along with my father and that's the first thing on her mind."[13]

For the very young, there is no world larger than the family. When parents are themselves emotionally ill, needy, or abusive, the child's life is made miserable and lonely. Parents are supposed to guide their children. In the above cases, the parents couldn't guide themselves, much less their children.

In some families there is a reversal in the parent/child roles. The child is expected, sometimes in subtle ways, to nurture the parent. In a letter to her beloved former teacher, Vivienne Loomis wrote of the terrible burdens her mother placed on her. Mrs. Loomis would come home from work exhausted, only to resume arguing with Rob, Vivienne's older brother. Her mother, according to Vivienne, came to her for help and advice. Vivienne complained about the pressure of being loaded down with family problems. She wondered about this state of affairs, mentioning that she is not even fourteen and that her mother is forty-eight. She said that among the reasons for her first suicide attempt was that she could no longer manage her mother's problems, her father's problems, her sister's problems and, most of all, her own problems.[14]*

Rachel R., the only child of a suburban Atlanta couple, became suicidally depressed at age twenty. She was extremely intelligent and had already been accepted at a leading medical school. Much to her classmates' and her father's surprise, she was seriously considering not accepting the offer. She had also told her roommate that she had been "turning over in my mind killing myself." The roommate told Rachel's father, himself a psychiatrist, who arranged for counseling.

---

* Psychiatrist John Mack, co-author of *Vivienne*, pointed out that, to a degree, family problems were imposed upon Vivienne, but "this assumption of the pain of others was a feature of Vivienne's depression." The doctor traced it back to her feeling of inconsolable grief when her mother's father died.

During therapy, Rachel admitted to a deep, yet until then un-expressed, resentment of her father, who had remained mute in the face of a long-standing very unhealthy relationship between his wife and daughter.

Rachel's mother was a well-bred drug addict, hooked on the tranquilizers her husband had been prescribing for her since shortly after Rachel's birth. Rachel felt responsible for her mother's problems—a feeling her mother encouraged. Over the years, Mrs. R. had hinted that Rachel was "unplanned" and an enormous physical and emotional jolt to her delicate constitution and to the once affectionate relationship between her and Dr. R. The unspoken message Mrs. R. sent was that Rachel should ac-cept the lifelong responsibility of caring for her mother. In a per-version of the parent/child relationship, it was the mother who had the terrible fear of separation.

Cynthia Pfeffer and her colleagues at the Albert Einstein School of Medicine found that parents of the suicidal children they stud-ied had several characteristics in common—characteristics that normally would be associated with children. They were very de-pendent, they lacked the ability to delay gratification, they were subject to intense mood shifts, they were incapable of com-municating with or guiding their children.

The children struggled to maintain communication with the par-ents by identifying and commiserating with their moods. When their parents failed to parent, the children felt hopeless and worth-less and blamed themselves for family problems. "They often believed that they could solve the problems in the family," Pfeffer said, "and depreciated themselves when met with disappointment. Fantasies of escape from such disturbing circumstances were prev-alent. Often death was evidenced as a means of eliminating stress and attaining peace and satisfaction."

Saying that some parents act like children does not really an-swer the question, Why the rising teen suicide rate? There have, after all, always been immature and disturbed parents. But today, at the same time that increasing numbers of parents are with-drawing from their children, children are becoming ever more de-pendent on parents. As neighborhoods disintegrate, as churches lose their hold, as families scatter over the country, the only adults, besides teachers, with whom children have protracted contact, are their parents—or, more and more frequently, as divorce rates rise, their *parent*. If a parent lets a child down, there probably is no favorite aunt or understanding uncle or grandmother nearby to comfort and, most important, to talk to the child.

Life for the average teenager is becoming ever more impersonal, aimless, and lonely. Children *and* adolescents know very well that they are not yet capable of caring for themselves—physically or emotionally. They are, after all, still children. They need their parents. Many parents, preoccupied with their own agendas, seem to forget this fact as they push their children—at increasingly early ages, to grow up, to stop making demands and mistakes, to become mini-adults. Children need nurturing and love and they'll kill—themselves—to get it.

In Chapter 7 we'll discuss how the changes in the way the American family lives today have contributed to the rising tide of teen suicide. The changes are many, as we'll see. But the overriding change is this: Teaching our children to be self-reliant is one thing. But teaching them that they can rely *only* on themselves is quite another. The latter, unfortunately, is the lesson too many teens are learning.

7

Feeling Rootless and Valueless

Ron T. was thirteen when he moved with his family from a suburb of Cleveland to a suburb of Houston. He had lived in Shaker Heights, Ohio, for just three years before the latest move—a move his father made reluctantly, only after being informed by his supervisor that if he wasn't willing to grab the promotion at the Houston branch someone else would.

Mr. T. was reluctant to move because Ron, his only child, had shown severe adjustment problems after the last move. He still wrote nearly every day to the boy who had been his best friend in New Rochelle, New York, where he was born. He also wrote diligently to his grandmother in Brooklyn, to whom he had been very close and who was now dying.

From infancy until the move to Ohio at age ten, Ron had spent almost every day with his grandmother in the big old house in which she had raised Ron's father and her seven other children. Mrs. T. would drop her son at her mother-in-law's—in an old, working-class neighborhood—en route to her office in Manhattan.

"Houston is even further from New York than Shaker Heights was," was all Ron said when his father informed him the family would be moving. "I'll never see Grandma before she dies."

He was right. His beloved grandmother died two weeks after Ron's family arrived in Houston.

Although Ron hadn't been told, his grandmother had been living in a nursing home in Staten Island for nearly two years before her death. She was healthy, but she had grown somewhat forgetful and her children feared she would harm herself if allowed to continue living alone. None of the eight children, all of whom, except Ron's father, lived in Westchester County, invited her to move in with them. They claimed she would prefer the "independence" of a nursing home. Apparently not. She had not been in the home a week when her health began deteriorating and continued to do so at an alarmingly rapid pace.

After a funeral service for his grandmother at her parish church in Brooklyn, Ron walked to her house, just three blocks away. He arrived at the wrong moment. A few weeks before their mother's death, her children, unable to sell the drafty old house, had decided to raise the money to pay the taxes by selling her massive antique furniture. They hired a woman to run a house sale which, at the time of her death, had already been advertised, and so could not conveniently be postponed.

Ron saw a stranger walking out with the grandfather clock that had been standing in his grandmother's front hall since she had married sixty years before. To Ron the clock was like an old friend. In his mind, it was being mistreated as his grandmother had been mistreated. "I bet some stranger came in and carried Grandma out too," Ron accused his father, "and then stuck her someplace where she didn't know anyone, and she got so lonely she decided to let herself die."

In the days that followed the funeral, nearly every relative remarked to Mrs. T. that Ron seemed morose. "It's called the joys of turning fourteen," she quipped.

Ron was visibly depressed after returning to Houston, especially when his parents decided to leave their furniture in storage in Cleveland. They rented a furnished house from an oil executive who was living in Saudi Arabia for three years. To Ron, the arrangement was a pretty good hint that this would not be the last move.

"Why even bother to make friends?" he asked his parents. They didn't know how to answer him. One teacher later described Ron as a "morbid loner." Several of his classmates described him as an "eastern snob." On the rare occasions when he spoke in class, he ridiculed Houston and the way of life it represented. "Houston sprang up from the dust and one of these days it'll be blown away," Ron said angrily one day in history class. Under his breath he added, "Unfortunately, I won't be here to see it."

At age sixteen, Ron T. hanged himself from the branch of a massive white oak in the backyard of his parents' rented home. "This is the only thing around here that has any roots," he wrote in his suicide note.

Since 1897, when Émile Durkheim (considered the founder of sociology) wrote *Le Suicide,* experts have agreed that the person who has strong ties to the community is less likely to kill himself.

In a radical departure from then current theory, Durkheim argued that it is not the individual and his unconscious that prompts suicide but rather the individual's sense of isolation from the community. Durkheim described three types of social conditions that trigger suicide. (See the close of Chapter 8 for a full discussion.) In the first type, egoistic, the category into which most suicides of all ages fall, the individual has loose or nonexistent ties with his family, his community, and various local institutions such as the church, schools, social clubs, political organizations, etc. He ends up relying exclusively on himself for nurturing and support. He is a person who is profoundly lonely.

Durkheim's theory, although nearly a century old, still works. During the last decade, when the suicide rate began climbing in the suburbs, the theory seemed especially presentient. Durkheim's description of the egoistic environment fits the contemporary suburb so well that he might have formulated it in 1980, not 1897.

A single family is ensconced within its own house, on a street that, more likely than not, has no sidewalks—no means of encouraging spontaneous communication between neighbors. A child cannot walk to a friend's house. He must be driven. The sense of community suffers as job transfers and divorce create a rootless, "here today, gone tomorrow" atmosphere.

The extended family, with two or three generations living under one roof, is a thing of the past. Children see their grandparents rarely. When they do, they probably have to board a plane or wait for a special occasion when Mom or Dad will drive them into the city.

Children, who develop their values and goals by observing their parents, care increasingly about improving themselves instead of the community. Solitary, passive television watching, for many children, has replaced community projects, volunteerism, and even sports events.

Not surprisingly. The golden years of the 1950s, when life revolved around the kids, have faded. Suburbs today are closing schools, canceling park district activities, shutting down libraries. Adults are simply refusing to pay the increased taxes to support these programs, no matter what the effect of their loss on the children.

Obviously, the main reason for this trend is that people feel they are being taxed into bankruptcy. But also, many parents consider children's activities less important, as they push their children to grow up faster and faster. It's almost as if they want to shorten their terms as parents.

This need to have "adult" children is not confined to teenagers. Many parents would reject out of hand a nursery school that didn't offer reading training. Just playing, they say, is a waste of time. Little League and hockey and football have turned into serious business. Play well and eight years down the road an athletic scholarship may be waiting. Even summer camp is no longer just plain fun. The trend today is for camps to offer specialized and rigorous training in basketball or foreign languages or music or even computer technology.

Teenagers, dressed like miniature adults in the latest designer fashions, compete, at age fourteen, for dates and sex and grades and status. But physically and emotionally they are still children. Many pay a terrible price for the rush. When they stumble, as they will, too many have neither values nor understanding parents to cushion the fall.

The Demise of the Extended Family

Take a look around any suburb and you'll notice immediately that old people are few and far between. One reason is the demise of the extended family—the old way of living in which three generations and, perhaps, a couple of aunts, uncles, and cousins thrown in for good measure, lived under one roof.

The extended family protected each member from self-destructive impulses. The nuclear family—often with father *and* mother working—or, especially, the single-parent family offer far less protection and support. When they can't get along with their parents or their parents are too busy, young people benefit immensely by having an aunt or an uncle or grandparents nearby to whom they can turn for advice and solace. Otherwise, they have no one to turn to but their peers or, in too many cases, themselves.

The child who grows up separated from adult relatives other than his parents has a tougher time establishing friendships with adults—friendships that are as important to the teen's mental health as are his relationships with his peers.

Since the extended family has gone out of fashion, no alternative institution has filled the gap. The church—the obvious substitute for or complement to the family—has actually declined in influence.

Like the church, the neighborhood could sometimes fill in where the family left off. But close-knit neighborhoods—especially the ethnic enclaves of older industrial cities—are also disintegrating. Some were in the paths of expressways and others changed hands as whites took off for the suburbs. A suburban subdivision, like the one into which Ron and his parents moved, with its high rate of mobility, is a pale reflection of neighborhoods as they once were.

America on the Move

Recently, a teen suicide epidemic struck suburban Morris County, New Jersey, one of the fifteen wealthiest counties in the United States. Statewide, the rate remained stable, but in Morris County it almost doubled. Officials blamed affluence and transience—fathers, and now also mothers, climbing the corporate ladder, relentlessly uprooting their families.

For children of all ages, moving can be traumatic. An extreme example is Kevin, a twelve-year-old only child who had attended ten schools in five years. By the time he reached Evanston, Illinois, he had become totally withdrawn. Charles, a five-year-old who moved recently from a suburb of Philadelphia to a suburb of Chicago, entered treatment for sudden severe depression. He told the therapist that he felt he had lost all his best friends when he moved. She asked him to describe those friends and he described a bench in a neighbor's yard, the tree outside his window, and the steps leading up to his family's front door. In typically childlike fashion he had endowed normally inanimate objects with names and personalities.

Ruth, who attempted suicide at age seventeen, had a strong attachment for her old city neighborhood, on the South Side of Chicago, and truly suffered after her parents moved to the North Shore. They couldn't understand their then thirteen-year-old daughter's lack of enthusiasm for what they considered "The Big Move . . . everything my parents had lived for, something my mother never imagined could be."

If she had stayed on the South Side, she claimed, she wouldn't have attempted suicide. "I loved the South Side. Everyone was lower-to-middle-class and working toward sort of getting along. And then I moved to the north suburbs and saw wealth like I'd never seen before. When your father is making all this money and you're living in a big house, where are you, as a kid, supposed to go from there? And then they want to give you everything so you can have more. What's more? The definition was: There is never enough. Whatever you have is not enough. I don't know anybody's parents who didn't say this. . . . One thing is sure. No way will I *ever* live in the suburbs again. The norms and values are absurd. Everyone is alike. There are hardly even any old people. There's a feeling of futility, yet you're raised to think you're lucky."[1]

Materialism as a Way of Life

When the Chicago *Tribune Magazine,* which is circulated widely on Chicago's North Shore, carried an article on teen suicide, writer April Olzak opened by posing this question: "What can you do to prevent your child from becoming suicidally depressed and committing suicide? Don't make too much money, and don't live in certain high-status suburbs. It could kill your child."[2]

That is an exaggeration, but like many exaggerations, it contains an element of truth. The North Shore, like affluent suburbs across the nation, has more than its share of teen suicides.

As one social worker put it, "A person is expected to achieve and be successful here. For those not willing to meet these norms, the North Shore can be pretty brutal. There are no alternatives. . . . That's one of the reasons for the high suicide rate."

With success and sophistication come higher expectations—and, inevitably, disappointments. "People here want more from their social lives, marriages and children," said psychiatric social worker Stanley A. Levi. "By the very nature of their lifestyle, they often get less."

This emphasis on acquiring—keeping up with the proverbial Joneses—is still very much a part of suburban living. For the child whose father loses his job or suffers a financial setback or really never could afford the suburbs in the first place, life can be pure torture.

Diane K.'s parents moved from the southwest side of Chicago, a working-class area, to one of the wealthiest of the North Shore suburbs. They carefully chose that suburb for its well-regarded junior high school. But the high school was the real drawing card—New Trier East, one of the most prestigious in the country. They lived in an apartment building—one of the few in the suburb—just outside the exclusive central shopping district.

Diane soon began manufacturing illnesses and excuses not to go to school. Her clothes, her parents, and especially her address were just all wrong. She was hopelessly out of her league. "It's hard enough to get into the little cliques at New Trier," she explained, shortly after her first suicide attempt, "without living in the same building as everyone else's maid."

Diane longed to fit in and felt suicidal because she couldn't. But for children such as Ron T. or Ruth, who have known and loved other values in other places and who studiously avoid fitting in, the move to the suburbs can be equally upsetting.

"If you live in (my suburb), there are no limits to what you should have or what you should want," Ruth explained. "Like being the first. I remember when getting your kids CB radios to put in their bedrooms was The Thing, and minibikes, and being the first to have a Cuisinart, and the first to buy a condo in Florida, but now that's schlock, of course—now it's condos in Mexico. There's all this pressure to be more, have more, do more, have all the advantages your parents never had. Well, *not* having those advantages is what got them where they are."

North Shore social worker Isadora Sherman agreed, "If it's all given to them and all done for them, how can they prove their own abilities?"[3]

Because it's all given to them does not mean, of course, that there's no deprivation. The deprivation here is emotional, not material. The young people have good schools, spectacular houses, designer jeans, but they lack support, love, and caring parents. It's more elusive, but it's as real to these kids as the physical deprivation found in the ghetto.

In September 1980, *Time* ran an article on teen suicide on Chicago's North Shore, an area it dubbed "the suicide belt." "We have an outrageous number of suicides for a community our size," said Laurie Pfaelzer, then nineteen, of Glencoe, Illinois, who knew one student who slit his wrists and two who ran their cars into trees. "Growing up here, you're handed everything on a silver platter, but something else is missing. The one thing parents don't give is love, understanding, acceptance of you as a person."[4]

Where Have All the Values Gone?

To lack of understanding and acceptance, she might have added lack of values.

A North Shore girl named Robin, eighteen, who had overdosed on her mother's antidepressant medication, had been in intensive care for twenty-four hours and was released from the hospital after three days. She was referred to the outpatient section of the hospital. When she did not show up for her appointment, staff members tried unsuccessfully to reach her. Ten days later, the police brought her to the clinic because of her bizarre and withdrawn behavior in a local bowling alley.

When first seen, Robin kept repeating, "Stay away from me. I don't want any help. Anyway you're all nuts. Only creeps deal with kids like me." Patiently, the psychiatrist kept inquiring. After an hour, Robin broke into tears and cried nonstop for fifteen minutes. Then she looked up and asked, "Why in hell do you do it?" and smiled.

In subsequent daily sessions, Robin showed an unusual curiosity about the details of the psychiatrist's office. She asked about the Freud collected works, about the children's books on the ledge, about the photographs, about the stack of mail on the desk, even about the bookends and the flowers. The doctor answered each question factually and followed by inquiring into Robin's own thoughts. Robin seemed surprised that the psychiatrist had so many roots in her office. She often said, "You like that book too? How come?" The child psychiatrist answered that Winnie-the-Pooh and Eeyore were part of her literary family. Finally, in disbelief, Robin blurted, "I never knew people really cared about one thing more than another."

As the months passed, Robin worked through her memories of her family's vicissitudes and came to understand how her father's head injury and her mother's cyclic depressions had affected the family. When all was beginning to make sense, Robin observed, "But the worst thing about our family was that nobody helped us know who we were and what we stood for."

It then became clear that her curiosity about the office reflected her own emptiness. As she began to clarify her own values, she became less depressed, more outgoing and, in time, a child with a future.

Over and over, the adolescents we talked to—children from families that appear completely normal—groped for words to describe what they felt was a void in their lives—the lack of anything to stand for, of an altruistic goal, of a push to improve the community, the country, the world, of, in two words, "meaningful values."

Although most parents cheered when the youth rebellion of the 1960s fizzled—their children, after all, were on the barricades—they cheered too soon. The movement gave suburban youth an outlet for grievances, a sense of direction. Today, they are more self-indulgent. Over the years, most of the hippies who gave up material goods in their struggle to redistribute the wealth have disappeared into corporations and law firms and business schools. To the suburban generation now coming up—many of whom are children of the 1960s hippies—any type of alternative lifestyle seems unattainable. There is an increasing stress on getting what your parents have. Changing the world no longer seems possible.

The teen suicide rate was lower in the 1960s, probably because of the sense of community the antiwar movement generated. There's simply nothing left to distract today's teen. Unlike their grandparents and parents who could rally around keeping the world safe from fascism and communism, and go to war to do it, today's teen has no great cause or ideal to preoccupy him; leaving him to brood over deficiencies in himself and his relationships.

(During past national wars, there was a significant drop in suicide rates among people of all ages. They were buoyed by patriotism, by purpose, and they could find a socially acceptable, even laudatory, reason for venting their aggression. The Vietnam War was a special case, but it too brought down the suicide rate—mainly because of the opportunity it afforded young people to protest, to strive for some goal greater than getting better grades, clothes, cars, and rock concert tickets.)

In 1981, the results of a poll of 160,000 teens were published in *The Private Life of the American Teenager*. When asked, "What do you want most in life?" only 9 percent said they wanted to "do something worthwhile for the world."[5]

Similarly, in a survey of nearly 300,000 college freshmen conducted in 1982 (by UCLA and the American Council on Education), 63.3 percent said that being well off was very important. In 1967, when the same question was asked, 43.5 percent said being well off was very important. In 1967, 82.9 percent chose the goal of "developing a meaningful philosophy of life," but in 1982 only 49 percent chose that goal.

Television—Breeding Passivity and Violence

After the move to Houston, Ron T., the boy described at the opening of this chapter, spent most of his time watching television —exclusively old movies, which seemed to give him the connection with the past, for which he so desperately longed.

Ron's television watching habits further alienated him from his peers. He had no time for athletics or riding his bike or playing video games or just hanging around. And because he refused to watch the new shows, he did not speak the same TV language as his classmates. They had one less thing in common.

Ron's is something of an unusual case. Unlike most children he did not grow up with television. His grandmother, with whom he spent so much time, did not own a set and stubbornly refused her children's offers to buy her one. (This was a present her children were eager to give her because their children balked at missing their favorite shows while visiting Grandma.)

Ron became addicted to television to fill a void in his life, to maintain a connection with the past—a connection that was becoming increasingly tenuous—and to keep himself from worrying about the future. Most children today become addicted to television before they even realize what they're missing by sitting, staring at a screen.

In 1975, Kenneth Keniston, chairman of the Carnegie Council on Children, denounced television as "this flickering blue parent occupying more of the waking hours of a child than any other single influence."

On the average, children between ages two to five watch television over thirty hours a week. A substantial number, measured in the millions, are glued to the set for sixty or more hours a week.

To put those statistics in context, in many homes, nearly all a preschooler's waking hours are spent watching television. Maria Piers, author with Genevieve Millet Landau of *The Gift of Play: And Why Young Children Cannot Thrive Without It,* wrote that the danger of television lies not in the quality of the programs children watch, but in the quantity. "As kittens naturally spend most of their first months playing—that is, practicing to be cats—so children naturally spend most of their first years playing—that is practicing to be mature human beings."[6]

Television substitutes passivity for play and "subjects the child to a bombardment of sound and pictures at a pace he cannot control or alter." When a child is read a story, he has to use his imagination to make up his own images of people and events. A child will often ask to go back and reread a section or to stop and talk about it. None of that, obviously, is possible when watching television.

Few thoughtful adults would claim that television is a boon to childhood development, but that doesn't make it a killer either. How is television related to suicide? First, let's consider how it's not related.

We hear occasionally about some grisly television-related death. In late 1980, for example, the Chicago *Tribune* reported that a suburban kindergartner hanged himself by accident while imitating the acrobatic stunts of one of his television heroes, the Incredible Hulk. The body of five-year-old Gregg Vogel was discovered in his closet bedroom by his father. Gregg's bathrobe sash was wrapped over a clothes rod. When his mother put him to bed the night before, he was wearing an Incredible Hulk T-shirt. He was still wearing the shirt when his father found the body.[7]

A tragic accident such as this is just that—an accident. Even incidents that can be more directly linked to television are isolated cases. Not many children commit suicide for the reason a Minneapolis youth named Eddie Seidel, Jr., did. When his favorite show, "Battlestar Galactica" was canceled, he said he had no reason left to live and jumped from a bridge two hundred feet to his death.

The link between television and suicide is less direct, but there is a link. Television creates a limited frustration tolerance. The viewer lives a lifetime in a half hour. A struggle that, in reality, would take three years to resolve, in TV land takes three minutes. Whatever the predicament, no matter how complicated, even unsolvable, it gets solved before the next prime-time show hits the air. Life just doesn't work that way.

Television leads children to expect quick answers. They don't understand that life is a struggle. It leads them to demand immediate gratification, to think that they can achieve any goal instantly without first working and failing and working and failing again. It leads to a decline in rational thought, analysis, reflection, and patience. (Researchers estimate that young people spend about 20,000 hours in front of the television and only about 11,000 hours in the classroom.)

A Nielsen survey agreed that a typical high school graduate has logged about 20,000 hours before the television screen—more time than he has spent on any other activity except sleep. At present levels, the researchers said, he will have been exposed to 350,000 commercials and vicariously participated in 18,000 killings.

Children who are relentlessly bombarded by video violence learn to accept violence in the most matter-of-fact way. Children may at first be frightened, just as they'd be frightened by a book with a violent story. But unlike reading, the child is powerless to stop the violence on the screen. The program proceeds at a predetermined pace, leaving him out of control and, eventually, numbed. Violence becomes a part of his everyday world.

On October 21, 1981, Dr. Thomas Radecki, a psychiatrist from Illinois, testified before a congressional committee investigating television violence. "I can comfortably estimate that 25–50 percent of the violence in our society is coming from the culture of violence being taught by our entertainment media, most strongly by the television and movie industries. This estimate is based on solid research findings."

When local television stations began airing *The Deer Hunter,* a movie about Vietnam that contains a scene in which U.S. soldiers and Vietnamese play Russian roulette with a loaded pistol, there were reports of people (mostly men in their teens and twenties) shooting themselves in the head within a couple of days of watching the movie. As of December 1981 there were twenty-seven documented cases of self-inflicted wounds. Twenty-four people died from their wounds.*

Television, as any hassled parent will admit, is the best and cheapest baby-sitter. Everyone knows the mother who chats on the phone while parking her children in front of the screen. Everyone knows the father who, left home on a Saturday to baby-sit, putters around the house while his children sit mesmerized by cartoons in the morning and old movies in the afternoon. Everyone knows the family that watches television over dinner, not talking to each other except to grunt, "Change the channel," or "Pass the beans."

The relationship with parents and siblings suffers. Research

* Dr. Radecki, who launched a crusade against television violence, attempted to pressure stations into either canceling the movie or deleting the Russian roulette scenes. To make his case, he presented to station managers documentation of the twenty-seven incidents. So far, he has gotten nowhere. He warned the station manager in New York. The film was shown anyway and two young men killed themselves. A similar sequence of events occurred in Washington, D.C., and in Chicago, where two young men, both sitting at their kitchen tables, shot themselves in the head. Both died.

conducted at the University of Minnesota has shown that families who watch a lot of television tend to exhibit a high level of inter-personal tension. The researchers suggested that many families use television as a means of escaping conflict.

The most insidious effect of television is that it inhibits children from flowering individually. It's what they don't get to because of television that should concern us greatly. In many families, there is no family game playing—TV is easier. There is no reading out loud, no book heroes or plots to worry over all week long, no characters to grow up with as cherished companions, as projections of one's own fantasies.

"Freedom's Just Another Word for Nothin' Left to Lose"

Rock singer Janis Joplin, who died at age twenty-seven of an overdose of heroin, after suffering through depression and terrible insecurity, belted out a line in her hit "Me and Bobby McGee" that teenagers innately understood. "Freedom's just another word for nothin' left to lose" can serve as an epitaph for this generation, children who are given much too much freedom much too soon.

Although any outsider would have found Joanne B.'s family perfectly normal, she was convinced that her parents didn't care about her. "They're both college professors, and they must have read somewhere that adolescents should have complete freedom—or maybe they just don't want the hassle of raising a kid. My friends are all heavily into drugs and I'm getting pushed that way too. We were smoking grass in the living room, and my dad walked right by, sniffed the air and went into his study. He didn't say a word."

The school psychologist spoke to Joanne's parents, following her near-fatal suicide attempt, explaining that they were giving their daughter everything but the attention and direction she craved. "They took him seriously," Joanne said, "I guess because he's an adult and he has a couple of degrees. When I went out last night, my mom actually asked where I was going—and listened when I told her."

A teenager asking for a curfew? Yes, most teenagers want their parents to be parents. They want guidelines, standards, stability, they want to know where they stand. Fewer and fewer parents are offering such direction. They can't decide between being their child's parent or his best friend. "The unhappiest kids in the world are those with the least parental supervision," said Bill Gregory, who, as Director of the Excelsior Youth Center in Denver, has seen more than his share of troubled youngsters.

A British nanny who worked for families on the North Shore of Chicago put it as well as any of the experts: ". . . Americans are afraid to discipline their children. They're terrified of losing the friendship of their children or of not being loved."[8]

Pediatrician T. Berry Brazelton, the Dr. Spock of this generation, said basically the same thing. "In the 50s and 60s parents were afraid of being disciplinarians. That left the kids high and dry. Now I think we have come to the realization that a parent's role is really to show the youngster discipline. . . . At the point their child gets provocative and the parent knows he or she is looking for a limit, the parent had better be sure to provide it. And the child will be reassured for having limits set. Children need limits spelled out for them. It is the only way they learn."[9] And, he might have added, the only way they build strength of character.

Too many parents expect that the minute children hit thirteen they should be capable of making it on their own. In reality, teenagers need as much support and direction at that time in their lives as they needed when they were toddlers.

"I hear kids complain all the time, 'My parents don't care what I do,'" lamented Susan Bender, a social worker on Chicago's North Shore. "Parents out here don't realize they need to say, 'Stop.' The kids will go further and further in testing us. They want us to order them to stop."

Susan Bevis, who works at one of the North Shore drop-in centers, observed, "Kids tend to be real clear about wanting limits. They want rules and regulations here and they want to be involved in setting them. (The drop-in center's board is split between adults and children.) They don't want carte blanche to tear the place apart. Many of them absolutely insist on rules because they just aren't getting any at home."

Lynn Joanis, another social worker on the North Shore, recalled one of the regulars at the local drop-in center. She was picked up by the police one winter night wearing only a halter top, very tight pants, and white boots, chomping on gum, with a cigarette hanging out of her mouth. The police, understandably, thought she was a hooker—a rare sight in this affluent suburb. Joanis explained that the girl's free-wheeling parents were her major problem. They allowed her to sleep with her boyfriend in her own bed and, when she threw a party, free access to her father's liquor cabinet.

John Dooley is the manager of a roller rink, Skate Castle, in Loveland, Colorado. In the county that encompasses Loveland, there have been twelve cases of adolescent suicide in the last eighteen months. "I call up some of the parents to come and get their kids," Dooley said sadly, "and this is the answer I get. 'You got 'em. They'll find their own way home.' "[10]

Parental permissiveness is an act of neglect, not love. It produces insecure children, not independent ones. It produces children who will continue to test their parents until they finally meet with resistance.

John, just sixteen, asked his father for the car while an ice storm raged. His father handed him the keys and John, as he skidded down the ice-slicked streets, was deeply hurt and insulted. Another boy we interviewed, eighteen-year-old Jamie, was devastated when he sent home a parental permission form required for a sky-diving course and received back the signed form by return mail.

Hurried Children

Carolyn P.'s mother took her daughter to a psychiatrist after finding a suicide note in her nightstand drawer. She happened upon the note while searching for a barrette for Carolyn to wear to an interview for private music lessons. It was characteristic of this mother's approach to child rearing that she first confronted the eleven-year-old girl with the note and, after the girl sobbingly admitted she wrote it—and meant it—made her go to the interview anyway. "We don't quit in this household," she said. "We carry through on our obligations."

Carolyn's most pressing problem was that she simply had too many obligations. Her schedule was exhausting. It left no time for napping or daydreaming or playing or making friends. She was taking, besides accelerated courses in school, ballet and cello and tennis and private French lessons. She was signed up for a private foreign exchange program which meant that, the next summer, at age twelve, she would be traveling alone to Paris to stay with a French family. She had been prepared for this experience by spending the last three summers—eight weeks per year—at a language camp in upstate New York; a camp at which only French was spoken. (The regimen really started at age three, when Mrs. P. enrolled her in a program that promised to instruct preschoolers to speak—and read—in two languages.)

Carolyn's father worked for the UN, and her mother, at age thirty-seven, was the first female partner in her Wall Street law firm. They were both very busy people, the father too busy to get involved with Carolyn or her thirteen-year-old brother, Carter, and the mother also, if only she had admitted it. Mrs. P. wanted to be a good mother but simply didn't have the time. Keeping her daughter fully scheduled, busy, busy, busy, was her way of resolving this basic conflict. In the bargain, she produced a daughter who was remarkably precocious and accomplished.

Several years earlier, Carter had rebelled against his mother and her plans and ambitions and was now spending all his free time hanging around with his friends and doing embarrassingly mediocre school work. Carolyn was too compliant by nature to rebel openly. Besides, it was very important to her to win her mother's approval—and the love she hoped would come with it.

Carolyn was one of the youngsters who described herself as feeling like a marionette, with her mother pulling, constantly pulling, the strings and screaming at her daughter, "Hurry, hurry, faster, faster, more, more!"

Sigmund Freud was, perhaps, the first psychiatrist to worry about parents pushing their children to grow up too fast. In 1910, during a discussion of "Suicide in Children" before the Vienna Psychoanalytic Society, the founder of psychoanalysis observed that teachers, in their zeal to wean children from early family life, often exposed the immature student too abruptly to the severities of adult life.

He would be horrified to see that today parents, more than teachers, demand that their children act like little adults. Too many parents are placing a dangerously high value on independence in children—a value that conflicts with our biological heritage. Children, as we'll see in Chapter 8, can suffer terribly if a parent tries to prematurely loosen the bond by sending a child too early to summer camp, to pajama parties, for weekends away.

Psychology professor David Elkind, who has written a book on the subject, explains that hurried children are peculiar to our times. Whereas spoiled children were the rule in the 1950s—children who were indulged, undisciplined, and babied—hurried children are pushed to grow up too fast, to achieve, to assume adult responsibilities at age twelve, thirteen, or fourteen, before they are emotionally and intellectually ready. Thrown into the adult world, these children are overwhelmed, terrified, and sometimes self-destructive. Consciously or unconsciously, their parents may want to be free of their dependents so they can pursue their own goals.

These are the parents who complain about nursery schools in which children do nothing but play and kindergartens that don't feature reading and math as part of the "curriculum." "I'm not a romantic or sentimental about it," one young father told us. "Winning is the name of the game and my son will be better off learning that lesson sooner rather than later." The son about whom he spoke was three years old.

With this sort of background, not surprisingly, the hurried adolescent is frequently the one suffering severe anxiety about academic success. He may salve this anxiety by using drugs or she may get pregnant to prove she can accomplish something adult. As these "remedies" make things worse, suicide may become another "adult" option.

Elkind, a professor of Child Study at Tufts University, pointed out that the "in" way to dress children today—in "miniature versions of adult clothing," such as Lacoste shirts, Calvin Klein and Pierre Cardin jeans—is a reflection of our need to see children as scaled-down adults. Thirty years ago, prepubescent boys wore short pants until they began to shave. Girls were not permitted to wear makeup or sheer stockings until they were in their teens. Clothing "set children apart. It signaled to adults that these people were to be treated differently, perhaps indulgently; it made it easier for children to act as children."[11]

The mother of a ten-year-old boy who attends an exclusive private school in Chicago complained that in her son's class, one girl tossed a birthday party at an ultra-expensive restaurant. Another hosted an overnight swimming party at a posh hotel. When they do those things at the age of ten and eleven," she asked, "what can they have to look forward to when they're older?"

"Drugs and sex" is one obvious answer. Not all young people are spending their afterschool hours studying the cello or ballet. Many more are searching for something grown-up and no longer clearly forbidden to give a kick, and some meaning, to their lives.

The statisticians tell us that almost one of every three teens in the United States can be classified as a problem drinker. When surveyed, 40 percent of high school students said they had five or more drinks in a row during the last two weeks. The age at which they started drinking is also dropping. Half of those teens who are classified as problem drinkers started drinking when they were thirteen.

Drug use is equally popular. Six in ten high school seniors have had some experience with marijuana. Thirty percent have tried cocaine. Ten percent of all high school seniors get high every day.

Eight in ten boys and seven in ten girls have had sexual intercourse during their teen years. One third of America's teenagers have had sexual intercourse by their fifteenth birthday. Forty percent of the girls who are now fourteen will be pregnant at least once during the next five years.

Like Carolyn, who was overdosing on lessons, the alcohol, drug, and sex abusers also become exhausted, jaded, and scared. Lisa Owens, director of Talkline, a Chicago suburban crisis hotline, said that many of the young people who call the hotline complain that "they've done it all already. They're fifteen years old and they've done drugs and had sex and it hasn't been all that it's cracked up to be." They too feel they have nothing to look forward to.

We recently saw a seventeen-year-old boy who was referred to the clinic by a youth worker in a drug center. She was concerned that "he had tried it all and was still depressed." The boy was taut, thin-lipped, ashen in color, and spoke of "two bad trips," years of drug abuse, no sense of family involvement, and the feeling that, "People who try to help are cardboard."

Many young people, instead of trying desperately to match an image held up by their parents, try to match one held up by the media. Erin, fifteen, was one of the suicide attempters interviewed on a recent television show on teen suicide. In her Omaha, Nebraska, junior high school gym, she swallowed thirty-six phenobarbital pills, climbed into her locker, and shut the door. If her gym teacher hadn't noticed the edge of her dress sticking out, she would have died.

Erin recalled that just before she took the pills, she looked at herself in the mirror and said, " 'This is it, you ugly bitch!' I said it right to myself. I said it right to the mirror. I just really—I felt that way."[12] Like her peers all over the country, Erin thought that, at age fifteen, she should have the poise and looks of a TV or movie star, of a cover girl. Another girl who had attempted suicide put it this way, "There's a lot of pressure in the media to be like Brooke Shields. You can't get away from that face on the billboards. I'm attractive, but I'm not going to be on any billboard. It's an unattainable goal."

The Gifted Child Is Still a Child

One of the myths of suicide, as we discussed in Chapter 2, is that there is a certain type of child who kills himself—the stereotypes range from the school dropout to the genius. In reality, all sorts of students from all sorts of families with all levels of IQ commit suicide.

But, still, it is true that many of the young people who attempt or complete suicide fall into the category of gifted students. The mistake that parents of these children frequently make is in assuming that intellectually precocious children are also emotionally precocious. They're not. The fourth-grader who reads at the twelfth-grade level is, emotionally, still in the fourth grade.

Bill and Jean Casey, whose seventeen-year-old son, Shaun,

killed himself, talked about the problems of raising a gifted child on a recent "Phil Donahue Show." "Unfortunately," Jean said, "with a gifted child . . . you say, 'Wow, they are gifted, they are intelligent,' and you put a label on them and you don't realize that they intellectually may be very intelligent but socially and emotionally they may be seven years old."

"I think that was our big mistake," agreed Bill. "He was a tall, strong, handsome kid, physically mature. He was obviously intellectually above his age level . . . but emotionally, you know, that aspect we didn't figure into it. He is a big, smart kid. He's an adult. He wasn't."[13]

Dallas Egbert shot himself to death at age seventeen. Even as a toddler, his brilliance was obvious. He knew his alphabet at age two, he could read at three, he finished high school at fourteen and he entered Michigan State University at fifteen. Intellectually he was a genius; emotionally he was a baby. His brilliance coupled with his physical immaturity (he regularly skipped grades in school) resulted in his being shunned by his classmates.

That fourth-grader who reads at the twelfth-grade level still needs other fourth-graders for friends. The problem, often, is that he simply can't relate to other nine-year-olds. And so he becomes a loner, preferring books or special interests to friends. The more he retreats into intellectual activities, the less chance he'll ever make friends.

After Dallas' death, his family received condolences from other parents of gifted children. One sympathizer was Mary Connelly, a mother of seven children whose IQs ranged from 130 to 150, five of whom had contemplated suicide. Another mother wrote of a six-year-old son who felt as if he were "in an iron cage" because his mind had developed so much faster than his body. Another told of a son who said he was so alienated from his peers that "he could understand just how Dallas Egbert felt." And still another described a son so troubled by his failure to communicate even with his own family that he killed himself four days before Dallas did.[14]

"When I talked to them at the L.A. County Suicide Prevention Center," Mrs. Casey said, "they said 10 percent of these gifted seniors and freshmen in college are walking around feeling suicidal. . . . The difference is a coach or a counselor or somebody. Another adult who relates to them . . ."[15]

"I should have picked up on it," said Dallas' father. "I just didn't see how he could be so brilliant and not be good at coping with social situations."

"Childhood's End"

In an essay entitled "Childhood's End," novelist Scott Spencer wrote that children today have lost their status, their élan. "What is it like to be a child at a time when society is virtually obsessed by the notion that there are too many children in the world? Whereas the postwar Golden Age of childhood occurred when babies were welcome and even the privileged classes partially measured their fortune in children, there is now an overwhelming, crushing consensus among nations that the world's resources cannot support continued population growth.

"Interesting enough, this desire to limit the number of children born is most fervently expressed in our own country, with its vast wealth, its open spaces, and its birthrate markedly down." History's fair-haired flower children have passed into middle age, and in their place "comes a changeling generation that may be the most disturbed and demoralized in this century."

Indeed, never in recent memory has it been less a privilege to be young in America.† "Parents who two decades ago were willing to suffer genuine material hardships in order to have and raise children are now judiciously balancing the needs of yet another generation against their own desire for a country house, a larger air conditioner, a microwave oven . . ."[16]

It seemed a regrettable but predictable sign of the times when, in the late summer of 1980, a New Jersey couple was arrested for trying to trade their fourteen-month-old son for a three-year-old black and silver Corvette valued at $8,800. They left the baby on the showroom floor while they negotiated the deal. The car dealer at first was going to make the deal but later changed his mind and called the police.

† Psychiatrist Derek Miller, chief of the Adolescent Program at Northwestern University's Institute of Psychiatry, said that for adolescents this is the worst time to be growing up since the Middle Ages when the bubonic plague created chaos.

And that was far from the only sign. In September 1980, an official of a welfare agency in the Washington, D.C., suburbs reported that troublesome children thrown out by parents (called "throwaways" by social workers) comprise a large and growing portion of their case load. The director of a shelter for runaway and throwaway kids said, "The whole sixties idea of 'do your own thing' has moved into the seventies and eighties with disposable relationships—if it doesn't work, if it's not perfect, I want something else." Sister Dolores Gartanutti of New York's Noah's Ark Shelter calls this "the Kleenex mentality." "We live in a society where we use things and just throw them away. I swear, a lot of people have this attitude toward kids."[17] "At least once a week," a social worker reported, "a parent drives up and drops off a child with a suitcase and a quick good-bye."

Robert Frost's description of the family in his poem "The Death of a Hired Man" is no longer accurate. "Home is the place where when you have to go there, they have to take you in." That kind of family is increasingly rare. If they don't like you in your family nowadays, you just might get kicked out.

The director of a runaway center in McLean, Virginia, observed that the average age of the throwaway child coming to the center has dropped from fourteen to twelve.‡ And there's another notable switch in the sort of child that people who work with runaways and throwaways are seeing. More and more are coming from "good" homes, from solidly middle-class homes. Carter P., the son of the diplomat and the lawyer, who rebelled against his father's neglect and his mother's ambition, eventually ran away from home and ended up, clear across the country, in a runaway shelter in the Bay area of California.

Richard G. was born and raised in Houston. His father was a middle-rung corporate executive for an oil company, his mother a housewife. Richard, his two brothers, and his parents lived in a spanking-new subdivision that hadn't even existed five years before. The family was solidly middle-class.

Unbeknownst to his family, Mr. G. had been having an affair

‡ According to the latest report from the United States Department of Health and Human Services, the average runaway is 15—a drop of one year from the 1976 average. It is estimated that each year more than one million youngsters between ten and seventeen leave or are forced to leave home.

with a secretary in his office. He had repeatedly promised the woman, who was supporting three of her children from an earlier marriage, that he would divorce his wife, marry her, and adopt her children. When she realized he never would, she went public with the affair. Mrs. G. eventually filed for divorce. The secretary created such a scandal in the company that she was fired, and Mr. G. was transferred to the company's Atlanta office.

Mrs. G., who was extremely religious and almost morbidly concerned about what others thought of her, made it very difficult for her ex-husband to see his sons. He seemed only too happy to accede to her wishes. For Mr. G. was practically broke. He had to take a demotion in status and pay to stay with the company, and he was being drained by alimony and child support. He had no reserve savings, for the money his wife thought was going into savings was really going into expensive gifts for his girlfriend and her children. Within a year after he moved out of the house, his visits and then his phone calls stopped. Soon the only contact Richard and his brothers had with their father was an occasional letter or, more likely, a postcard.

Even after the scandal had ceased to be much of a scandal, Richard, who was fourteen at the time of the divorce, felt terribly humiliated. He felt that everyone was laughing at him, or, worse yet, feeling sorry for a boy whose father didn't love him enough to stick around. He ran away several times to escape the imagined gossip and also the responsibilities newly thrust upon him. Richard's mother and her relatives repeatedly told him that, as the eldest, it was his responsibility to be the man of the house, to take care of his mother.

What bothered Richard most and what finally triggered his first suicide attempt was the feeling that he had lost his father forever—not through death, which would have been relatively easy for the boy to accept, but through divorce, through his father's free choice. The loss, Richard decided, was simply more than he could bear. He would rather die, than live with the feeling that his father didn't love him.

In the final chapter of this section—"An Unbearable Loss"—we shall discuss several cases like Richard's, in which the child who loses a parent through death or divorce comes to feel an emptiness that is, quite literally, lethal.

8

An Unbearable Loss

In analyzing the multitude of reasons why a child kills himself, one reason is omnipresent. The young person suffers a loss that, in the moments before he swallows the pills or puts the rope around his neck, seems to make life empty of meaning, hope, of reason to go on.

The loss may be a literal one, the death of a parent, a best friend, a sibling. More likely, though, the loss is less literal. Parents get divorced or both mother and father become totally absorbed in their careers. The child feels a loss of their full-time love.

Examining case histories of children who commit suicide reveals a striking commonality. They frequently have lost the one and only person in the world they feel they can confide in—the one person they feel understands them, cares about them. Often the person has not died. He has, worse yet, rejected the teenager or moved away or begun giving all his love to someone else.

The loss does not necessarily have to be another person. The young person may feel that he is losing the part of himself that made him worthwhile; that made him competent and admirable. He may feel, for example, that he has lost his identity because his life and status and goals revolved around being a star football player. When he gets permanently thrown off the team for cheating on an exam, he feels stripped down to nothing. "I may as well be dead," he says, and means it.

Divorce—a Nightmare for the Children

The United States now has the highest divorce rate in the world, one divorce for every two marriages. If we look at the statistics for divorce and teen suicide, we see a startling and shocking parallel. In the last twenty years in the United States, both the number of divorces granted and the number of young suicides committed have tripled.

Coincidence? Probably not. Too many carefully conducted studies show that most young suicides are children of divorce. In one recent study, 71 percent of young suicide attempters came from broken homes. An even higher percentage came from "disturbed" homes in which families moved frequently, quarreled, had severe financial problems, homes in which one parent was absent, alcoholic, or institutionalized, or homes in which there was conflict with a stepparent.

Dr. Joseph D. Teicher of the University of Southern California conducted research on young suicides in Los Angeles County. He found that:

- 72 percent had one or both natural parents absent from home.
- 84 percent of those with stepparents wanted them to leave.
- 58 percent had a parent who was married more than once.

A study at New York's Bellevue Hospital of 102 teens who attempted suicide showed that only one third of them lived with both parents. Psychiatrist Barry Garfinkel studied the family backgrounds of 505 young suicide attempters who were treated, over a seven-year period, at the Hospital for Sick Children in Toronto. He compared their family lives with a control group of youngsters admitted to the same emergency room for non-suicide-related reasons. More than half of the families of the suicide attempters had an absent parent. In one quarter of these families both parents were absent.

For an adolescent, divorce is harder to accept than death. Death is final—an irrevocable separation. Divorce means tortuous memories lingering for years, the beloved parent dropping in and out of a child's life, and the child's terrible fear that he was somehow responsible for the split; that if his parents really loved him they would have stayed together. "Did Dad leave because he didn't like me, because I was too demanding, why?" the child asks. Divorce means a reopening of the wound if Dad dates other women, and a twist of the knife in the wound if he remarries, especially if the woman has her own children.

Even the smallest children are aware of tensions and disputes between their parents. (They are particularly sensitive to their mother's moods.) Debbie, age four, and toilet-trained since age two, started wetting the bed and becoming increasingly irritable and dependent during her parents' divorce. Craig, age five, had been sleeping through the night since he was two months old. Suddenly he started waking repeatedly.

We are talking about huge numbers of children who are under some divorce-related stress. Sixty percent of the couples getting divorced each year have children under eight. In August 1982 the Census Bureau released figures showing that one of every five children younger than eighteen lived in a one-parent home—54 percent more than in 1970. Statisticians predict that during the next decade, 48 percent of schoolchildren will have lived a portion of their childhood in a one-parent home.

No matter how sensitively handled or amiable a divorce (most divorces, of course, are neither sensitively handled nor amiable, as parents struggle with their own wrenching problems), a child feels awfully guilty. And too often he feels guilty for good reason, as one or both parents blatantly or subtly accuse the child of being a cause of the divorce.

Jennie is a fourteen-year-old we interviewed recently. Her parents were getting divorced and she blamed herself. "I have dyslexia (impairment of the ability to read) and my parents had to put me in a private school that costs a couple of thousand a year. When they fought it was almost always over money." Jennie's father regularly mentioned her dyslexia as one of the most intolerable expenses. "Finally, my Dad got fed up and left," Jennie explained.

Some parents use the threat of divorce to control a child's behavior—which invariably makes the child feel responsible when the
split comes. John Killinger described Tommy, who was only five
years old the first time he heard his parents discuss divorce. Realizing he had overheard the conversation and that he was utterly
terrified, his mother used that knowledge as a weapon to keep
Tommy in line. "Now, Tommy, you must be quiet and not annoy
your father, or he will go away and leave us." When his parents
did divorce, five years later, Tommy was certain he was responsible. Two years later, twelve-year-old Tommy made his first suicide
attempt. He was unhappy, he later told his therapist, because he
was failing in school,* he didn't have any friends, and he was tired
of moving (his father was constantly late with the child-support
payments and his mother moved her family frequently—to ever
smaller apartments and drearier neighborhoods).

Divorce can hold no end of horrors for a child. In the battles
that precede the breakup, a father, for example, may attack his
wife by attacking their child. Adults seem to believe sometimes
that children—even teenagers—won't hear or won't understand.
They almost always do.

Shortly before the divorce, the father of Bart, sixteen, accused
his wife of having done a totally incompetent job of raising Bart.
"I never realized how much my father hated me," Bart said, "until
he attacked her for the job she had done with me. According to
him, I was dumb, cowardly, lazy, undirected—unattractive in every
single way." When Bart attempted suicide a year later, he blamed
himself for the breakup of his parents' marriage and said it proved
he was "worthless" and "harmful to the health of anyone unlucky
enough to know me."

On the ABC "Nightline" program on teen suicide, newsman

---

* Failure in school, a problem that frequently plagues suicidal children, is
more common among children whose parents have divorced. In a 1980 study,
researchers compared the behavior and achievements of 18,244 students, some
from one-parent and some from two-parent homes. Thirty-six percent of the
children from two-parent families were high achievers, compared to only 9
percent of the children from one-parent families. Twenty-two percent of the
children from two-parent families were below average; 41 percent of the children from one-parent families.

Children from one-parent families were also more likely to be discipline
problems. They were three times as likely to be suspended from school and
twice as likely to drop out of school.

George Strait reported on another fallout of divorce by describing the suicide attempt of one boy who felt his parents were forcing him to choose sides. "So you feel," Strait asked, "like you had to . . . choose between your mother and your father?"

"I sort of feel sometimes," the boy answered, "that the fights that go between my Dad and my mother . . . pull me apart. . . . So it's like I've got to choose sides. . . . I can't—it's difficult for me to just stay in the middle . . . and be pulled from side to side. . . . I was asking for help . . . by attempting suicide. . . . And that's why I told my mom, you know, sort of asking for help in a way."[1]

A ten-year-old North Shore girl, in treatment for depression, called divorce "emotional cancer" in this poem which she wrote and showed to her therapist.

> Divorce shakes you off the ground,
> Divorce whirls you all around,
> Divorce makes you all confused,
> Divorce forces you to choose.
> Divorce makes you feel all sad.
> Divorce pushes you to be mad.
>
> Divorce makes you wonder who cares,
> Divorce leaves you thoroughly scared.
> Divorce makes a silent home,
> Divorce leaves you all alone.
>
> Divorce is supposed to be an answer
> Divorce, in fact, is emotional cancer.

Few things are as important to the healthy development of an adolescent as a strong self-image. In the aftermath of divorce, unfortunately, a self-image can get battered to the point of terminal weakness.

As Doctor Sula Wolff has observed, when a parent dies, it is rare for the surviving parent to speak ill of his mate. If anything, the dead parent's bad qualities are forgotten and some good ones amplified. The child's self-image is protected, even enhanced by the memory, the glorification really, of his dead parent. Divorce is different. Because the children still usually stay with the mother, the father is often presented to his children as bad. The bitterness does not necessarily diminish as the divorce becomes final, so the child is left not only without a parent but with the image of a "bad" parent. The child of the same sex as the "bad" parent invariably identifies with him. The mother often fosters this identification in a negative way by, every time the son does something distasteful to her, charging, "You're just like your father."†

Ira H. was twelve when his parents divorced. Theirs was an extremely bitter breakup, with a protracted battle over custody of Ira and his younger sister, Amy.

Eventually Mrs. H. won custody but not before a court battle in which her lawyer tried to prove that Mr. H. was an adulterer and gambler. It was a bittersweet victory for Mrs. H., because she did not enjoy taking care of children. Several relatives and neighbors testified that Mr. H., despite his alleged moral lapses, was a far more loving, giving parent.

Having to go out to work to support her family did not sweeten Mrs. H.'s opinions of her ex-husband. She seldom missed a chance to tell her children how rotten their father was. Amy seemed oblivious to the comments and enjoyed her Sundays with her father, who always took the children to an exotic spot and then out for their favorite food.

But Ira was different. Although he adored his father, and felt much more comfortable with him than with his mother, he also felt guilty, terribly guilty, for not sharing his mother's opinion of his father—for not being able to commiserate with her, for not feeling more appreciative of the financial and social sacrifices she made to support the family.

As the years passed and the physical and personality resemblance between father and son grew stronger, Mrs. H. went into more explicit detail about Ira's father's deficiencies. Ira suspected that the attacks were really attacks on him. He began to fear that his mother "saw through" him and hated him—especially as she took to noting similarities in character flaws.

After Mrs. H. convinced Ira that his father was "obviously a bad influence" on him, Ira stopped accepting the Sunday invita-

† The child of the opposite sex is not necessarily safe from this emotional battering. The mother may foster a negative identification by trait. For example, looking at a daughter's unruly hair with distaste, she might say, "Your hair always reminds me of your father's."

tions and so had to bear loneliness in addition to his deteriorating self-image. He made his first suicide attempt when he failed two courses his senior year and was informed he wouldn't graduate. He had no one to comfort or guide him. All he had was his mother's comment—"You're on the same road to ruin as your father. He didn't graduate from high school either."

"My Parents Don't Love Me."

Brickman, a syndicated cartoonist for the late Washington *Star*, draws "The Small Society." In a recent cartoon, two adults stand talking, as they watch a hunched-over, dejected-looking teenager. One adult says to the other, "He was an only child—and even then, wasn't his parents' favorite."

A loss even more devastating than the loss of a parent through divorce or death is the loss of love. In many cases, the child didn't lose love, he never had it to lose. The children who are the most unfortunate—sometimes from the most conventionally stable families—are the ones who grow up feeling unloved. These children can blame no particular crisis, such as divorce or death, for their dilemma, so they begin to see themselves as unlovable, as unworthy of love. They grow into prime candidates for suicide.

Typically, they become increasingly angry and depressed. Francine Klagsbrun describes the terrible irony in that the more angry, the more depressed, they feel, the more they need their parents. Young children simply can't accept the fact that their parents don't love them. To survive they must twist reality to blame themselves rather than their parents. "If Mom doesn't love me, it's because I'm so ugly and dumb and bad," one seven-year-old named Stacey assured us. By the time they reach adolescence, children such as Stacey usually can no longer deny the truth. They become furious with their parents but also guilty. They turn that fury inward where it festers and may eventually explode into suicide.

"I felt that they really weren't loving me," said Erin, fifteen, who survived a serious suicide attempt. "They (her father, a banker and her mother, a housewife) could have been feeling that they were, but I didn't feel it. So, I just faced it off. I figured,

'Well, if my family doesn't love me, that's it—everything's gone.'"[2]

Barbara, eighteen, has attempted suicide several times. She no longer lives with her parents. She has friends, she told a panel on a WFYR call-in radio show, but she misses her parents. "I can think straight about my problems. And I know what I need. I need my parents. Sometimes I feel like I've missed my childhood because my parents rejected me."[3]

Even the very youngest child can sense ambivalence; can sense if her parents, despite their protestations, don't really love her. Suzie is now eighteen years old and hospitalized following her third suicide attempt in three years. She described to us an incident that occurred when she was five. She was outside playing, watching her mother talk on the kitchen telephone. "I started feeling angry. I was such a little kid and she hadn't even once said 'Just a minute' and looked outside to make sure I was still alive. I snuck inside, and crawled out the bedroom window to the garage roof where I could still watch her. A long, long time passed before she came out to call me in for lunch. She called a few times, looked around quickly, shrugged her shoulders, and went inside. I couldn't believe it. She got back on the telephone. She was smiling, so I knew she wasn't calling the police. I was depressed for days after that. I felt the most terrible insecurity. I had suspected she didn't love me. That confirmed it."

Herbert Hendin described a case similar to Suzie's. Bart, then a college student, recalled one day as a very young child playing alone outside. When his mother came out to look for him she couldn't find him because he had climbed a tree, from which he could observe her. She looked for him perfunctorily, gave up, and returned inside. As soon as she slammed the door, he fell—probably jumped—out of the tree and broke his arm.[4]

Children like Barbara, Suzie, and Bart—children who are ignored—develop a need for stimulation. Like most hungers, the more it is unfulfilled, the more it grows, and soon it hardly matters to the child whether the stimulation is positive or negative. "It's easier to beat your head against the wall than it is to get someone to hold you," said Dr. Jackie Schiff, a psychotherapist who works with suicidal children. This addiction to negative stimulation can become life-threatening because a child has not yet developed a sense of consequence.

In many middle-class families today, the problem often is not so much neglect as self-involvement, not so much abuse as selfishness. Metro-Help is a twenty-four-hour hotline in Chicago for young people in trouble. Executive Director Cynthia Myers talks to thousands of troubled young people. "In many families," she observed, "it has become potluck for kids, with families operating in an atmosphere of self-involvement or indifference. The child feels isolated and without contact; many feel out of control of their own lives. That is why the suicide rate for teenagers is increasing."

When *Chicago* magazine sent a writer to interview English nannies working for wealthy families on the city's North Shore, the nannies' analysis of life in suburbia, U.S.A., was not very flattering. One nanny, named Jane, told of the Glencoe couple who left on vacation knowing that their two sons, ages five and two and a half, were seriously ill with croup. "I mean, they didn't have to go away—it was a trip they easily could have put off."[5]

Kathy M.'s parents expected her to do spectacularly in school, almost as a matter of course—after all, she had highly successful parents. But their goals for her, like most everything in their household, were vague. Mr. and Mrs. M. lived as if they were single, attending busily to their own professional and emotional concerns and ignoring the growing depression of Kathy, fourteen, the older of their two children.

They apparently believed that a shopping trip each season to buy new clothes was sufficient attention. They provided little academic, emotional, or moral guidance. They sneered at parent-teacher conferences as a waste of time—for "parents who like to socialize with other parents because they haven't got anything better to do." They persuaded their daughter to get involved in extracurricular activities, as a means of keeping her busy after school, but ignored Kathy's requests that they come to see her perform in the school play or exhibit in the craft and science fairs.

It was typical of this household that what would have been a suicide attempt for most children ended as a "successful" suicide. Kathy took prescription allergy pills after dinner one night when her parents were home. They rarely said good night to her and this night was no exception. They didn't discover her until seven-thirty the next morning, when it was too late. She had been dead for only a couple of hours.

Sandy was the salutatorian of her high school class. At sixteen, she was one of the youngest in her class of five hundred, and known as a colorful, humorous, and fun-loving girl, part of a group of four very close girlfriends. She jumped from the roof of her town's most exclusive hotel, the night before graduation.

Sandy's father, a physician/researcher, was a stern and, according to one of Sandy's friends, a "black" man. The friend could not remember his ever wearing a bright tie. Sandy's mother was pleasant but, according to another of Sandy's friends, "never seemed to have a mind of her own. Harold (the father) obviously made all the decisions." Sandy and her friends stayed away from her home whenever possible because the atmosphere was dark and strained and the adults seemed to take no pleasure in Sandy, her friends, or her two brothers.

Margy, another of this group of friends, recalled that two hours before the suicide, Sandy had given her a beautiful brooch—Sandy's own that Margy had long admired. That same afternoon, Sandy told Margy that her father wouldn't be at graduation to hear his daughter deliver the salutatory address. He had an important meeting at the Academy of Sciences.

The hotel from which Sandy jumped was located near the clinic in which Sandy's father worked. Her body dropped in the street beneath his laboratory window.

It is reasonable to speculate that this girl felt such a terrible loss, a void—a lack of love—that she decided she didn't want to live.

There are too many children today who are growing up feeling that their parents do not really regard them as a source of pleasure. As Herbert Hendin put it, "Children who see they are not a source of pleasure to their parents become unable to be a source of pleasure to themselves, and have few expectations of happiness with others."[6]

Even in the case where a parent appears to be conscientious, he often communicates a sense of joyless duty. There is a feeling today, in these narcissistic, hedonistic times, that anything done for another person must result in some immediate personal gain. To many parents, a child is worth it only if his successes provide them with immediate gratification. Anyone who has raised a child knows that immediate gratification is seldom one of the joys of child rearing.

When families lived on farms, the entire family worked together. When families ran small businesses, it was assumed sons would follow in Dad's footsteps. Children were the most valuable of assets. Today, many people consider them a liability—in the most literal sense.

Newspapers are full of estimates of the exact number of dollars required to support a child from infancy through college. (The most recent estimate is $254,000 per child for the first eighteen years—*not* including college.) The articles are aimed at people deciding whether to have children. But, undoubtedly, people who already have children read them and think the once unthinkable—that their children have turned out to be simply not worth the expense.

Working Mothers, Distracted Fathers

Rarely a week passes when the newspaper reader isn't confronted with the grisly tale of a welfare mother who beat or burned or starved her child to death. Eight-year-old Pam was such a victim. Clarice, her still teenaged mother, admitted in court that she had seriously considered "dumping" her daughter "in the garbage can." When Pam was seven she was placed in a foster home. A couple of months later, she ran away from the also abusive foster parents. When the police found her she gave them her mother's address. Through a bureaucratic foul-up, Pam was allowed to stay with Clarice, who, one night a couple of weeks later, beat her to the point of unconsciousness "for botherin' me."

There will, unfortunately, always be Pams—children whose lives have been uninterrupted horror stories of abuse and abandonment. But there is a new and growing group of adolescents in the United States who any social worker or census taker would conclude live in normal families.

These adolescents would completely disagree. Although they may be lamenting their conditions in a cheery suburban bedroom instead of in a rat- and roach-infested tenement, they feel abandoned. Their parents, who may be sitting downstairs in the living room watching television, are, in a sense, as unavailable to them as Pam's.

Today, 65 percent of all mothers of teenagers work. So what? you might respond. Teenagers aren't home that often. They don't need full-time mothers. But 41 percent of women with babies under three also work. By 1990, the Department of Labor estimates, 65 percent of women with babies under three will be working. Only 14 percent of the population lives in the traditional way —a family in which the husband works outside the home and the wife works inside.

Many of us see the shifting state of the American family as a major reason for the escalating suicide rate. There have always been absent, uninvolved fathers, but, for a great many children, mothers were always there. If Dad couldn't always or even often be depended upon, Mom always could be—no matter what.

The feminist movement seems to have left us with mothers who are striving to be more like fathers, with fathers who are as inattentive as they've always been, and with children who are definitely left out in the emotional cold. Many children end up losing twice. Instead of an anchoring mother, they're cast adrift with a preoccupied-with-business Dad and a preoccupied-with-business Mom.

It is certainly true that many women work because they have to. Looking at the enormous increase in households headed by a woman (a jump of 51 percent in the last decade) makes this obvious. But many of the suicidal children we see are from families in which the mother works because she wants to. We saw one woman recently who did not have a job but so disliked her baby she placed him in a day-care center for twelve hours every day, and found a menial job to fill her time.

We see an increasing number of women who work not to fulfill their ambitions or to escape from the family, but to escape from the dreaded "just-a-housewife" stigma. "I worked until I went into labor and I was back in my office three weeks later," is a badge of prestige today instead of a warning sign of a woman who has probably failed to bond with her baby.

There is a certain shame attached to raising children full time, as if one were too lazy or incompetent to do anything else. Women whose images are not strong enough to resist this latter-day peer pressure often work in jobs that are not nearly as interesting, rewarding, or challenging as raising children—while they pay out most or all of their salary to an often mediocre day-care center or housekeeper. Children from families such as these may feel, with some justification, that in the scheme of things, their happiness and needs come last. Miles, a suburban Chicago boy who hanged himself last spring, had been raised by his grandmother and an ever changing series of maids. He was bitter, he wrote in his suicide note, that his parents never committed themselves to him as they did to their work—and to each other.

Browsing at a magazine rack, one is certain to find several women's magazines bannering articles assuring mothers that, in raising emotionally healthy children, what matters is not the quantity of time spent with them, but the quality. This advice is intended to sell magazines by salving the consciences of couples such as Jean and Bill Martin who arrive home from work at 7 P.M., have a calming drink, and spend fifteen minutes reading to junior before his 8 P.M. bedtime. When he awakes the next morning, the baby-sitter is standing over his crib.

Articles such as these are frequently sneeringly condescending in tone. They imply that the average housewife could be at her baby's beck and call twenty-four hours a day, but because she isn't too bright (if she were, she'd be out working), little of that time is "high quality." A bright mom or dad could accomplish in fifteen minutes what took her all day. How convenient, how comforting, how untrue!

Edwina and Mary, both English nannies working on the North Shore, said they were shocked by the limited amount of time their employers spent with their children. "These people see their children as infrequently as they can. They see the kids before they go off to school, and occasionally, they'll eat with them. I know it's supposed to be quality versus quantity of time, but they just say that to ease their consciences." Mary worked for a couple who were gone from seven in the morning until six-thirty at night.

"When they came back from work, they wanted to sit around and drink. They saw their boy for about half an hour each day. Then they'd lose their temper if he was bad within the half-hour time limit."[7]

There is no substitute for spending a lot of time with children, for being with them when they are fussy and boring and dirty and inconvenient and sick—as well as when they are a joy. We will discuss in Chapter 9 why mother-infant bonding is so important. Bonding doesn't happen in once-a-day fifteen-minute segments. To learn, to thrive, children need a parent who has an absolutely irrational commitment to them, upon whom they can depend always.

American parents, studies show, spend less time with their children than parents of any other nation in the world—and this goes double for American fathers. Dr. Urie Bronfenbrenner, the child development authority from Cornell, conducted a study during which he attached microphones to the shirts of small children from middle-class families to learn the exact amount of contact they had with their fathers. The average contact was thirty-seven seconds per day. Another study showed that fathers spent only ninety minutes a week with children between the ages of six and ten. Not surprisingly, a third study showed that 44 percent of 156 preschoolers said they preferred watching television to being with their fathers.

For most children, the father is a shadowy figure. Despite all we hear today about shared child rearing, fathers of the 1980s are as absent as fathers of the 1950s, a decade when child rearing was dismissed as women's work.

In too many families, the father has shrunk to a negative presence—someone to avoid. When psychiatrist Grace Ketterman and Rev. Truman Dollar surveyed teenagers for their book *Teenage Rebellion,* they asked, "If you could change one thing about your father, what would it be?" The most common answer was that the father "would not become so angry."[8]

On the ABC "Nightline" program on teen suicide, host Ted Koppel closed by asking Dr. Pamela Cantor, clinical psychologist and professor at Boston University, "All right, we have half a minute left. You've described the litany of ills that exist. Is there anything that can be done about it short of changing our society inside out?"

"Well, I don't think you should say 'short of,'" Dr. Cantor answered. "I think that's what's necessary." Apparently realizing that her answer was vague and impractical, she added, "One practical factor that we could talk about . . . would be in some way to legislate, mandate that fathers spend more time with their children, that there be a division of time between parents."[9]

Recently, I suggested in a speech to mental-health professionals that pregnancy be available only to the licensed, the licensed being those who could demonstrate their commitment to child rearing. Any unlicensed person who got pregnant would have to give up the child for adoption.

Legislate that fathers spend more time with their children? Require a license for child rearing? These suggestions sound outrageous, even a dangerous impingement on the individual's privacy and rights. They are suggestions that could only have been made by a psychologist and a psychiatrist, people who, every day, see the awful damage parents can inflict on their children.

Loss of Identity or Status

Although they usually don't express it in these terms, suicidal children frequently complain that they feel that they have no identity, or that they have a "bad" identity.

Some teens seem to be constantly trying on identities for size. Most eventually find one that fits; that gives them a sense of security, direction, of knowing who they are and what they should work for in life. Other teenagers switch identities as they switch outfits before an important date. They simply can't find one that feels right. "I'm a nothing," they may conclude in desperation, "and killing a nothing is not such a big deal."

If they do finally find an identity, and that identity gets snatched from them before they feel secure and worthwhile, suicide may be the means they choose for coping with the loss. Searching for reasons for Mark Cada's suicide, his mother and younger sister recalled his desperate search for an identity. "He never really felt like he fit in anywhere," his mother said. "He wasn't into athletics, he didn't get the recognition in grades."

Teenage boys, his sister added, are under intense pressure from their friends to be in a group—"either a hood, or a roper (cowboy) . . . or a jock, and Mark never felt right in any of the groups. He asked for a pair of cowboy boots for Christmas. He tried to fit in with the ropers but he didn't feel right with them and so he tried on another group." After abandoning the cowboy boots, he assumed another identity—this time as an outdoorsman. "He bought a pair of hiking boots with red laces," his mother explained, her voice still tinged with exasperation, "and then he wore them a couple of times and then he didn't wear them again either."

Finally he found a pair of shoes that fit—roller skates. A good skater, Mark felt terrific when he was at Skate Castle. Shortly before his death, a newspaper reporter writing an article on the rink asked Mark, "Is Skate Castle like your second home?"

"No, it's like my first home," Mark answered.

He told his sister, "I got cowboy boots, I got hiking boots, I got tennis shoes, but I don't feel right in anything but my skates."

"He found attention at Skate Castle," his mother explained. "It was just like being Fonz at Archie Arnold's in 'Happy Days.'"

Going to Skate Castle was a privilege that hinged on Mark's grades. His grades turned out to be poor that quarter, and his privileges were revoked. When the reality of being grounded from Skate Castle sank in, he told his sister he was going to kill himself. The morning he put the rifle to his head and pulled the trigger was the one on which his parents had ordered him to call his friends and tell them he wouldn't be seeing them at the rink until his grades improved.

And so his latest and greatest identity was lost. Shooting himself was his response to a loss he felt was simply too great to bear.[10]

Jody was luckier. He had other identities to fall back on, and so his suicide attempt appears to have been more a cry for help than a serious effort.

Ever since he was old enough to put on his own shoulder and knee pads, Jody's goal was to make his high school's varsity football team—a prerequisite, he knew, to becoming a college and professional star. And that was the one achievement that mattered in his family, both to his two older brothers, off to college on athletic scholarships, and to his father, the head football coach at a Big Ten university.

His family's life in a small college town revolved around football—around players coming to dinner and a pep talk, a never-ending game of tackle on the front lawn, Saturday afternoon football games at home or away, Sunday afternoons and Monday evenings in front of the television set.

In Jody's family no other kind of success mattered—certainly not academic success. Getting grades good enough to play football was, according to his father, "the name of the game." Jody told his high school coach that he really didn't think his father would pay for college if Jody weren't able to win an athletic scholarship. "To Dad, college *is* football. It's got no other purpose."

The most intellectually well-rounded of his family, Jody was smart and inquisitive. He had a hundred interests besides football. There was about him a sense of hyperactivity, as if he feared that, because of the enormous amount of time football consumed, he wouldn't have enough left to pursue photography, which he loved, and history and politics (he was a member of the Student Council and a volunteer in John Anderson's presidential campaign).

He was also a football hero at his high school and he was counting on an athletic scholarship to another Big Ten school—a good football school but also one at which he felt he could fulfill his academic goals.

When two teammates got scholarships and he heard nothing, he asked his father to use his clout and connections to check with the university's head recruiter. His father was shocked by the recruiter's reply, "Your son is good, but not good enough. I knew right away when I asked him what his other interests were and he mentioned a whole bunch of things other than football. He claims he lives and breathes football but he doesn't really. He's missing that killer instinct. I wish we could recruit boys like Jody. I really do. He's a terrific kid and he'll be a very successful man, but his success won't be on the field. It'll be in business or law or teaching."

A week after Jody got the bad news from his visibly upset father, he tried to kill himself by driving his mother's car into the brick wall of his high school. He had suffered a total, unexpected loss of self-esteem. The suicide note he left in the glove compartment read, "Without football, I'm nothing to myself and to the family. What else is there?"

Fortunately, Jody survived (he had braked at the last minute, crashing, but without deadly impact) to reflect for a while. With the help of a psychiatrist who shared his love of photography, he answered his own question. "There's plenty."

He's now at the stage of feeling anger toward his father (and his mother, for going along) and his brothers. "They're just one-dimensional men." He has overreacted, totally losing interest in the game, except to scorn those who can get "all hot and bothered by a bunch of fatheads knocking their skulls together."

Although it is rarer than suicide over a loss of identity or status, some young people kill themselves after losing an ideal that gave them a sense of purpose. Nathan was a young man from Shaker Heights, Ohio, who shot himself through the head with a Saturday Night Special after a Senate candidate he had tirelessly worked for lost the election. In a long suicide note, Nathan explained that the candidate, unlike his opponent, was a strong proponent of gun control. "I don't want to live in a state that elects a man to office who condones the murder of innocent children and mothers. I hope that my death will stop the killing. P.S. I bought this gun at a Cleveland pawn shop. No questions asked."

A Death in the Family

Dan, who attempted suicide at age sixteen in the bathroom of his Omaha, Nebraska, high school, had never come to terms with his mother's death. He mourned her still, grief that was exacerbated by a poor relationship with his father and stepmother. "I was four when my mom died, four years old. It was rough for me when I was growing up, you know, to look and face the problem that, 'Listen, she is dead.' That's real hard for me to accept. I guess it still is. The day of the funeral . . . my shoes came untied, and I wouldn't let anybody tie them. And I kept on walking around saying, 'No, no, Mom is going to tie them. Mom is going to tie them.' And they tried to explain that Mom wasn't around anymore to tie them."[11]

Max was eleven when his mother was killed in an auto accident. He was twelve when he made his first suicide attempt. "I couldn't get used to her being dead. Never, never, I knew I'd never get used to it. Life was completely different without her. It was like the house was filled with . . . well, nothing—like no cookies after school, no one to find my socks, no one to make me study. I mean, Dad tried to but he didn't know how, cause Mom always did it."

(Actually, in this case, the father seems to have made a valiant effort to "mother" Max, but Max, as so often happens, stubbornly rejected him—until his father lost patience. Max said, in therapy, that he figured that if he didn't let anyone else "pretend" they were his mother, "Mommy might see how lonely I was and come back.")

A similar case involves Mary Jo, who was fifteen, attractive, and well groomed, when she was first referred to the clinic for treatment. "If she will talk to anyone I think she may talk to you," her sister told Dr. D., an older woman psychiatrist. When asked why, the sister replied, "Because you remind me of our grandmother."

Mary Jo greeted Dr. D. in the waiting room, but as soon as the office door closed she sat with her head bowed, saying nothing. Gradually she started sharing drawings and poetry created at home, but still said nothing. The psychiatrist free-associated, made up hypothetical ideas about Mary Jo's plight, commented on opinions of family members, spoke of other adolescents and their conflicts. She got nowhere.

After four months, a change was obviously necessary, and so weekly sessions with a family therapist were tried. Mary Jo remained mute. When Dr. D. suggested hospitalization, Mary Jo said, "No, please," and nothing else. When her inability to talk continued, Dr. D. expressed discouragement. Following this session, Mary Jo burned her arms from wrist to elbow with more than one hundred burns. She explained that she could not stand the thought of hospitalization.

The next day Mary Jo brought in some poetry. Only after the therapist and the girl read the poems together could Mary Jo begin to express her pain. Only then was it possible to focus on her longing to "return" to her mother who had died when Mary Jo was seven. She had developed a fixed idea that if she spoke not at all about her mother, magically, her mother would be returned. In the older therapist, Mary Jo had found a grandmotherlike figure who she expected could somehow fulfill her longing.

Stanzas from two of Mary Jo's poems follow:

To Whom This May Concern:

. . . I wanted it to be me that died
Not one who was great and faithful
    inside.
I lov'd her so very much
And in my mind there is no such
A person to ever take her place. . . .

I struggle and fight
Trying to pull myself up.
But all that's accomplished
Is a torn and ripped self—
Till I'm worn, and I stop.

After all my trys and attempts
To become one as a whole
I fall—and all that's left for
    me to do . . .
Is give up and die.

I lower myself to this way out
Only as a call for help and
    a way to escape
The sadness surrounds me!
I'm tired of living!
I'm sure I'm right.

She

. . . I sit in my room—all alone with the fear
Of the threat of sadness—coming too near
How can I go on—when a life
    stops—I stop.

Now that she's gone
there is no dawn
there is no sun to shine on her
Every single day, when she's away
It seems the day will never end.
She knows there's no one else—
And—all over again—she's
   by herself.

Through the hours of uncertainty
She feels the need of someone close
A person, who understands the pain
   To listen to
Suffering the facts—only to sustain
that—her love is gone.
These times are so sad, but so true
She was up before—but now descends
It's too late to try—too late to do . . .
So now she will leave and find her end.

Mary Jo burned her arms as a way of assuring herself that she still had feeling even though she had tried to repress it. If she felt, she reassured herself, she could therefore still hope.

Mary Jo remained in therapy for four years, passing through periods of acute suicidal preoccupation, during which she cut and burned her arms and wrists. She was eventually sent to a residential treatment center in another part of the country.

Maureen was fifteen when, one June evening, her mother took the dog out for a bedtime walk. Maureen was already asleep and her father was away on one of his frequent business trips. Several hours later, Maureen was awakened by the dog scratching at the front door. When Maureen called her mother and got no response, she ran downstairs. She saw the light on in the garage and found her mother slumped over the steering wheel, dead of carbon monoxide poisoning.

One year later, to the day, Maureen attempted to asphyxiate herself. She was discovered in time by the housekeeper her father had hired to, in Maureen's words, "replace my mother." In her suicide note, she advised her father, "Don't worry, I'm sure you can find someone to replace me, just as easily as you found Mattie to replace Mom."

Maureen's mother had been hospitalized several times for severe depression. During the last hospitalization, which ended a month before her suicide, Maureen, busy with school activities, had visited her infrequently—a fact about which she felt very guilty. "Mom must have thought we didn't love her. Dad was always away and I was always busy."

We have described suicidal children who come from monstrously unstable or insensitive homes. Sometimes, however, children with no history of emotional problems become suicidal. These are "crisis suicides" and they frequently are triggered by the loss of academic or athletic status, as we discussed above, or by the loss of a loved one—especially when that loss is by suicide (studies have shown that people who had a suicide in their families are nine times as likely to commit suicide themselves as those who did not), and most especially when that loss occurs in the young person's life before he reaches adolescence. The young child is likely to view the death of a parent as abandonment. When he reaches his teens, the still-festering wound is aggravated by some other loss, such as the loss of a boyfriend or girlfriend or even a pet.

Researcher D. M. Palmer reviewed the backgrounds of twenty-five consecutive cases of attempted suicide and found that 84 percent suffered from the death or absence of a parent or sibling. Sixty-eight percent lost parents before the age of fourteen.

Psychiatrists Leonard M. Moss and Donald M. Hamilton analyzed the case histories of fifty seriously suicidal patients. They hoped to identify commonalities in the patients' backgrounds. The most consistent feature they found was a "death trend" in 95 percent of the cases—involving the death or loss under dramatic and often tragic circumstances of individuals closely related to the patient, usually parents, siblings, or mates. In a whopping 75 percent of the cases, the deaths had occurred before the patient completed adolescence.

Sue B. is a seventeen-year-old girl from Chicago's North Shore, whose father died in a car crash when she was eleven. She had known that her father, to whom she was very close, had been depressed, a depression her mother told her had started years before Sue's birth. Deep down, she had always sensed that her father killed himself, but it hurt a lot less to accept the family line that this was a "tragic accident."

During her early teens, she began catching stray comments that confirmed her intuition. At a point in her life when nothing—not her school work or her social life—was going well, at a time when it appeared she would neither get a date to the prom nor an acceptance letter from the college of her choice, she became fixated on her father's probable suicide. She thought about him morbidly, longed for him, decided that if only he had not "left" her, she would be a better person, a more attractive person, a more outgoing person.

She had a tenuous tie to her mother who, Sue complained, ignored her. Mrs. B. worked long hours to support the family. Her husband had left grossly insufficient insurance coverage. Sue had devised her own psychological explanation of the poor mother/daughter relationship: her mother was furious with her husband for killing himself and subjecting the family to such public humiliation and economic strain. Sue and her father were so alike in personality and looks that Mrs. B. transferred her anger to her daughter.

There was nothing or no one in Sue's life to keep her mind off her problems and her dead father. She fantasized incessantly about killing herself, feeling confident, she said, that it was not too late to "join him in a better world."

Sometimes she got angry and turned that anger against herself. "If Dad could abandon me, I figured I wasn't worth sticking around for." She took an overdose of pills but at literally almost the last minute, panicked and called the crisis intervention center at the local hospital.

Sylvia Plath killed herself at a point when she felt abandoned by her husband, poet Ted Hughes, who left her for another woman. That loss reactivated all the anguish she had felt when her father died when she was nine years old. She had come to see his death as an "abandonment," a "betrayal."

Besides grief, the major emotion that the death of a parent triggers is guilt. Children tend to feel responsible.

After all, what child hasn't harbored resentments, jealousies, ill will toward the dead parent? What about the child who has envied

Dad's relationship with Mom and wished Dad dead? Imagine the guilt if Dad dies.

These young people suffer what psychiatrist Robert Jay Lifton calls "survivor guilt." "What did I do to make my mother want to kill herself?" or "Why did Dad die while I stayed alive?" The child tortures himself with such questions. Sometimes he becomes furious with the parent who has abandoned the family so abruptly and then he feels terrified and guilty for having such thoughts. When, during adolescence, the child experiences other profound emotional and physical changes, these feelings may erupt into depression or suicide. The young person may come to believe that he had no right to continue to live. He may try to keep the parent alive and preserve the relationship through his own death.

In an essay for a Harvard College course on "Death and Suicide," a student whose father had died of lung cancer when he (the student) was four years old wrote, ". . . I have kept him alive in my head, sanctified and consecrated him, begged forgiveness of him. . . . I am afraid . . . of my father in me as death . . . I am afraid of aggression . . . somewhere in my head aggressive thoughts killed my father . . ."

He explained at the opening of his paper, "Over the last three years I have become convinced that as a four-year-old child I believed the illusion that I killed my father. . . . The part of me which so depended on his company and his love looked in utter horror at my supposed complicity in the event." The result, he found, once at Harvard, was that he could not allow himself to succeed in any area. "Any glimmer of life was a threat. . . . My fear of success grew so strong that I had to seek failure. . . . It is aggression turned inwards, cruel self-persecution. Self-hate."[12]

Baltimore television reporter Susan White-Bowden told of the effect the suicide of her ex-husband had on her son, who, two and a half years later, also killed himself. The Whites had divorced after a nineteen-year marriage. Shortly after the split, John White, an affluent construction company owner, came home to ask his ex-wife for a reconciliation. She said no. "Well, then, kiss me good-bye," he said, and went upstairs and shot himself in the head.

Five minutes before he shot himself, White had been standing beside Jode in the kitchen. They hugged each other and the father told his son, "I'm very proud of you." Jode had sensed something strange and had pushed him away. Five minutes later his father was dead. "And do you know what that child, who was only fourteen years old, had to live with?" asked White-Bowden. "Number one, 'why did my father leave me?' and two, 'Did I have anything to do with it? Wasn't I good enough? Didn't I provide enough?' And five minutes before, I pushed him away. I rejected him!"[13]

A Deadly Role Model

A parent who commits suicide provides a deadly role model for his child. He teaches the child that when things get rough suicide can be the solution. The child will be less fearful of suicide. Someone he knew and loved has already charted the waters, obliterated the mystery and the sheer terror of the act. The child may even believe he is predestined for suicide.

"Had his father not set the example," said Susan White-Bowden, "I really don't think he (Jode) would have done it." She believed her son identified totally with his father. Jode wasn't getting the girl he wanted (the reason for killing himself Jode gave in his suicide note) just as his father hadn't gotten back the woman he wanted. Jode "thought he was sharing his father's experience. . . . By killing himself in the same way (shooting himself through the head), he felt he would thereby be reunited with his father."[14]

Denise, thirteen, was referred to a Chicago-area mental health clinic after her teachers noticed that a year after her father's death by suicide, she was showing no signs of interacting with her classmates. Like many twelve-year-old girls, she had believed herself in love with her father. His abrupt death made the love a permanent fixture instead of the normal and passing phase it really was.

She wanted only to be left alone to nurse her love for her father. She convinced herself that she would soon die of a broken heart and decided to hasten the process. She died at age thirteen—one week after her first session with the clinic psychologist—of a knife wound to the chest. "I am drawn toward death," she wrote in her suicide note, "like a bee toward honey, like Juliet toward Romeo, like a baby girl toward her Dada."

When a Classmate Commits Suicide

On December 11, 1981, Herbert K. Beer, eighteen years old
and a 1980 graduate of Wheeling (Illinois) High School, went
into his bedroom and shot himself to death. When his mother entered the boy's room to tell him to turn down the stereo, she found
the body.

The following Monday, the day of Beer's funeral, Jack C. Stillson, seventeen years old and then a student at Wheeling High,
came home from his good friend's funeral and told his grandparents, with whom he lived (his parents were divorced and Jack,
since age four, had lived with his grandparents), that he wanted to
be alone. He was extremely despondent over his friend's death
and he retreated to his bedroom with his dinner. At about 8 P.M.
his grandmother heard a blast and went to her grandson's room.
She found him close to death, a .38 caliber revolver next to his
body. He died two hours later at a nearby hospital.

A month earlier, on November 8, 1981, another student at
Wheeling High, a senior, had killed himself by carbon monoxide
poisoning. Thus, this suburban high school north of Chicago
suffered three suicides in five weeks. (At nearby New Trier West
High School, four classmates killed themselves within four
weeks.)

When a classmate kills himself, his suicide may appear, for a
friend who is also having problems, a legitimate way of dealing
with those problems, instead of the fantasy in which so many
young people occasionally indulge. While the dead child's parents
may be horrified and profoundly embarrassed at the public statement a child's suicide makes about the quality of their family life,
a classmate, in most cases, does not feel personally responsible.
Unlike the dead child's parents, who might deny that their son or
daughter had problems, the friend can identify and sympathize
with his problems, even magnify them. He can brood over how his
dead friend was really too sensitive to live, too good for his imper-
fect family, community, and school.

And, he may begin to feel, as did Terri, who is described next, that he "owes it to his friend" to "join her in death"—especially as other students and parents and teachers dismiss the suicide as "crazy" or seem to continue with their lives as if nothing had happened. The surviving friend may become furious at the indifference. As his friend achieves nothingness instead of immortality, it may become increasingly important to make the death "count" through his own.

There is no doubt that one suicide in a school can be contagious—in the same way a suicide in a family can be contagious. For we have seen too many cases to believe that the Wheeling and New Trier West incidents were isolated or particularly unusual.

Terri, fourteen years old and a North Shore resident, was feeling suicidal after her best friend, Amy, killed herself. Terri called herself "the victim's victim" and said she longed for the same kind of "peace" her friend found and a "fateful accident" to achieve that peace.

"Today I found out the worst news of my entire life," she wrote in her diary. "It was the news of a death. My best friend is dead—Amy. I baked cookies, brownies with her yesterday. I really loved her."

Nine days later, she wrote, "Things have calmed down greatly at school. My one main feeling is that everything is so full, but I'm so empty. Why, why, why? Some people say Amy was screwed up, but to me she wasn't. She wasn't. Did her death change anybody's feelings on dope? That may not have been the purpose of her death, but shouldn't it affect some people? Oh God, doesn't it?"

Terri was considered the "well-adjusted" member of her group. No one perceived how upset she was. She went to school, did her work, got good grades. At lunch, she sat beneath the same tree she and Amy used to eat under. When the snow came and she had to go into the lunchroom, she couldn't bear it. She couldn't tolerate the fact that life went on; that Amy's death was soon simply forgotten. She rushed home every day and hid out in her room.

A year later, on her fifteenth birthday, Terri wrote,

> Another birthday
> but my birthday
> is not a time of joy anymore

> two weeks before
> is the anniversary
> of Amy's death, how
> can I be joyous when
> I am so sorrowful
> I don't understand
> confusion—me.

Although she perceived herself as being all alone, Terri was not the only friend of Amy's who felt suicidal. Another friend went to a therapist because she was depressed and, when she couldn't muster the energy or motivation to get out of bed, she was hospitalized. A second friend partied day and night, as if she were afraid to confront the pain. A third flunked out of school and transferred to a private school. A fourth, after cutting her wrists a few times, was placed in a residential treatment center.

A similar case involves four boys, also from the North Shore, all friends who committed suicide within a seven-month period, the first in February 1977 and the last in September 1977.

The first boy, Chuck, a student at a Catholic high school, hanged himself. He was a friend of Tom's, whose parents had just divorced. After constant quarrels with his mother, Tom moved in with the Thompsons, a local family, with whom he stayed for two years.

During that time he was much happier and more successful in school. But, at this point, his mother began to demand that he return home. He slid downhill quickly, was thrown off the football team, quarreled irreconcilably with his girlfriend. He pleaded to return to the Thompsons', but by this time they were having their own marital difficulties and refused to take him back. After a violent argument with his mother, Tom rushed to the Thompsons' and became extremely menacing toward Mrs. Thompson, holding her hostage in the bedroom and threatening to kill or rape her. Instead, he went out to the garage and hanged himself with a piece of rope he had bought the day before.

Scott, a friend of Tom's, came in from college for the funeral. He returned to school, and a few weeks later his roommate shot and killed himself. When Scott returned home for the summer, he hanged himself at work.

Mark, who was a friend of two of the boys described above, had a record of speeding and drunk driving and had an accident with the family car a short time before he went out of state to college. Friends reported that he seemed terribly depressed about the accident. After a few days on campus, he lay down on the railroad tracks and waited to be crushed to death by a commuter train.

In the small community of Ridgewood, New Jersey, four teens, all students at Ridgewood High School, killed themselves in close succession, including two sixteen-year-old classmates who hanged themselves within the same week. Jeffrey Hunter hanged himself Sunday evening and Christopher Mathiesen hanged himself the next Wednesday evening. Mathiesen was discussing Hunter's suicide with a group of classmates when he suddenly jumped up, said there was something he had to do, and rushed home to hang himself. Another young man in the community, who would have been the fifth suicide, was saved while trying to follow Hunter's and Mathiesen's examples.

The Contagion Factor: News Coverage of Suicides

Sometimes the adolescent who kills himself is not even acquainted with the teen whose suicide sparked his own. Reading about a suicide victim in the newspaper or hearing about him on the radio or evening news is enough to push some young people over the edge.

In 1979, sociology professor David Phillips found that news stories of suicides stimulate a wave of imitative acts. He set out to investigate the supposition that some fatal traffic accidents may be caused by people bent on suicide. Checking Los Angeles traffic records for periods immediately following locally publicized suicides, he discovered that for three days after a suicide report in the Los Angeles *Times,* auto fatalities increased by 31 percent. (He later found a similar surge in Detroit, following front-page coverage of a suicide.) Although it's impossible to prove that the increased auto deaths were suicides rather than accidents, he did notice that in the three days following the news report, a higher-than-usual proportion of auto collision fatalities involved single-car accidents, the type of crash in which a person who wanted to commit suicide would most likely be involved. Moreover, people fatally injured on those days lingered for fewer days than other car-crash victims. Phillips postulated that their injuries were more severe because, in an effort to kill themselves, they were deliberately accelerating rather than braking. They also might have lingered fewer days because they were not fighting to live, as would someone who wanted to recover.

Phillips further postulated that some of the crash victims in the days after a suicide news story might have identified with the suicide victim. Three days after a suicide report, the ages of those killed on the road were closer to the ages of the suicide victims than were the ages of people killed in crashes on other days. Phillips also found that the more days the story of a suicide remained on the front page, the higher the national suicide rate climbed. (Conversely, researchers have discovered a drop in suicides in cities experiencing extended newspaper blackouts—for example, a city in which a strike has shut down the paper.)[15]

On July 25, 1980, twenty-five-year-old Frances Kryzwicki, a newspaper reporter, jumped 160 feet to her death from the Chesapeake Bay Bridge. Her suicide was almost an exact replay of a suicide she had covered in April 1979 when she was a reporter for the Annapolis *Evening Star*.

Kryzwicki left the key in her car's ignition. She then abandoned the car against a guardrail at the top of the bridge. On the front seat she left the name and number of a psychiatrist.

In her story about the other woman's death, she wrote, "The key was in the ignition. Inside a handbag on the front seat was the name and phone number of a psychiatrist. Police believe the woman drove the car near the top of the bridge before abandoning it."

In analyzing the suicide, Kryzwicki wrote, "Many (women) may perceive the act of jumping into the water as a swallowing into a watery grave . . . one is gently swallowed by a giant wave." She obviously saw great comfort and serenity in the act. Stu Samuels, the Annapolis *Evening Star*'s city editor who assigned her the story, recalled, "She was fascinated, almost fixated, by her coverage of the bridge suicide story." Elizabeth George, twenty-three, a friend and fellow reporter, said, "I think a fire was lit in her when she wrote that story a year ago and it just grew into a rage to die."

Frances ended her report by warning, "It seems the mere fact of publicity about it (bridge leaping) might trigger something in the person to try something like this."[16]

Frances obviously identified with the other woman—a stranger—who had jumped from the bridge. But even news stories about people with whom one is unlikely to identify can trigger suicides. On November 20, 1978, the day on which twenty-one-year-old Tom Kane killed himself, the first reports of the mass suicide of hundreds of followers of Jim Jones in Jonestown, Guyana, were made public. Tom hanged himself early in the evening. The roast he was preparing for dinner was still in the oven. Did the lead story on the evening news, which seemed to prove just how cheap life can be, give this depressed young man the final impetus he needed to kill himself?[17]

Celebrity Suicides: What Hope Is There for Me?

Statisticians have long been aware that the suicide rate rises after the always heavily publicized suicide of a prominent person or a celebrity. When a celebrity, someone who seems to have it all —fame, money, enormous success in the "real" versus the "school" world—commits suicide, think how many young people must agonize: "If he who had everything to live for killed himself, what possible hope is there for me?" The youth suicide rate was up, for example, after twenty-three-year-old Freddie Prinze, who skyrocketed to fame as star of the television series "Chico and the Man," shot himself to death.‡

Although John Lennon was a victim of murder, not suicide, still the teen suicide rate increased after his death. Many young people felt they had a long-standing relationship with him. Losing him was like losing a member of the family.

‡ Although her death probably did not trigger many teen suicides, in the calendar month after Marilyn Monroe overdosed on sleeping pills, the national suicide rate rose by 12 percent. A number of suicides, in the notes they left behind, linked their deaths to the movie star's presumed suicide.

Anniversary Reactions

Suicides don't always occur within days or weeks of the suicide of a parent, friend, or celebrity. Psychologist Carl Tishler of Children's Hospital in Columbus, Ohio, is one of many researchers who have documented what psychiatrists call "anniversary reactions." The anniversary of a suicide places tremendous stress on the survivor, sometimes stress sufficient to prompt him to kill himself.

In Atlanta, a seventeen-year-old named Jeremy killed himself a year to the day after his father, a prominent sportsman and philanthropist, hanged himself. Jeremy titled a creative writing assignment turned in the day before his death "An Open Letter to my Dad." Although he didn't reveal his plans in the body of the paper, he wrote in a footnote, "So Dad, I've lived this year out hoping that things would get better, that I'd find some meaning in the whole mess. I don't want you to think I don't respect you for what you did. I do, oh yes, I do. You did the manly thing because you too could find no meaning in any of it. Tomorrow I'll dedicate my death to you."

A youngster who is suffering but unable to talk about the suicide of someone close seems especially prone to commemorating an anniversary with her own death. A high school senior from Wilmette, Illinois, one of the North Shore suburbs, slashed her wrists on the second anniversary of her friend's suicide. She survived to explain. "There was a part of me that wanted to say, 'Hey, I do feel bad,' but I was never able to let anybody know."

Why Do They Do It? Theories of Freud and Durkheim

After all the years of studying suicide, there are still only two comprehensive, "textbook" theories that attempt to explain why some people defeat the basic human drive to survive. Both theories were formulated around the turn of the century.

Sigmund Freud (1856–1939) looked inside the individual to find the cause of suicide. His explanation is a psychological one. Émile Durkheim (1858–1917) looked outside the individual, to society, to explain suicide. His is a sociological explanation.

In 1917, in his paper "Mourning and Melancholia," Freud postulated that people who kill themselves are actually killing the image of the parent within them—a parent whom they both hate and love and, most important, identify with. Because it is horribly taboo even to contemplate killing one's own parent, when the rage and despair become overwhelming, these young people try to kill the parent within them by killing themselves; an act that serves a dual purpose because, through the suffering and embarrassment the suicide causes, they punish the parent. Freud commented in 1920 that he doubted that suicide could take place without the repressed desire for matricide or patricide.

Murder, Freud said, is aggression turned upon another. Suicide is aggression turned upon the self; retroflexed anger. Freud called suicide "murder in the 180th degree."*

The famous psychiatrist Karl Menninger (born 1893) is probably the best-known proponent of Freud's theory. In his book *Man Against Himself* (1938), he expanded upon Freud's ideas. "One frequently reads in the news," he wrote, "that a young boy scolded by his father for some minor offense hanged himself a few hours later. We are accustomed to explain such actions as revenge. But the boy went further. The hate was so great that he was willing to sacrifice his life to vent it. It must have been his father whom he really wanted to kill. He loved his father too much to kill him. Or perhaps he feared him too much or feared the consequences. He killed the father that existed within himself."[18]

Émile Durkheim's interest, as stated in his book *Le Suicide,* was not in the individual but in the forces of society that affect the individual. It is not the individual and his unconscious that trigger

* Freud's clinical experience with suicide was apparently limited. He described in detail only one patient who actually made a suicide attempt—a Viennese woman who threw herself down a railway embankment. She tried to kill herself after she met her father on the street in the company of a woman with whom she was homosexually infatuated. Her father rebuffed her during the meeting, causing her excruciating humiliation.

suicide, Durkheim argued, but rather society's strength or weakness of control over its members.

Durkheim's theory was radical. In saying that to understand why an individual committed suicide it was necessary only to trace the social conditions under which he lived, Durkheim, the French founder of sociology, turned the study of suicide on its head. Until then, suicide was considered a highly individual phenomenon.

Durkheim isolated three varieties of social conditions that could cause people distress sufficient to want to kill themselves:

> • egoistic: Most suicides are of this variety, in which the person has few ties with his community, with his family, his church, a political party, or any other institution that imparts a sense of belonging. In other words, the individual is not sufficiently integrated into his community.

Over the years, Durkheim's theory has repeatedly been shown to be valid. Statisticians know, for example, that more individuals, especially men, who are on their own kill themselves than do family or church members. The suicide rate, in fact, is much higher among the unmarried, the divorced, and the widowed than among the married. Protestants are more likely to commit suicide than Catholics because Protestantism encourages free will and allows divorce, while Catholicism insists on greater subservience to ritual and doctrine and forbids divorce. (Thus, Catholic countries, with the exception of Austria, tend to have low suicide rates.) Similarly, those who live in anonymous urban settings are more likely to kill themselves than those who live in rural areas where the community and the extended family exert a stronger force.

> • anomic: The individual's adjustment to society is suddenly disrupted, for example, by an economic depression, or, on the other hand, by winning a million dollars in a lottery. The person can't adjust. A sudden, shocking, "effective-immediately" loss of a job, a divorce, loss of a wife, a close friend, or a fortune are all possible causes of anomic suicide.

In the case of a young person, getting thrown off the football team or being replaced as editor-in-chief of the school newspaper could cause an anomic suicide—if football and journalism were central to these students' sense of self; if losing these positions would leave them with no anchor or purpose in their lives.

In anomic suicide, instead of the individual's society being too loosely or tightly structured, it suddenly seems not structured at all.

> • altruistic: The opposite of egoistic, altruistic means the individual is overly integrated into society. The group's authority over the individual is so overwhelming, so compelling that he loses his personal identity and sacrifices his life for the community—as would a soldier on the battlefield.

The Japanese custom of hara-kiri (ritualized suicide in which the person voluntarily disembowels himself, usually as a form of political protest) and the Hindu custom of suttee (a widow willingly is cremated on her husband's funeral pyre) are other instances when the rules of society demand suicide.

In the last four chapters we have discussed a multitude of reasons why young people kill themselves. These, however, are precipitating reasons. We are becoming increasingly convinced that there is one basic, overriding cause of teen suicide, no matter if the precipitating cause is the death of a parent, too much pressure, or whatever. Nearly every suicidal child we've seen has suffered a break, a problem, in the mother/infant bond. The child who has a healthy, dependable bond with his mother can, we believe, survive almost any blow that adolescence may bring. The child who doesn't, sometimes can't survive.

So vital is the mother/infant bond that we have devoted the next chapter to it.

PART III

Bonding

9

The Key to Good Mental Health

Emergency-room physicians at a large suburban hospital serving Chicago's North Shore suburbs have treated, in the last year, a shockingly high number of would-be suicides. The majority have been college-aged or younger. Interviews with several of these young people and their parents lead to a striking conclusion.

Their problems started not in late childhood or in their teens and certainly not in their college years. Their problems seem to have started in infancy when their mothers, for a variety of reasons, failed to bond with them.

Paula G. was seventeen at the time of her suicide attempt. She was her mother's third child (and daughter) in four years. Born nine weeks prematurely at a time when neonatology* was still an uncharted subspecialty, her first month was a desperate struggle to breathe through underdeveloped lungs. Her mother, who had little help at home, cut short her hospital stay to return home and resume caring for her two older daughters, both of whom, at one and two and a half, were still in diapers.

During Paula's three-month stay in the hospital, her mother's visits were few and far between. Her father's were even fewer. Mr. G. owned a small restaurant near Northwestern University at which he toiled daily from dawn until after midnight. He saw his

---

* The care, treatment, and study of the human infant until it is out of risk —usually one month for normal children, longer for children born prematurely or with other problems.

new daughter in the hospital twice—the day after she was born and the day, three months later, when he took her home.

He made no secret of the fact that he was "disappointed" that Paula was "another girl." He admitted, seventeen years later, that he had been "hoping against hope" for a son.

Once home, Paula was reasonably healthy but subject to frequent colds and respiratory infections. These proved a big strain on Mrs. G., who recalled "having no energy left to give to another baby." And Paula was not an easy baby. She seemed to have a hard time adjusting to her new home. Although she had been a calm, good-natured baby in the hospital and had slept for four- to five-hour stretches during her last week there, at home she kept her mother and her increasingly angry father up all night.

When Mrs. G. held Paula she stiffened and wailed, sometimes refusing to eat. After a couple of days, her mother gave up and for most feedings just propped the bottle up in the crib. The little girl would become so famished and agitated that the disembodied bottle of lukewarm formula soothed her.

Mrs. G. recalled how she felt at the time. "I had three children in four years. I was just exhausted by the time Paula was born. I just couldn't accept any more responsibility. I had wanted a son—not for myself but for my husband because I thought it might make him take more interest in the children—and when I had another little girl I thought, 'Oh, God, what have I done?' I felt like running away."

Joshua was twenty-one at the time his second suicide attempt landed him in the hospital. His mother, Marie, was a concert pianist in demand for appearances around the world. His father was an impresario who also had a hectic travel schedule.

After years of unsuccessful attempts, Joshua's mother had him when she was in her early forties and his father in his late fifties. They had both resigned themselves to a childless life and threw themselves, with prodigious dedication, energy and talent, into their work. As so frequently happens, when they stopped trying to conceive, they succeeded.

The pregnancy was a delightful surprise, but Marie was already booked for four years running, including a debut with the Berlin Philharmonic and a commitment for two years to long stints at the

Edinburgh Festival—commitments she felt she couldn't break. Besides, she was no longer a wunderkind. Younger artists were beginning to capture the media attention and an increasing number of the most prestigious bookings. At forty-two, Marie, for the first time in her career, was finding herself competing hard. This was no time to let up.

Joshua was born between engagements. Marie stayed home with him for a month, refusing, against her husband's protests, to hire a nurse. She attended lovingly and tirelessly to the boy. She breast-fed him at a time when most women didn't. She was obviously enjoying motherhood immensely. She sobbed when she handed Joshua to a newly hired housekeeper and boarded a plane for Vienna, the first stop on a six-week European tour.

By the time she returned home, exhausted, jet-lagged, and still taking medication to relieve mastitis (a breast infection sometimes caused by a sudden cessation of breast feeding), she was less exuberant about baby care. Besides, in the absence of both mother and father (Josh's father was off booking concerts on the West Coast), the baby had become attached to the housekeeper. He would nap only if she rocked him to sleep and he would tolerate his bath only if she did the honors.

The housekeeper became a surrogate mother, and Josh, for the first seven months of his life, seemed to thrive under her care. But while Marie was in Edinburgh, the housekeeper quit. Josh's father called an agency and two days later a new woman was installed in the apartment, much to Josh's distress. Although he cried hysterically at first, he learned to barely tolerate this woman and the string of others who followed over the years as he became increasingly belligerent and uncooperative.

His parents, accustomed, as they put it, to "dignified and gentle artists" felt increasingly alienated from their son. For Josh resisted culture as if it were boiled spinach. He seemed to get a kick out of being rude to their friends. During their frequent dinner parties he played rock music at ear-shattering volume.

Joe's mother, Suzie, was barely eighteen and his father, Tom, just twenty when he was born. They had married, at the insistence of Tom's parents, two months before the baby was due.

Neither had any job skills and the marriage was a disaster from the start. Although Tom and Suzie stayed together for ten years, the tiny apartment that Tom's parents rented for the young couple was filled with tension and hostility. Shortly after the baby was born, Tom began to beat Suzie and came close, at least twice, to beating his newborn son. Tom was always disgusted with himself afterward, and to control these violent urges would leave his wife and son for weeks at a time.

Suzie had no experience caring for a baby and had no warm memories of her own mother's care. She had been abandoned in infancy and raised in foster homes. She came close to getting adopted several times but was always returned to the orphanage by prospective parents who couldn't handle the increasingly wild, destructive girl who told such preposterous lies.

She had been excited about having a baby. In fact, without Tom's knowledge, she had stopped taking birth control pills. She longed for a family and felt that having the baby would mean finally having someone to love her. But the reality of the tediousness of baby care struck her like a ton of bricks. She couldn't cope. She made an effort for the first couple of weeks but increasingly ignored Joe's cries. Although she fed him somewhat regularly, she failed to meet almost every other need.

Paula, Joshua, and Joe were three very unlucky people. As a result of circumstances beyond their control, they were denied one of life's greatest and most far-reaching experiences. For no matter what the vicissitudes, the obstacles, the disappointments the child faces later, if he bonds with his mother, if he has a loving, dependable relationship with his mother† he will survive and, probably, thrive.

What Is This Thing We Call Bonding?

When hospital routines allow the mother to hold and cuddle

† Throughout this chapter, we will write as if we're assuming that the mother is the person who is bonding with the baby. The "mothering" figure or, in psychological jargon, the "primary care-giver," could be a father or a grandmother or a housekeeper, as long as that one person devotes herself—or himself—to the baby; as long as the care is constant and consistent.

and breast-feed her just-born child, bonding begins. The process seems almost mystical, as if mother and baby had known each other previously. The description that springs to mind when one watches an eager mother with her new baby is that the two appear to be falling in love. There is a rhythm to it, a reciprocity—the mother talks to the baby, the baby nuzzles his cheek against her breast, their eyes lock—they gaze at each other as if they would be happy to be the only two human beings on earth.

Dr. Silvia Feldman, a psychotherapist, family counselor, and mother of three, wrote of bonding: "The major reason for the rapid adaptation to the routines and responsibilities of motherhood is the psychological and biological phenomenon called bonding, which transforms ordinary adults into motherly and fatherly types."

She described the seemingly strange behavior of new mothers who may once have been the most committed career women. Women who have bonded with their babies "find staying home with a baby a joy. It's being away from baby they can't bear. They have a constant longing to get back even on rare evenings out. Their genuine enjoyment of interminable hours of baby care is surprising to outsiders, considering their previous lifestyles and unfamiliarity with babies."[1]

At the start, bonding, which occurs in species down to the lowest rungs on the evolutionary scale, is largely a physical phenomenon—a hormonal spurt that triggers, immediately after birth, a burst of maternal interest. About one day before a rat mother gives birth, about ten days before a sheep mother, and about three weeks before a human mother gives birth, their levels of progesterone decline sharply and their levels of estrogen rise. This dramatic rise in estrogen levels triggers maternal behavior.

In addition to the physical aspect of bonding, there is also a psychological aspect that leaves bonding fraught with possibilities for failure. In their experiments with rats, Drs. Jay Rosenblatt and Harold Siegel of Rutgers found that although hormones triggered a maternal response, the hormones didn't maintain the response. A certain amount of close, sustained contact with the rat pups in the first days after birth was necessary for bonding.

Those days after birth really do make a difference. Cleveland pediatricians Marshall Klaus and John Kennell studied two groups of mothers (both from the same socioeconomic level and with similar IQs) and their babies. In one group, the mothers got the traditional sort of maternity care—not much contact with the baby after birth and on subsequent days. The other group of mothers and babies were left together for an hour after birth and were again together for five or more hours on each of the first three days after delivery.

Starting a month after birth and continuing through the next five years, Klaus and Kennell compared these groups and found striking differences. The women in the bonding group picked up their crying babies more, fondled them more, were more reluctant to leave them with a baby-sitter, and reported that, when they did go out, they couldn't stop thinking about the baby.

After two years, the bonding mothers used richer language in speaking to their children, issued fewer commands, asked more questions, and continued to speak to their children when adults came into the room. (The mothers from the other group were more likely to interrupt conversations with their child to talk to the adult.)

Although the study is still in progress, it is reasonable to speculate that the children of mothers who were given the opportunity to bond will fare better than the children whose mothers were not given that opportunity.

Ironically, human beings, whose offspring are the most dependent in nature, are the only species that has managed to subvert bonding by creating hospital rules and regulations that, even today, separate mother and infant almost immediately after birth. The minutes after birth are prime time for bonding—and nature intended them as such. We call this a "maternal sensitive period," when the mother is primed by her hormones to care for the baby and the baby is more alert and responsive than later on.

Researchers, not to mention parents since time immemorial, have observed that the newborn, during the first hour or so of life, remains in a state of rapt attention, of intense alertness. His eyes are bright and wide open, he is capable of focusing on objects, especially faces.

The newborn's amazing responsiveness elicits in most parents a state of ecstasy. It is an emotional high whose presence promotes bonding and whose absence inhibits it. When it is completely denied to parents, the results can be disastrous.

Klaus and Kennell noted that a disproportionate number of "preemies," who were saved against enormous odds and sent home thriving, ended up in hospital emergency rooms battered and abused by parents. The doctors concluded that the immediate, routine, and prolonged separation of mothers and premature infants sometimes irreversibly blocked bonding.

Although today mothers and full-term infants (in some cases, even premature infants) are allowed time together, bonding is still interrupted in innumerable ways. Many mothers and infants are separated for at least twelve hours after birth. Unfortunately, anthropologist Ashley Montagu's description of the moments immediately following birth is still accurate. The baby's cord is cut, he is exhibited momentarily to his drugged mother, kept out of reach of his father, and then whisked to the nursery to be weighed, measured, numbered, and "put in a crib to howl away to his heart's discontent. The two people who need each other at this time, more than they will at any other in their lives, are separated from one another, prevented from continuing the development of a symbiotic relationship which is so critically necessary for the further development of both of them."[2]

Many mothers postpone bonding until they are home and away from hospital schedules and formula feedings. But frequently, by the time they arrive home, to household chores and demands of other children, bonding is a lost opportunity.

Most parents who have failed to bond never physically batter their children (according to the National Center for Child Abuse, three of every hundred infants need medical attention for injuries suffered at the hands of parents), but many, as we've seen, end up battering their children psychologically. These young people start out feeling neglected, then misread, then not accepted for themselves, and, finally, battered.

What's almost always missing in the relationship between mothers and psychologically battered children is responsiveness— and responsiveness, as we'll see, is the primary ingredient of bonding.

Responsiveness—the Key to Bonding

From the newborn's point of view, bonding is exclusively a matter of responsiveness; of a magic person who always comes when baby cries, who cuddles, soothes, and reassures him, who always knows what baby wants and gives it immediately. Responsiveness makes the difference between a baby who grows up feeling helpless and one who grows up feeling competent and confident.

Psychologist Michael Lewis, Director of the Institute for the Study of Exceptional Children, illustrated the importance of responsiveness by describing the experiences of two infants, Toby and Sharon. It is clear that the earliest experiences of these two little girls—experiences totally out of their control—will leave them with stunningly unequal chances in life.

One morning Sharon awoke wet, hungry, or perhaps just lonely. She cried. Nothing happened. She cried again—still no response. She continued crying for several minutes, but no one came. Finally, she fell asleep exhausted.

On the same morning Toby awoke, also crying. Within seconds her mother was at her side, offering her a warm hand, a smile, and the milk or dry diaper she needed.

Toby's world was a highly responsive one. Her behavior got almost immediate results. Sharon learned that making an effort to change her condition was useless. Things happened or they didn't, but what she did was meaningless. Toby learned the opposite; that her efforts were worthwhile, that what happened depended upon what she did.

By being responded to, gently and lovingly, the baby develops what psychoanalyst Erik H. Erikson called "basic trust." Because the baby discovers that a caring person always comes when he cries, he gradually develops a trusting attitude toward the world.

Crying as Communication

Infant crying, we now know, is much more than a distress signal. It is a communicator. Dr. Lewis and other researchers have shown that infants as young as eight weeks appreciate their ability to make things happen through crying. "Ideally, crying should teach the child optimism about the environment, which he learns when his cries are answered," Lewis explained. If a parent's response is unpredictable, the infant feels confused and powerless. "There is no causality to teach him a sense of his own competence."

By crying and eliciting or not eliciting his parents' response, the infant begins to shape a concept of the environment. He will develop patterns of competence or helplessness that may persist throughout his life.

"To claim that crying is good for the baby's lungs is like saying that bleeding must be good for the veins," said Dr. Lee Salk, a psychologist and magazine columnist. "Children whose cries are answered learn . . . not to whine or whimper. . . . A baby repeatedly left to cry alone ultimately learns to give up and tune out the world. This is learned helplessness, and possibly the beginning of adult depression."

Psychologists Silvia Bell and Mary Ainsworth conducted a study of the effects of responsiveness on crying. They observed interactions of mothers and their infants during the first year of the child's life. The most responsive mother responded 96 percent of the time; the least responsive only three percent. Many parents would predict that the first infant would cry constantly. Not true. The child who could control his environment by crying soon learned to use more subtle means of exerting control. He also learned to do things for himself.

Susan Crockenberg, associate professor of human development at the University of California at Davis, asked pregnant women whether or not they believed they would spoil the baby by picking him up each time he cried. She later observed these same mothers with their infants and found that the mothers who feared they might spoil their babies if they responded too consistently had babies who cried more than the others.

The Newborn: Much More Competent Than We Thought

Only in the last twenty years have we come to realize that John Locke, who considered the newborn a *tabula rasa* at birth, a piece of clay to be molded entirely by his environment, and William James, who considered him a "blooming, buzzing confusion, a blank slate to be written on by his world," vastly underestimated the competence of the newborn. The newborn is extremely competent. He can think, feel, sense, and process enormous amounts of information about the world around him.

That the newborn is senseless at birth is a belief that died hard. In 1895, Dr. J. P. C. Griffith insisted in his book *The Care of the Baby* that "When the baby is just born . . . it is . . . very little more intelligent than a vegetable. . . . It is, in fact, not directly conscious of anything." Fifty-one years later, when Dr. Spock's *Common Sense Book of Baby and Child Care* was first published, the famed pediatrician called the baby ". . . just a bundle of organs and nerves during his first month." (Long after Dr. Spock changed his mind, countless pediatricians are still giving mothers the same misinformation.)

If these experts of their times were to be believed today, a woman who wanted to return immediately to work would have no conflict. A newborn, she could console herself, neither knows nor cares whether his mother, a maid, or a machine answers his cries. He is, after all, just a blob of drives.

For the neonate, the mother is much more than a machine that magically fulfills his drives. Although the experts used to assure mothers that their newborns couldn't see, hear, or smell, we know now that all three senses are moderately to very well developed at birth.‡ Not only that, the neonate uses his senses to discriminate his mother from all others, to recognize her, to respond to her, to bond to her.

‡ They are fully developed by three to four months.

The just-born baby can fix his gaze and pursue an object. He can discriminate visual patterns of relatively fine detail and tends to prefer areas of high contrast or movement. An infant consistently will gaze longer at a patterned poster than at a plain one and will do so at one week, as well as at one and six months.

As early as the second week, an infant will reach for a three-dimensional object rather than for a photo of the same object, indicating that he sees the world in a three- rather than a two-dimensional fashion. The newest baby instinctively recognizes and responds to the human face. At delivery, babies are more likely to track a human face than a string of bright beads. At two weeks, a newborn prefers a line drawing of a face to a series of random dots. The human face, it seems, holds compelling fascination for the infant from the moment of birth.

Not surprisingly, in tests that have been restaged repeatedly, a two-week-old infant who has bonded with his mother would much rather gaze at her than at an unknown female. Some infants will even avert their heads if faced with a stranger. It is obvious watching a baby interrupt his sucking to gaze at his mother's face that his gratification is as much related to the person who gives the food as to the food itself.

Estimates of the age of an infant's competence in specific skills get younger all the time. The famous Swiss psychologist Jean Piaget placed the ability of an infant to imitate facial gestures at about eight to twelve months. Two psychologists at the University of Washington now claim to have discovered, after making faces systematically at eighteen infants, that babies can copy facial expressions at twelve to twenty-one days. (So young are estimates of competence becoming that we are now beginning to think that even the fetus is somewhat attuned to its environment—reacting to voices, light, and perhaps even to its mother's moods.)*

* According to Dr. Brazelton, who has been doing intrauterine research using ultra-sound and bright lights, fetuses can hear as well as see. He cites reports from pregnant women that their fetuses "dance" during concerts and move differently to classical music and to rock. He also cites the experience of a concert pianist who was learning a concerto during her pregnancy. She had to practice one passage repeatedly. After the baby was born she was too busy to practice until he was three months old, then she put him in a playpen next to the piano. He kicked and gurgled until she reached the passage she had practiced so hard before his birth. He became absolutely still, gazing wide-eyed at the piano. "He *knew* that bit!" Brazelton concluded.

A baby's sense of hearing is also quite well developed at birth. It is especially sensitive to the female voice. If a baby is placed within earshot, but out of the line of vision of a man and a woman talking simultaneously, the baby will invariably turn toward the female voice. Researchers have also discovered that the baby will nurse longer if its mother's voice accompanies the feeding than if a stranger's voice rewards its performance. The baby thus shows a remarkable ability to discriminate—an ability that is transforming the experts' view of infancy.

A newborn's sharp sense of smell also allows him to recognize his mother, even when his eyes are closed. In one study, his mother's breast pads were placed on one side of a newborn's head and another nursing mother's pads were placed on the other side. Babies as young as five days old consistently turned toward their mother's pads.

At Boston University in the early 1970s, two pediatricians filmed adults talking to eleven newborns. They wanted to find out if there was a correspondence between an adult's words and a newborn's body movements. By slowing the film down, they showed that the babies' bodies were actually moving in synchrony with the words. In one instance, a baby's body undulated in synchrony with the words, "I love you." Also, when the adult's voice was light, the child fluttered; when it was heavy, the child slowed.

Anyone who has observed a group of mothers and babies will recognize that there is a sort of universal baby talk—a high-pitched prattle that's appropriate to the infant's sensitivity to high-frequency ranges. This talk has its own rhythms, rhymes, and intonations. Women seem almost instinctively to use these abnormally high, "kitchey koo" tones, and then return to their usual pitch when talking to older children or adults.

Conversation Without Words

We can think of bonding as a conversation without words—a predictable, rhythmic, synchronized process; a turn-taking sequence in which each partner first acts and then attends to the activity of the other. When the mother responds to the baby she gives meaning to his actions and helps the child understand the world and believe in a sense of the predictable. For newborns are social animals and mothers who are left to do what comes naturally relate to them as if they were exactly that.

Mouthing and vocalizing at the baby will cause him to respond with conversationlike expressive gestures. He will open his mouth, circle and purse his lips; his body will quiver and his head thrust forward. (His response to a toy is entirely different. He will follow it with his eyes and make grasping or kicking movements with his hands or feet.) Adult and infant are soon able to regulate their joint activity harmoniously and produce an adequate simulation of mature human discourse. Because the mother assigns meanings to the infant's activities, the infant begins to demonstrate degrees of intention. A prelinguistic form of communication evolves. In this interaction, language skills have their roots.

If the mother does the unexpected—maintains a blank expression, for example—the baby may turn off and eventually turn angry and distrustful. Pediatrician T. Berry Brazelton, a pioneer in neonatal research (now an associate professor of pediatrics at Harvard Medical School), asked mothers of infants between two and twenty weeks not to respond in their usual way. He asked them to stop themselves from instinctively imitating and mirroring their infants' responses. They were instructed to stay still and maintain a cold, hard expression. He described each infant's distress when, looking for himself in his mother's face as if it were a mirror, he could not find himself.

First the baby tried, with increasing urgency, to elicit the customary response. He smiled, stared, waved his arms and legs, pleaded with her to respond. Nothing. Then the baby tried his biggest ploy—to lean forward in the baby seat as if to fall. Still nothing. After repeated failures the baby simply gave up, withdrew. "We've had babies spit up," said Brazelton, "have bowel movements—it's so horrible, so traumatic. The system is *so* powerful."

Brazelton noted similar expressions of stress, helplessness, wariness, and aversion in a group of babies who were failing to thrive (i.e., gain weight). He soon discovered that their mothers were not picking them up or responding to their cues. When, as a result of treatment, the mothers became less depressed and withdrawn and learned to respond to their children, the infants became more lively and started rapidly to gain weight.

A baby who is failing to thrive can come perilously close to starving itself to death. (This might be considered the earliest form of suicide.) An infant is diagnosed as failing to thrive when no physical cause for his chronic lassitude can be found. The cause is purely psychological.

Dr. Daniel Rosenn designed a scale that can predict an infant's weight gain by plotting the degree of his responsiveness to the therapist treating him. Within a day or so after the baby begins really responding to the therapist, he begins gaining weight. The development of his physiological mechanism for gaining weight seems to depend on his first being served rewarding emotional experiences.

The Mother Is the Natural Bonder

When asked, "Is the mother really the best person to bond with the baby? Can't a father or an aunt or a grandfather or even a dedicated day-care worker do just as well?" child-care experts of both sexes are likely to answer, "Sure, yes." Rhapsodies about bonding have a pie-in-the-sky, even a reactionary, ring to them, they'd probably say, especially when faced with the realities of women's new role in society, not to mention the hard economic times and the dramatic increase in families headed by women.

But even in cases in which a woman has a husband who is making an adequate salary, we "experts" have become wary of urging mothers to make baby care their full-time job for a few years. If the experts are men, they're afraid of being labeled sexists; if they're women, they're afraid of being damned as traitors to their sex.

Unfortunately, it has become hopelessly unfashionable to even suggest that women have a natural advantage as bonders. The phrase "maternal instinct" is seldom uttered in polite circles. But the fact remains that, in most cases, the mother is still the natural choice.

She has, after all, one undeniable advantage. She usually can breast-feed—an activity that creates the ideal atmosphere for bonding. Babies and mothers, allowed to do what comes naturally, seem to yearn for each other. The reason is partly physiological. The mother produces a lactational hormone, prolactin, that creates a vague craving for contact best soothed by suckling. Another hormone, oxytocin, which is produced to "let down" the milk—open the ducts to make the milk available to the baby—also provides a physical stimulus for close contact.

While Mother is in the hospital—in those crucial days for bonding—feeding the baby provides him with the only meaningful contact he's likely to get. Breast feeding is a repeated, goal-directed, unambiguous activity; an activity with psychological and, of course, physical benefits. As she feeds the baby, the heat of her body keeps him warm, while her breast milk satisfies his hunger, builds his resistance to infection, and offers immunity to certain illnesses.†

Bonding Takes Time and Consistency

As we said in Chapter 7, going back to the bank or the law firm or even to an office job within weeks of the baby's birth has become a badge of prestige for many women. Such a schedule does not leave much time for bonding.

Bonding is often described as "magic." In reality, there's nothing magic about it. Like most things worthwhile, bonding takes time, patience, and just plain devotion. It is a cumulative process that requires consistency of care. Consistency means one person

† In a study done in 1973, one group of mothers was allowed to nurse their newborns while still on the delivery table. Mothers in the control group were not allowed to nurse until several hours later. The mothers in the first group were not only much more likely than mothers in the control group to continue breast feeding, they also had a more positive attitude toward their babies. When asked to report on their babies' progress, they consistently described them as more advanced, even though, at this stage, an outside assessment showed babies in the two groups were progressing at equal rates. (At one month, however, babies in the first group *were* significantly more alert.) In later months, the mothers in the first group reported fewer sleeping and eating problems and consistently described their children as "better than average."

sticking with the child full time for, ideally, the first five years of life—that's *years,* not months.

In 1979, with 40.9 percent of all mothers of children under three working and estimates that by 1990 that figure will increase by 65 percent, bonding is often thwarted—with probable long-term consequences.

That children need a mother's full-time care for the first five years is a controversial—even counter-revolutionary—opinion. Researchers only recently have begun to study the effects of bonding deprivation. For instance, while Dr. Brazelton warns a two-career couple against "ducking out" on the infant too early, he is not disturbed unduly by a woman who returns to work four months after childbirth. He also does not agree with the notion that one person should be the primary care giver. The ideal, he says, is for the mother and father to share baby care and, one hopes, for the baby to bond with both parents.

In Brazelton's opinion, it is only the first four months that are "sacred," the "most critical time for parents to begin to feel attached to that child. . . . If the parents have to share (with a housekeeper, day-care center, etc.) their babies before that time, I think it's really dangerous in terms of the development of their relationship with the child." Mothers *and* fathers, he urges, must be home with their baby during the first four months. He recommends that parents lobby for obligatory maternity *and* paternity leave.

Because of the large amount of research being done on bonding deprivation (ironically the most pioneering and extensive conducted by Dr. Brazelton), this esteemed pediatrician is becoming a minority voice in support of working women and shared child care.

Dr. Urie Bronfenbrenner asked in an article in *Psychology Today,* "Who is caring for America's children?" "There has to be at least one person," he wrote, "who has an irrational involvement with that child, someone who thinks that kid is more important than other people's kids, someone who's in love with him and whom he loves in return. A colleague of mine once said, 'You can't pay a woman to do what a mother will do for free.' You can't pay for an irrational commitment. And yet a child needs that. He needs somebody who will not just be there certain hours and then say, 'I'm off now. I work nine to five.'"[3]

Vanderbilt University professor John Killinger, author of *The Loneliness of Children,* placed the choice, for most women, between their children's needs and their own. Dr. Spock reached the same conclusion but, in good liberal fashion, argued that the government should pay mothers to assume the full-time care of their children. Uncle Sam should pay a salary to parents to stay home and care for their preschoolers, "for children should not be deprived of the parental attention which creates security and sound character just because of the family's financial needs."[4]

Psychiatrist Arnold Tobin warned that a time bomb can be set ticking in a child's infancy if bonding is disturbed by a mother's returning to work too early, leaving her children with multiple sitters or in a day-care center. "I have strong feelings that a woman who has a baby has agreed to a full-time job. If a woman just wants a toy, she is going to pay a price."

It is not only men who caution that four months of full-time mothering are not enough. Many women, like Maria Piers, former dean of the Erikson Institute for Early Education, said that the child, not the mother, should signal when it's time to loosen the bond.

We agree. The mother is important to the two-month-old. She is irreplaceable to the two-year-old. Career women need to be encouraged in their hopes and plans but they also must be educated to the risks. It may well be that in finding themselves they are losing their children and limiting their potential. The child needs to signal the mother when he is ready to begin to break the bond—and that may be at three years old or it may be at seven. When the break comes it should not be at the whim of the mother's career opportunities.

Weaving the mother-infant bond, like weaving a fine tapestry, takes time. In the old days the assumption was that the woman would work until she got pregnant and then the couple would go back to living—sometimes just scraping by—on one paycheck. Today many couples no longer consider that an alternative. They assume they'll continue a lifestyle that requires two incomes and maintain the standard of living they enjoyed when both worked.

There's scant thought given to lowering their standards for the benefit of the baby.

People should plan for children and part of the plan should be for the mother (or father) to take a few years off, to sacrifice some luxuries. Telling women it's just fine to trot right back to work may be nice for the mother, but it's not so nice for the child who will lose the main person who can read and interpret him. (It may not be so nice either for the mother who misses a glorious experience.)

Outside Care—What's Wrong?

In October 1980 I gave a speech before the North Shore Mental Health Association titled "The Ecology of the Family."

"I have two pictures to show you," I told my colleagues. "The first is a picture of a handsome mountain goat known as the Kabul Markhor. He is physically a member of an endangered species living in Afghanistan and Pakistan. There are fewer than two thousand of these lovely beasts and they remain only in isolated refuges in these two countries. The current invasions of Soviet troops into their mountainous terrain endanger them even more. Many will undoubtedly be destroyed for food by the Soviet army.

"The second picture is of baby Lisa, a child of nine months. She is psychologically an endangered species. She is charming in appearance but under the pressures of society, under the sociological priorities of today, and the narcissistic thrust of our time, she is as endangered a species as the Kabul Markhor. She will survive physically but whether or not she will survive psychologically is in the balance. She has had four caretakers; mother, father, grandmother, and aunt who have split their time, without any particular pattern. She has been cared for physically but not psychologically."

Think back to the description of the conversation without words and it should be obvious why continuity in care giving is so essential to early human development. For an adult to establish a means of communicating with a preverbal infant takes seemingly endless hours of interaction—and the pattern will be very idiosyncratic until the child starts to talk. If the mother suddenly starts disappearing every morning, the infant will be set back to square one, robbed of the one person with whom he's beginning to establish all sorts of shared understandings.

A baby who is quiet and requires a lot of stimulation to bring him out will especially benefit from one person making a single-minded commitment. But any child needs routine, consistent care —not haphazard care; not a strange baby-sitter recruited at the last minute when the housekeeper who has been around since the baby's birth quits. If the baby is hungry, wet, fussy, or afraid, he needs to be able to depend on some one person for comfort.

What's wrong then with bringing the child to the same day-care center every day? That's consistent care, isn't it? Well, maybe, but not particularly attentive or enthusiastic care; not the sort of care that results in a strong self-image, in the feeling, "I am a special person." In even the best centers—and these are few and far between—one adult, and not always the same adult, shares responsibility for several children.

Anyone who spends much time around toddlers knows that they adore applause. Praise, especially from a beloved mother, makes them smile ear to ear, clap their hands, and generally feel good about themselves. Burton L. White, who spent twenty years researching what makes a mentally healthy child, says that the one conclusion he is sure of is that a "sure sense of pride in achievement" is a characteristic of good early development.

White uses the example of watching a toddler take his first steps to illustrate how even a first-rate child-care worker can't match a parent. Parents await the event with enormous pleasure. They become so excited that when the child finally does it they "envelope him in praise," solidifying his sense of "personal security and worth." A day-care worker could never match such enthusiasm and excitement. ". . . when you've seen 200 babies take their first step, your reaction to the 201st cannot reflect the excitement typically present in the response of the baby's parents."[5]

Although so far studies comparing babies raised at home with those raised in day-care centers haven't shown any startling differences, the centers studied tended to be unrepresentative. Most were nonprofit and university-affiliated, a far cry from the sort of center in which the majority of children are left.

"I would not think," concluded Burton White, "of putting a child of my own into any substitute care program on a full-time basis . . . If I don't believe full-time substitute care during the first years of life would be in my own child's best interest, how can I recommend it to other parents?"[6]

Signs of Failed Bonding

Even in the smallest babies it is possible to detect signs of bonding deprivation. Such signs include failure to make eye contact, lack of interest in the world, refusal to eat, constant crying or sleeping, even repeated vomiting. Take Tony for example, one of a hundred infants at a mental health research center in Adelphi, Maryland. Dr. Stanley Greenspan studied these infants to learn whether babies who have bad relationships with their parents can be identified and helped before their intellect and emotions are permanently damaged.‡

Tony, only four months old, had a noticeably worried expression. When his mother tried to hug him, he arched his back, held himself away, and stared stubbornly over his shoulder. He refused to look at her face or any other human face. He needed a mother with great patience and determination. To his mother, who had herself been abandoned and beaten as a child, his rigidity meant only one thing: that her baby, like everyone else in her life, was rejecting her. She became nervous, then angry. When Tony cried she ignored him—sometimes for hours.

Billy was a healthy eight-pounder at birth. Five months later, when he was referred to the Child Development Project at the University of Michigan, he had dropped from the seventieth weight percentile to the twenty-fifth and had gained no weight in the preceding three months.

Billy's parents were very young, had moved from their home-

‡ Greenspan concluded that the answer is definitely yes. He is one of a growing number of psychiatrists who is successfully treating infants *and* their mothers. Treating the pair is essential, Greenspan explains, because "some of our mothers were not nurtured adequately themselves by their own mothers, and literally don't know how to give support to a child."

town, and were in great financial distress. The father seemed ambivalent toward Billy. During the therapist's weekly home visits,
he would tease his son, "Billy, do you want to go home with her?"
The mother, Kathie, overweight and lethargic, had only recently
emerged from an extremely unhappy childhood. The therapist described her as "an unfinished adolescent" who had "become a
parent while still in need of a mother."

Kathie complained that Billy vomited after every feeding, that
he didn't like to be cuddled, and that he turned away from her
when she held him. The therapist noted that on the rare occasions
when Kathie held her son, she held him facing away from her.
When she fed Billy she put him and the bottle on the floor. The
famished infant crept urgently toward the bottle, and, after several
misses, finally grasped the nipple in his mouth and sucked voraciously. "He likes it that way. He likes to have his bottle alone on
the floor," Kathie explained.

As soon as Billy finished drinking, Kathie rushed him to the
bathroom and suspended him over her arm, head down over the
sink. The upside-down baby promptly vomited. She then explained that his after-meal vomiting so revolted her that she
wanted to make sure he made it to the bathroom in time. She further explained that when she added solid foods to his diet the hue
and texture of the vomit repelled her even more and so she
abruptly stopped almost all solids.[7]

One setting in which signs of bonding deprivation are unmis-
takable are poorly staffed institutions. Children living there tend
to act subdued and apathetic. In a now famous thirty-five-year-old
study, psychiatrist René Spitz described signs of bonding deprivation among children in an orphanage. Children placed in a traditional orphanage during infancy invariably developed severe intellectual and emotional disturbances, often becoming, if they lived,
retarded or unbalanced. The death rate among babies in orphanages was tragically high.

To see what exactly it was about institutional care that deprived
babies, Spitz compared two orphanages. The major difference between the two institutions was that in one children were given the
chance to bond with their mothers, and in the other they weren't.

At the Nursery, an experimental orphanage attached to a

women's penitentiary, children were given plenty of toys, lived together in a large room where they were able to chatter with one another in a preverbal way and where their mothers, who were serving prison terms for prostitution, came to visit. They visited daily and fed, bathed, and cuddled their infants. These babies had the proper skills for their age, had big appetites, and enjoyed people. They were also physically healthy.

At the Foundling Home, children had no toys, each was isolated in a small cubicle where it lived in virtual solitary confinement. There were no visits from mothers and one nurse was overburdened with the care of eight infants. When these children reached two they acted only like ten-month-olds. They couldn't walk or talk, cried frequently and never smiled, they weren't toilet-trained or able to feed themselves. They were extremely susceptible to infection and had a high death rate.

The Foundling Home children had little else to do but sleep or stare at the blank walls. According to Dr. Spitz, "these children would lie or sit with wide-open, expressionless eyes, frozen immobile faces and a faraway expression as if in a daze, apparently not perceiving what went on in their environment."

We Reap What We Sow

The infant whose physical and psychological needs are satisfied develops a sense of well-being. He learns from his mother whether the world is a soothing or a hostile place, whether he is in harmony with the world or in conflict with it. Because he feels good about himself and his world, because he has known gratification in the past, he can anticipate it in the future. If, in adolescence, he meets with hostility or rejection, it does not match his own feelings about himself and he can shrug it off.

Bonding is the foundation of a child's life. It is the quality of that foundation that will determine whether a child topples sometime before adulthood or whether he thrives as he anticipates each new story of growth.

In his latest book, *Suicide in America,* Herbert Hendin described the case of a fifteen-year-old girl whom he saw after a suicide attempt. She had a history of failing in school, lying, stealing, abusing drugs, and continually fighting with her parents, who considered the girl's sixteen-year-old sister the family's model child. Hendin discovered that the younger sister had been a problem for the family since her birth. She was born in a period when her father was away from home often and her mother was tense, irritable, and insomniac. The mother, in turn, saw her younger daughter as tense, unwilling to sleep, and unbearably demanding.

Her parents related the following incident to Hendin as if it were nothing more than an amusing family anecdote. They took a trip when their younger daughter was a baby, but only after they were in the taxi for the airport did they recall they had left her behind. They were insensitive to the fact that, for their daughter, this incident, which they told regularly at family gatherings, summed up exactly where she stood in the family. She soon began to act obnoxious and defiant so they would never again be able to forget her existence.[8]

Vivienne Loomis, the fourteen-year-old Massachusetts girl who killed herself, had problems with her mother that went back, literally, to her birth. Bucking the trend of the times, artistic, gregarious, and showy Paulette insisted on natural childbirth for her third child's birth. She ordered music instead of anesthesia and permitted "crowds" of hospital personnel to observe the birth. Paulette "seemed as much to be launching the creation of a work of art as giving birth to an infant."

In infancy, Paulette recalled, Vivienne made very few demands and required less of her mother's attention than the two older children. In the summer of 1961, when Vivienne was two, Paulette and David (Vivienne's father) went to Europe for ten weeks. They took their older son with them but left their middle child, Laurel, and Vivienne with a baby-sitter. When they returned, Vivienne seemed not to recognize her mother and for several days would have nothing to do with her. By Vivienne's third birthday, Paulette felt that the little girl had "already tuned us out."[9]

Psychologist Annette Reser interviewed twenty-three adolescent patients at the Wilson Center in Faribault, Minnesota, a private mental hospital where disturbed teens are treated for an average of two years each. She also interviewed their parents and discovered a startling commonality in their early lives. From the start, there had been problems with the mother/infant relationship. Consequently, these children lagged months behind in a milestone most children reach between two and four months, recognizing a face as human and smiling deliberately. Two thirds lagged in a milestone for eight-month-olds called "stranger anxiety," failing to show that they perceived the difference between their parents and other adults. Once in preschool, these children continued to show a surprising lack of anxiety at being separated from their parents. But once they reached kindergarten, they showed distress at going to school—the start of a long line of emotional problems.

Separation Anxiety

When mother and infant have bonded, the baby shows an intense, emotional attachment to her—an attachment that is clear at six or seven months, but reaches its peak of intensity during the second year. Until the eighteenth month, nearly everything the child does is directed toward a single goal: keeping Mom as close as possible.

Obviously the child whose mother rushes back to work or is frequently away senses somehow that he has failed at the most crucial task of his young life. John Bowlby, the English psychoanalyst and pioneer in the study of bonding or, as he called it, "attachment," showed in his experiments that young children are upset by even brief separations from their mothers. When the child notices his mother's absence, he will first react with crying or tantrums. That is his protest. If crying fails to bring her back he begins to despair of her return although he'll continue his protest intermittently in hopes she'll reappear. Eventually, his despair gives way to detachment, equivalent to an adult's decision not to expect anything in order not to be disappointed. If the mother returns within a reasonable time, the child will abandon this detached mood. But if the separation is prolonged, the child may adopt a permanent air of detachment that will affect all his relationships in later life. He may never feel confident enough to attach himself securely to anyone. "I'll just be hurt again," a sort of inner censor warns.

Professor Killinger described Mickey, age three and a half, whom he met during a visit to a day-care center. Mickey would hardly talk. He stood and stared, repeating constantly, "Mama." Asked where she was, he said she was "workin'." Mickey had been coming to the center for a year. At first he threw terrible fits when his mother left him. Then the protests began when he got out of bed. Eventually he accepted his fate stoically, no longer running to meet his mother when she came to pick him up. He seemed as indifferent to her coming as her going.

"One can only speculate," Killinger wrote, "in a case like this, that the child's ability to form deep and lasting attachments to other persons may well be impaired for life. He will not blame the mother. Small children do not question the right of adults to behave as they do. He will blame himself. He will believe he is not good enough, not worthy enough, to command his mother's attention. And even after he matures and knows better he will still feel unworthy."[10]

Bruno Bettelheim's *The Uses of Enchantment* deals with the compelling power that fairy tales and myths have over children. Even at a time when children are offered on TV and in children's books shallow but explicit explorations of the most sensitive social problems and, at least on television, murder and mayhem in full color, they still love fairy tales. It is Bettelheim's contention that they love them so because the myths embody their strongest hopes and fears. One of the fears that is almost universal in fairy tales is the fear of being separated from one's parents.

Children are absolutely terrified but also riveted by the episode in "Hansel and Gretel" in which the brother and sister are abandoned by their parents—taken to a forest and lost there because their parents can no longer provide food—and nearly stuffed into an oven by the wicked old witch. "There is," Bettelheim wrote, "no greater threat in life than that we will be deserted, left all alone. Psychoanalysis has named this—man's greatest fear—separation anxiety; and the younger we are, the more excruciating is our anxiety when we feel deserted, for the young child actually perishes when not adequately protected and taken care of."[11]

If we had to generalize in a description of the "typical" suicidal adolescent, we could say he is likely to be a teenager who very early in life was literally separated from important relationships or who never experienced a real trusting relationship. Thus he remained alone to cope with the stress and strain of growing up.

Recently we interviewed a sixteen-year-old girl who nearly killed herself with an overdose of diet pills, pills she had started taking the year before when her mother decided her daughter was "unattractively" overweight. When Shelley was three years old, her mother, recently divorced and without any salable job skills, sent Shelley to live with her aunt while she got herself back on her feet.

The divorce, as it turned out, was not the only reason for Shelley's being shipped off to her aunt. When Shelley was ten days old and again when she was seven months old, her mother had left her baby daughter with her aunt. At the time, she recalled, Shelley was an "inconsolably pesky and demanding child."

The separation at three years old was the most traumatic for the little girl. She soon decided that her mother had sent her away because she was a bad, overly demanding girl—that her mother was right and good and she was wrong and probably irreparably bad. She learned very quickly not to make demands of anyone; to think of herself as a person who should not express herself and should not expect anything from anyone. She was terrified of being rejected if she let her demands be known.

Like any child who commits suicide, Shelley lacked a sense of respect for her body, a sense that should be present by six months of age. Since infancy, her mother had convinced her that she was generally unappealing and specifically ugly and misshapen. Choosing an overdose of diet pills as her weapon of death was deliberate.

She believed that her personality was totally unattractive and that her "ugly" exterior was a reflection of an "ugly disposition"—an opinion she based on her mother's obvious lack of responsiveness and love. Shelley had a sense—and an accurate one—of her body and soul never having been cherished and protected, even as an infant. Understandably, she jumped to the conclusion that she didn't deserve to be cherished and protected.

Another young woman who made a suicide attempt at age seventeen had a mother who was home and who, although she never literally abandoned her daughter, paid scant attention to her. Margie C.'s mother aspired to a position of social leadership in her community and was singleminded about reaching her goal. Most afternoons were devoted to teas or committee meetings to plan other teas or luncheons. She was encouraged in these pursuits by her husband, a lawyer, who called his wife his most valuable client-getting asset.

Margie was left in the afternoons with a housekeeper who didn't like children, especially infants, but whom Mrs. C. kept on anyway. In the mornings, Mrs. C. generally stayed with Margie, but she was much more absorbed in household activities and telephone calls than in her daughter.

When Margie was hospitalized after her suicide attempt she seemed happier than her parents had ever seen her. In the private, well-staffed hospital she got an enormous amount of attention and coddling. She became quite attached to several of the older nurses, women whom she cast in the role of surrogate mother.

When she left the hospital for home she tried to maintain the friendship with two of the nurses, both older and maternal women. When they suggested to her that it was best she develop friendships with young women her own age, she became suicidally depressed. She was readmitted to the hospital. When, if ever, she will be able to relinquish this forced and false security is uncertain.

Searching for a New Mother

We see over and over again the case of a young person who attempts suicide immediately following a breakup with a boyfriend or girlfriend. When Lane's girlfriend dumped him he reacted by weeping uncontrollably and walking around in a gloomy mood for months. His parents scolded him to grow up. "She's just a girl," his father pleaded in exasperation. "There's plenty more where she came from." His father didn't realize that the depth and persistence of Lane's grief sprang from a much earlier period when he felt his mother didn't love him.

One of the main tasks of adolescence is to separate from parents. But the child who hasn't had enough nurturing to develop a sense of self has nothing when he separates from his parents. He will constantly search for the idealized parent figure. But his sense of self is entirely dependent on another, so when a youthful romance breaks up, he is left with nothing. "I feel like I lost part of myself," he may complain. For the teenage romance may have been all that was left in his life.

We know that depressed people often become obsessively and overbearingly eager to please one specific individual—first the rejecting mother who is usually impossible to please and then a girlfriend or boyfriend who typically tires of the intensity of the relationship. A twenty-year-old girl hospitalized after a suicide attempt admitted, "My isolation . . . was often self-chosen. . . . But when I did discover a rare soul I'd throw myself totally into the relationship realizing the other person could not handle the burden of me caring for them." These relationships become as important to the young person's ability to live as is milk to an infant.

Writing in *Good Housekeeping,* Alice Chase described the case of fifteen-year-old Ellen, who killed herself with an overdose of sleeping pills. Her mother found her sprawled across the bed, "her hands flung out as if in one last protest against the world." A suicide note propped on the bedside table read, "I'd rather be dead than stop seeing Tommy. He's the only person who really cares about me. You and Dad never have—that's for sure. Anyway, from now on you won't have to worry about my sneaking out to meet him. You won't have to worry about me, period—because I won't be around anymore."

Ellen's parents had forbidden their daughter to see Tommy because he was two years older than she, from the wrong side of town, and unattractive. From the moment Ellen's mother met him, she called him "that awful boy" and refused to let him into the house.

When they discovered their daughter was sneaking out at night to see Tommy, they threatened to have her sent away as an incorrigible delinquent. They scared her enough to make her stop seeing him, but not to make her stop thinking about him. It wasn't just Tommy she missed, but the attention and love he gave her—attention and love that had always been in short supply at home. "For a brief period," Chase wrote, "Ellen had felt she was important to somebody. When that good feeling was taken away from her, her life seemed empty and meaningless—so she ended it."[12]

Bonding: The Foundation of Life

It is essential that we begin a loving relationship with our children from the earliest possible moment. We must realize that the suicidal impulse can be ingrained within the first few months of life. Breaking up with a girlfriend, failing chemistry, any problem in the child's life may precipitate a suicide try, but the underlying causes frequently can be traced to emotional scars inflicted during infancy.

We must accept the fact that infancy is like the composition of a musical theme. The rest of life is a variation on the theme. Those subsequent variations *are* important. There's no question that the child needs to have ongoing, supportive, creative relationships. But without that first bonding experience, without that clarification of the major theme, the composition of the adult personality will be difficult to pull together.

We know that ratings of a mother's behavior on dimensions such as affection, rejection, protectiveness made in the first three years of life are the best predictors of the child's later behavior. Alan Stroufe, professor of child development at the University of Minnesota, found that infants who were judged "securely attached" at eighteen months were better problem solvers at age two. They were also better able to elicit the help of their mothers to solve problems too difficult for them. Stroufe claims it's possible to predict which children will be successful preschoolers by studying the relationship a child has with his mother at twelve to eighteen months. Children with a secure relationship can function better in nursery school at a younger age than children without one.

Burton White and his colleagues followed the progress of forty children, beginning at age one or two. Researchers visited the homes of these children every other week, twenty-six times a year. They concentrated on the interactions of infants and mothers and concluded that a close social relationship "was a conspicuous feature in the lives of the children who developed best."

If a child experienced more deprivation than gratification in early relationships, he will have an especially difficult adolescence. Observers of human development and human nature throughout the centuries have reached the same conclusion. Plato said, "And the first step, as you know, is always what matters most, particularly when we are dealing with those who are young and tender. That is the time when they are taking shape and when any impression we choose to make leaves a permanent mark." Freud, who lived over two thousand years later, made the same point: "The very impressions we have forgotten have nevertheless left the deepest traces in our psychic life, and acted as determinants for our whole future development."

We do not mean to say that parents cannot reverse a bad start. If we believed that, we would not have written this book. And if that were true, the suicide rate for young people would be ten times higher than it already is. For many parents *are* able to reverse a downward slide.

The most important point we can make in this chapter is that the earlier a parent recognizes a destructive pattern, the better the chances of changing that pattern.

One pattern that is becoming increasingly common—that parents *must* learn to recognize—is depression. For many of our young people, a life that starts with bonding deprivation ends with depression—depression that is every bit as life-sapping and shattering as that which afflicts adults. Depression is a factor in so many teen suicides that we devote the entire next chapter to the subject.

10

Depression: It Strikes Children, Too

When Beverly, twelve, informed her parents that she would not be joining them on a long-planned European vacation, they were confounded. "Should we force her?" they wondered, as the departure date neared and Beverly seemed to alternate between wild, exuberant behavior and immobilizing gloom. Because they were at a loss for what to do, they took Beverly to a psychiatrist—despite their distaste for psychiatry.

After two sessions with Beverly, the doctor called in her parents to suggest starting family therapy and to inform them that their daughter was seriously ill—depressed, and perhaps a manic-depressive. They informed him that twelve-year-olds don't get depressed, that their daughter was just spoiled and that she would go on the trip, like it or not. This was, they said, the last time the doctor would see them or their daughter.

They were wrong. Two weeks later, when Beverly arrived at the hospital nearly dead of a drug overdose, the same psychiatrist happened to be on call.

It's understandable why Beverly's parents thought the psychiatrist was crazy for diagnosing depression. Just twenty years ago, even psychiatrists believed that depression was a malady of mid-life or old age; that childhood was the one time of life that was truly happy, innocent, and free of the scourge of depression. Besides, we assumed that children were so resilient that even if they did get depressed, they would snap right out of it.

We now know that children are no more likely to snap out of it than are adults. We now know that even infants get depressed; that some infants get so depressed they stop eating and starve to death. One girl was referred for treatment after bouts of crying for no apparent reason, refusal to eat, and a series of accidents that included broken bones and deep gashes. At the time of her first appointment, she had just turned four.

We also now know that children can suffer from all varieties of depression, including manic-depression, with its peaks of euphoria and valleys of despair. The sudden mood swings, the manic highs and depressed lows are not, as we once thought, typical of adolescence. They are typical of manic-depression—a disease that can push teenagers, as well as adults, over the brink into suicide.

Rarely a week passes when I'm not treating a depressed young person. The North Shore is no different from the rest of the nation. In a study of seventh- and eighth-graders at a suburban Philadelphia parochial school, nearly one third of the youngsters were significantly depressed and had suicidal thoughts.

Estimates of the numbers of depressed young people seem to increase with every new study. Researchers for the National Institute of Mental Health estimate that one in five children may suffer from depression. In a recent study of 5,600 high school students, depression was second only to colds, sore throats, and coughs in frequency.

Although many young suicides do not seem to be depressed—rather their self-esteem is tenuous and totally dependent on others' approval—still depression is undoubtedly the single most common cause of childhood and teen suicide—just as it is the single most common cause of adult suicide. To cite just one of several recent studies that supports this point: Psychiatrist Frank Crumley, from the University of Texas Health Science Center, studied forty adolescents in treatment with him following suicide attempts. Thirty-three of them, or 80 percent of the sample, were depressed.

For impetuous, impatient young people, depression is a particularly dangerous affliction. Dropping out of high school, having a baby without wanting to, getting arrested, suffering a crippling injury as a result of unreasonable risk taking, are all forms of "masked" depression that can blight a young future.

Young people aren't used to dealing with stress, and so they can more easily convince themselves that no other person in the world has ever felt so awful. They are so afraid, so profoundly lonely in their suffering. They have not had enough experience with depression to know that, as dreadful as it feels, it will end; they *will* feel better. Too often, they see suicide as the only exit from their suffering.

As one college student put it, "When one of my friends who was a little younger committed suicide, my first reaction was, 'Why didn't you *wait* another year?' I saw so many kids going through what I went through—for a while I'd been so depressed I thought about killing myself, too—and I wished they could have known things would be better if they had waited it out. I know of someone who killed herself when she was fourteen. Fourteen! You haven't begun to know the most meaningful things in the world yet!"[1]

How It Feels to Be Depressed

Syndicated columnist Bob Greene reprinted a letter he received from a suicidal student at Northern Illinois University. The young woman offered an interesting perspective on how it feels to be depressed: "I've known for a long time that there was something different about me. But it's only here, at college, that I've really begun to realize how truly unbearable that difference is. I feel as if I'm missing some important part of personality that shows a person how to be happy. Every time I look in the mirror, I despise the person I see. Outwardly, she's a normal 19-year-old sophomore. But inside, she's a person writhing in anguish over her total worthlessness."[2]

When David's parents got divorced, this high school student from a North Shore suburb got depressed, and stayed that way. His mother took him to a local psychologist who asked David to complete a diagnostic tool called the Mooney Problem Checklist. Of the 210 problems listed, David checked that he was troubled by 113—that he was plagued by problems ranging from not getting enough sleep to missing someone very much.

The psychologist pointed out to David that he had checked

more than half the items on the list, three times the number checked by the average teenager. David did not regard this as unusual. "It was almost as if David thought it was natural to be burdened with all kinds of troubles and liked it that way," the psychologist wrote in his report. David later committed suicide by shooting himself in the head.

Depression hurts—a lot—as several people who survived that grim ordeal recalled:

- "I had thought depression meant simple sadness," said one young woman. "I didn't know one felt crazed, insane, dumb, dead, numb, enraged, hysterical, all at once. Depression is a killer."
- "The best way that I can describe what it felt like was that it was like being dead. Except that one had to go through the motions of being alive . . . and it was—pain."
- "Prison would be infinitely better. A person in prison would want to break the wall, because he wants to get back to the world. A depressed person very seldom runs away from the hospital, because he sees no need to take off."
- "I would rather have all the bones in my body broken one by one, than to go through *that* again. My nerves were screaming; it was constant, never-ending torture. Every single minute of every hour was torturous; I ate practically nothing; eating was an unspeakable chore. I had to force down every single bit. Couldn't sleep, cried; oh, I wept and I wept! . . . I was just so utterly defeated and down. . . . I just wanted *out*."

When a nineteen-year-old college student killed himself in the North Shore garage where he was working for the summer, he explained in his suicide note, "I'm sorry. I didn't want to live with these feelings."

Anyone who has been severely depressed would understand what he meant—a no-exit, psychic suffocation, a dark cloud that settles around its victims and drains them of emotion, of control, of the will to live, that makes life seem meaningless, futile, and hopeless. Even the smallest expenditure of effort is torture. One twenty-one-year-old woman said being depressed is "like dragging a ball and chain around with you, everywhere you go. Everything you do is an effort; getting out of bed is my big effort for the day."

There is no respite, no gratification, no zest, no hope that the mood will lift. Depressed people frequently describe themselves as feeling as if they had terminal cancer—but worse, because they know their disease won't kill them. And so they decide to kill themselves.

Most of all, a depressed person feels trapped, totally out of control, cut off from life by a curtain through which he can see others enjoying themselves but never join in the fun. It matters not where he is. He's in his own private hell—in Sylvia Plath's words, a "bell jar." Whether lounging in a café in Paris, in the most dreadful of state hospitals, or at home, Plath wrote, "I would be sitting under this same glass bell jar, stewing in my own sour air."[3]

The Warning Signs

When worried parents brought their eleven-year-old son Jonathan to a psychiatrist because he seemed unhappy and apathetic and also complained of headaches and stomachaches, the psychiatrist advised them to take Jonathan to his pediatrician. Unable to find a physical cause for the complaints, the pediatrician prescribed a sedative, assuring the parents that their son was merely going through an anxious time, "as all children do from time to time," and that the sedative would "calm him down and help him get through it."

The sedative, as is typical with this kind of drug, increased rather than relieved Jonathan's depression. It also gave him a few nights of good sleep and therefore the energy to kill himself. Three days after it was prescribed, he swallowed the remaining contents of the bottle.

While Jonathan was in the hospital recovering from the suicide attempt, a staff psychiatrist prescribed a course of antidepressants and family therapy. The medication continued for three months; the family therapy for thirteen. Now in high school, Jonathan is doing well academically and socially and has not had a relapse.

Too many doctors and even psychiatrists still consider depression and childhood a contradiction in terms. Frequently, it's not until the first suicide attempt that the depression is recognized and treated. The danger, of course, is that first suicide attempt may be "successful," and so parents should learn to recognize the signs of depression.

Besides a general air of unhappiness, apathy, and unsociability (avoiding friends and family), a depressed child will show several of the following symptoms: in younger children—sudden bedwetting, whining, clinging, frequent crying, sudden onset of nightmares, complaints of stomachaches or headaches; in children of all ages—difficulty concentrating and a slide in school performance, trouble sleeping (yet chronic fatigue), appetite or weight problems (refusal to eat favorite foods), feelings of extreme guilt or self-reproach, loss of pleasure or interest in daily routine, hyperactivity or listlessness, and recurrent talk of suicide or death. In general, activities, toys and people that used to make the child happy no longer do.

The warning signs of depression are basically the same as the warning signs of suicide (see Chapter 3). But in cases of teen depression, there is a unique emphasis. Whereas adults tend to become immobilized by depression, many teenagers become reckless. Depressed adults usually act sad and lethargic; depressed teens act angry, unreasonable, rebellious, and incorrigible.

School is typically the setting for this "acting out" behavior. (In fact, many, if not most, school problems are, at their core, reactions to depression.) The depressed teen may talk back to or threaten the teacher, set fires, fight with or tease other students, become the class clown. He may regularly cut classes or skip school altogether.

Not surprisingly, parents are more likely to react to this sort of misbehavior with anger and frustration than with understanding and offers of help. The depressed teen's behavior—fast driving, drug and alcohol abuse, running away from home, stealing, sexual promiscuity (many of the teenage girls who get pregnant are depressed)—is irresponsible and dangerous.

It's a good bet that the young person who is perpetually breaking bones, sporting black eyes, bruises, and cuts, who is, in other words, extraordinarily accident-prone, is also depressed.

Depressed children have a characteristic appearance. Their eyes look like burnt sockets. Their faces seem immobile, static; their expressions don't change. They're often skinny and ashen-colored; their voices sound flat and their words don't jibe with their tone. Their speech seems colorless, as if they're deliberately deleting all adjectives.

Even if a depressed child has no immediate plan for suicide, he will often give his most prized possessions to a friend because he has simply stopped caring about them. Even the youngest children leave "wills." When the parents of one eight-year-old girl, who had seemed "down" for several months, found her "will," they arranged for immediate psychiatric help:

I want to not
live no more.
Mickey gest my
bank and Mommey my stamp book.

Masked Depression

In this chapter and, indeed, throughout the book, we describe youngsters who have a variety of symptoms, some of them not clearly depressive. Many children with learning problems of psychic origin, many low achievers, many children exhibiting antisocial behavior are basically children struggling with depression, a depression hidden by inhibitions or acting out. Only when a clinician focuses on the basic problem does the nature of this masked depression become clear. Lurking behind is always the potential for suicide—suicide that may occur before the depression is unmasked.

This group of basically depressed children and teenagers are all too often misdiagnosed. The low achiever or the child with uneven learning skills may be seen as an educational problem in need of educational therapy. This child may indeed need such therapy, but what he needs first and most is to be treated for depression. The child who acts out will be viewed as a behavior problem and treated with behavior modification or a system of limitations and restrictions that only aggravate the acting-out behavior. Parents, teachers, and physicians must remember that behind any school or behavior problem depression may be hiding.

Debi's is a case of masked depression that appeared to be an obsessive-compulsive neurosis. Only after delineation of all the symptoms did it become clear that the compulsive rituals were part of her depression.

Fourteen-year-old Debi was referred for consultation by Mrs. C., the school social worker, because of severe rituals.* The social worker was concerned because Debi would soon be moving into high school, and so the two would have to sever their relationship.

Debi was a gifted child, an A student, yet lacking animation about her learning and lacking the usual curiosity of a gifted child. In fact, Debi showed no joy in any of her endeavors. She was a talented pianist, yet refused to play in a recital or for fun. She wrote well, yet refused to share her poems and short stories. She resented being in classes for the gifted and was infuriated when her well-meaning teacher announced to the class that Debi had earned a grade of 105 by virtue of getting all answers correct *and* doing additional work.

Debi had a pattern of waking at three in the morning and rarely returning to sleep. She also had a history of recurrent appetite and weight losses.

It was clear that Debi's was a case of masked depression. She had developed a ritual—in her case, a ceremonial sort of attention paying to her bedclothes and also the ritualistic touching of objects—in an effort to keep her depression in check.

When Debi was confronted with the reasons for her rituals, she burst into tears and said, "So that's what it's been about!" As therapy, with this focus, continued, Debi described her cache of pills, her plans to swallow them and then go to the lake for a last swim. "And if that didn't work," Debi explained, "I would have lain across the train tracks. I had a friend who did it that way."

Masked depression can be seen in younger children as well. Chad's is a case of masked depression that appeared to be a straightforward behavior problem. At age ten he was referred for evaluation of behavior difficulties at home and school. He spoke

* Compulsive acts that have a ritualistic quality to them, such as excessive hand washing.

of not being able to concentrate, of not caring about the work, and of being a dummy anyway.

During an interview with Chad's mother, she described severe obstetrical problems that persisted through the first six months of her son's life. She had suffered from continuing vaginal bleeding. As she put it, "He came so fast he ripped me apart."

Mother was not only physically unavailable for Chad's care, she also unwittingly blamed him for the damage done her. The result was that Chad, as an infant of one to six months, had probably suffered from infantile depression.

When all this was explained to Chad, he said, "Now things make some sense." He then was able to understand his mood swings, his sense of discouragement, which he later called depression. He began to have crying spells, but his behavior problems subsided.

Once the mask was removed, the boy could focus on his central problem, namely depression. Later in his therapy, he said, "I think the way I felt was the way kids who kill themselves must feel."

What's the Best Treatment?

There are basically two types of depression that strike children —reactive and biochemical; the same two types that strike adults. Biochemical, however, is much more common among adults than children.

Biochemical, also called endogenous depression, results from a chemical imbalance that numbs the brain's pleasure center and is normally treated with antidepressant drugs, and occasionally with shock treatment (both of which are described later in this chapter). We do not know why adults are afflicted with this type of depression so much more frequently than are children.

When a child gets depressed, his depression is usually reactive— triggered by some event or ongoing problem in his life. Examples of such problems might be the death of a parent or the child's unshakable feeling that his parents are disappointed in or don't really love him.

We will occasionally use an antidepressant to treat a reactive depression in a child—especially in cases in which the child is so profoundly depressed that trying to reach him with words is an exercise in futility. The antidepressant will lift his mood to the point where he's receptive to talking. But, most often, the sole course of treatment will be psychotherapy, sometimes including family therapy, because most conflicts that trigger teen depression center in the family.

Psychotherapy—What Is It?

Parents invariably have many questions about psychotherapy, even if they don't quite know how to ask them. "What is psychotherapy?" "What goes on in a typical session?" "How could just talking possibly help lift a depression?" "My son won't talk to me. Why should he talk to a perfect stranger?" "My daughter says nothing's wrong and that's all she'll say. So what's there to talk about?" "How long will it take before we see some results?"

In this section we'll try to anticipate and answer those questions and more, first by describing the case of Alicia, a depressed teenager, who underwent a typical course of psychotherapy.

Diane M., a social worker/therapist at a North Shore family service agency, called the clinic one Saturday to request that I prescribe an anti-anxiety drug to a girl whom the therapist had been seeing regularly for two years.† Ms. M. explained that seventeen-year-old Alicia had recently become more anxious and depressed. She was currently living alone in her family's twenty-room house while her parents were in Africa on a safari.

The social worker noted that previously, whenever the parents left town, Alicia had been anticipatively pleased and then very anxious when they actually left. The girl's intense fear when the burglar alarm went off at night bringing the police precipitated the Saturday call. No intruder had been found, and the alarm was ap-

---

† Only M.D.s can prescribe drugs, so many non-physician mental health workers, such as Diane M., work with psychiatrists. If they think one of their clients needs medication, they call the psychiatrist to examine the person and prescribe the drug.

parently an electrical malfunction, but Alicia was extremely frightened and increasingly talked of suicide.

I met Alicia that day in an emergency consultation. She was very boyish-looking, cynical, verbal, and anxious about managing for another two weeks alone. She said she was grateful for the availability of her boyfriend. However, in a very somber voice, she added, "If anything happened to him, it would be curtains for me."

She showed no physical signs of depression, was sleeping well, and had not lost weight. She had no history of suicide attempts, nor did any member of her family. We decided that she should continue to see Ms. M., that I would be available in an emergency and would continue to prescribe an anti-anxiety drug.

I was surprised when Alicia called me twice over the weekend, and then daily during the next week. Each time she reported that the medication was of "no help." (I had seen her on Monday morning and switched her to an antidepressant.)

Obviously, this girl was looking for something more than medication. With the full cooperation of her therapist, we decided on a "second opinion"—that is, I took a full psychiatric history to get a complete view of this adolescent's needs.

It became clear that Alicia had never felt accepted by her parents. "They never listen to what I want to explain. Whatever I choose for school they tell me is wrong." She related incidents from her early childhood that illustrated her view that her family had always favored boys. The result, she said, was her own conscious effort to act and "be like" a boy. "It was a bit difficult when I began to grow these," she added, smiling and pointing to her breasts.

She began to talk about dreams—a staple of psychoanalysis—but then mentioned, "My therapist (Ms. M.) doesn't want me to work on them (dreams) but I want to. I have the feeling they would help in figuring me out."

Alicia raised the possibility of my working with her to help "figure" herself out. She noted that she had worked out many of her adolescent problems with Ms. M., but she wanted a new therapist with whom she could work out "more basic and earlier things."

After considerable discussion with Ms. M., we agreed that Alicia would enter a course of psychoanalytic psychotherapy. "Talking therapy" seemed the right course for her because of her symptoms of anxiety and depression, because of her capacity to be introspective and psychologically curious, because of her sense of responsibility for her own adjustment.

Then came the toughest part—convincing her parents to support the therapy. Alicia came to the first session after their return from Africa and reported their total disapproval of her seeing a "shrink," of using medication, of her needing anything more than common sense and some discipline. As she described her parents' reaction, she became more and more depressed, shaking her head and saying, "Nothing is going to work; they will just make me blow it."

I scheduled a family session for the following day. The mother immediately called to "dismiss" me. I insisted that she and her husband come in. The banker father could not make it "for at least ten days," but the mother did come. There followed a poignant session in which the mother presented herself as a pawn in the hands of her aggressive husband.

Eventually the father also came, and slowly over the next three months, they became involved in their daughter's therapy. We stopped the medication, relying solely on interpretive psychotherapy.

With ongoing therapy, Alicia's prognosis is good. We are working on helping her understand her basic problems of suppression of anger, low self-esteem, poor gender identity, and her pattern of handling anxiety by attaching herself in a dependent fashion to the helpers and boyfriends in her life.

In light of what we said about bonding in the previous chapter, it's interesting that, in that first emotional session with the mother, she recalled being unable to relate to Alicia in infancy. "She didn't seem like one of me," the mother said. "It's as if she had come from another family."

Psychotherapy is a term that refers to the talking psychiatry widely used by clinicians within the mental health field. It is based upon the value of clarifying, in considerable detail, the biographical facts of a patient's life, and then seeking the hidden forces that have shaped that life, but which have been outside of the patient's conscious awareness. For the process to work, the patients must not only be introspective and curious about their psychological life, but also willing to face issues that may be unpleasant or embarrassing.

In turn, therapists must be able to focus in a singular fashion upon patients' experiences, empathize with their plight, and yet remain curiously observant about the unknown factors that may be focal to their symptoms. These may include the subtleties of parental relationships, mother-infant interchanges that set the stage for later problems, early losses of significant people, disappointments and self-recriminatory experiences, and many other highly idiosyncratic facts.

Children must be helped to understand what has made their parents or siblings become what they are, in what way things might be changed, and which things in their home life they must simply learn to accept.

Like Alicia, most young people being treated with psychotherapy would see a therapist two to three times a week for forty-five to fifty-minute sessions—except, of course, in an emergency, when they might see a therapist ten minutes, five times a day or, perhaps, two hours, five times a week. Treatment schedules are highly individual, especially with adolescents.

We said in describing Alicia's case that we needed to involve her parents. What we meant is that we needed to get them working with us, rather than against us. They would not sit in on therapy sessions. (Therapy in which parents are regularly involved is called collaborative or family therapy.) Rather, parents would serve as a resource—people who know that child better than anyone else does and who could offer guidance and answer questions. They would also encourage the child to understand how therapy can help and they would make sure that the child keeps his appointments and arrives on time. As we discuss later in this chapter, a parent who is skeptical of or hostile toward therapy can sabotage it.

In Alicia's case, therapy continued for two years—longer than normal. The average length of treatment for an acutely suicidal patient is ten months. Sometimes treatment is as short as twenty-one days—the length of most programs used in treating young people who have attempted suicide and ended up in hospital emergency rooms. (Unfortunately, many patients discontinue therapy after the emergency passes.)

Once Alicia's therapy started in earnest, she was treated without medication. Psychotherapy was her sole treatment. As we said earlier, most adolescents and children can be helped without drugs.

"My son won't talk to me. Why should he talk to a perfect stranger?" "My daughter says nothing's wrong and that's all she'll say. So what's there to talk about?" These are certainly legitimate and common questions.

The answer is simple: a perfect stranger is often just the person to get beyond that "Nothing's wrong" nonresponse—especially if that stranger has been trained in knowing what questions to ask and how to ask them. Psychiatrists, psychologists, and social workers have patient loads full of young people who desperately want to talk—to someone who is not the cause of or in any way connected to their problems.

Although most young people can be helped by psychotherapy, some are better candidates than others. Alicia is the sort of person who does best—a person who has the capacity to be self-observant and introspective and who has the wish to change; a person who can, in psychological jargon, "engage with a clinician and later disengage"—in other words, develop a relationship with a therapist and later end that relationship.

Obviously most little children have not yet developed these capacities. Such children may need what is called supportive therapy —a relationship with a kindly, supportive, and interested "teacher-therapist."

Therapy with children often takes the form of play—through which even the smallest children can communicate their worries and their sense of depression. By joining children in play, the therapist builds rapport with them, gets invited into their private world, encourages them to express themselves. Children might use puppets to reflect their moods and the interaction of the puppets to express their understanding of family relationships. Crashing toy cars might be the means by which they describe family tension or violence. Block-building, storytelling, painting, or drawing provide other outlets.

Why Not Analysis?

We hear all the time that someone or other is in "analysis"—today a status symbol in the same class as owning a foreign car or a country home. The person referred to is invariably an adult, because psychoanalysis usually must be modified for use with children or adolescents. It is classically a technique that requires a relatively intelligent and well-integrated adult patient. A child analysis variant on the classical technique has been used with well-integrated children, but for the most part children and adolescents require a much more active involvement of the therapist and much more of a dynamic relationship. Also, depression requires active and immediate intervention by virtue of the possibility of suicide.

There are many similarities between psychoanalysis and psychotherapy—especially because many psychotherapists use a psychoanalytic orientation. They use talking therapy as a tool—to get at unconscious forces which have been central in the person's life and problems but often are not remembered. As in psychoanalysis, dreams often play a key role in psychotherapy because they contain condensations of important problems.

By definition, only graduates of psychoanalytic institutes can do psychoanalysis. In practice, most clinicians use varying levels of psychotherapy. Certainly nonpsychiatrists make excellent therapists. In fact, much of the best work is done by psychiatric social workers who have had additional training and experience in child and adolescent therapy.

Therapy Begins at Home

Nobody is more important in determining therapy's success or failure than the parent. Unfortunately, time and again, consciously or unconsciously, parents sabotage their child's treatment.

Some parents have a steadfast belief that therapy is shameful and they communicate their embarrassment to their child. They tell him that they are "disappointed" in him and imply that if he were *really* mature, or *really* smart he could solve his own problems. Some even imply that therapy is punishment for the years of trouble and worry the child has caused.

Some parents discuss with their child their doubts that therapy can ever help and/or their lack of confidence in the therapist.

Some parents expect instant results from therapy and show their impatience when the depression lingers. Not only has the therapist failed, these parents suggest, but so has the child.

Some parents insist on knowing everything that transpires during sessions, subjecting their child to intense cross-examination. Some even coach their child on what to say—or not say—to the therapist.

Other parents do the opposite and refuse to become even minimally involved. They tell the child, in essence, "If you need therapy that's your problem. Handle it yourself. I don't believe in therapy. I am embarrassed by it and I don't want to hear about it."

What *should* parents do? They should assure the child that therapy is nothing to be ashamed of, that, on the contrary, it is an opportunity to get in touch with one's feelings, to become happier and more sensitive. They should allow the child privacy but be available to talk and listen when the child is ready. During the course of therapy, they should be accepting of the new behaviors and attitudes that the child will undoubtedly want to try out. They should always remember that the child's problems took several years to build to the point of trouble and will take time to solve.

Biochemical Depression

"I wonder why I've come to hate myself so much," asked that nineteen-year-old sophomore from Northern Illinois University quoted earlier. "I've led a life pretty much like other teenagers. I have two loving parents who've always given me their time, praise, and unstinting affection. I've never had any major tragedies or deprivations in my life that might cause emotional upheaval. So why do I find myself playing with razor blades, wondering how much I would bleed if I slashed my wrists?"[4]

Occasionally, long, deep depressions, such as this girl's, are biochemical in origin; mixups in the brain chemistry. Called endogenous depressions, they are stubbornly resistant to good news or to getting accustomed to a disappointment or failure. For the biochemically depressed, time certainly does not heal all wounds.

The person suffering from endogenous depression—the college student quoted above is a good example—usually can't single out any reason for the depression—any particular thing that happened to cause it. These depressions really do seem to occur out of the blue.

In one experiment that illustrates how chemicals affect mood, convicts, known for their aggressive behavior, were injected with a substance that disturbs the brain's chemical balance in a manner that we believe is analogous to the way some depressions disturb that balance. Within minutes, the prisoners plunged into a full-scale depression. They felt suicidal, apathetic, and, most of all, helpless. They described their condition as "miserable" and said they were powerless to do anything about it.

Biochemical Depression: What Is It?

Until the middle of this century, we considered the causes of depression to be exclusively psychological. But even in ancient times, scientists suspected that some depressions had a physical as well as a psychological origin; that there was some imbalance in the body chemistry. Hippocrates (460–355 B.C.) blamed "black bile."

Scientists today also believe the culprit to be a kind of black bile—delicate chemical compounds called amines that are manufactured and stored in the nerve cells and that help send messages from nerve cell to nerve cell in the brain. In some people—and we don't know why—depression is caused by the inability of the brain to transmit chemical messages. Antidepressant drugs, which we'll discuss next in this chapter, simply help get those messages through.

The brain is composed of millions of nerve cells called neurons which think and sense by sending messages to each other across gaps called synapses. The message bearers are chemicals called neurotransmitters, which are composed of the amines described above. Neurotransmitters are released via electrical impulses.

After the chemical message is transmitted from cell to cell, the neurotransmitter is returned to and reabsorbed by the neuron from which it came. We believe that depression is caused when certain neurotransmitters, particularly two called norepinephrine and serotonin, are depleted at the points where they are needed near the synapses. (In cases of manic-depression, during the mania phases there may be too much of these compounds.)

The Major Antidepressants: How They Work

Two types of drugs seem to relieve depression by increasing the supply of these chemicals at the synapses. One group of antidepressants called Tricyclics work by partially inhibiting the amount of chemical neurotransmitters that are reabsorbed, leaving more available for use in neurotransmission. The other group, the monoamine-oxidase inhibitors (known for short as MAO inhibitors), slow action of an enzyme called monoamine oxidase which breaks down serotonin and norepinephrine and results in a greater supply of chemicals at the synapse.

Most Tricyclics require two to three weeks to take effect. Progress zigzags, with good periods followed by a fleeting return of the symptoms. If, after several weeks on one or more of the Tricyclics at maximum dosage, there is no response, the doctor will probably try an MAO inhibitor.

The newest Tricyclic, a drug called Asendin, was used in Europe and other countries before being approved for use in the United States. It *appears* to be an improvement over the older Tricyclics in two important ways. First, it works faster. In many patients it produces a significant antidepressant response within four days. Second, it *appears* to be almost completely free of the side effects, described later in this section, that plague users of the older Tricyclics and the MAO inhibitors. Parents should ask their child's doctor about Asendin, but keep in mind that, while the other Tricyclics have been available for nearly two decades, Asendin is a relatively new drug.

The third type of antidepressant is lithium, used to treat bipolar or manic depression, a disorder that accounts for 5 percent of all depressions. Lithium, a salt, is a deficiency medication. The manic-depressive has too little of this naturally occurring salt in his system. Giving him lithium gives him what he lacks, just as giving insulin to a diabetic compensates for inadequate secretion of that hormone. Like all antidepressants, lithium has potentially toxic side effects.

Are Drugs the Answer?

Most child psychiatrists avoid medicating children and even, when possible, teenagers. We would much prefer to get at the underlying family problems that cause the depression and to attempt to help the child understand these problems and learn to solve them or to live with them. For example, the child who has always turned anger on himself will typically feel more alone than his more outgoing sibling. He must recognize the characteristics of this pattern and the vicissitudes of behaving in this way. Only then is change possible.

But parents should be aware that antidepressants—which should be administered in combination with psychotherapy—are an option. They should ask their child's doctor about antidepressants, especially if psychotherapy doesn't seem to be working.

And so we have included here descriptions of how antidepressants work, their side effects and the opinions and research of experts who believe very strongly in them. A word of warning: almost all the research on the efficacy of antidepressants has been conducted on adults. We still don't really know how effective antidepressants are with children. We do know that these drugs don't always have the same effect on children as on adults. This is a new field of research that awaits exploration.

Most studies show that approximately 65 percent of depressed patients (remember, we're talking about adults) will respond to the first Tricyclic they're given. And after a course of these drugs, many people never suffer a second bout.

Wina Sturgeon, a West Coast radio and television writer who wrote an Emmy Award-winning television documentary and later a book on depression, is one of many people who says that antidepressants saved her life. Although she had an IQ of 147, her behavior during most of her childhood, teens, and early twenties was erratic. She was horribly lonely, couldn't make or keep friends, and held twenty-one different jobs during her first eighteen months away from home. She had a breakdown when she was twenty-five and at that point was prescribed her first course of antidepressants. The drug, she says, reversed the deterioration of a "mind that had been possessed by chemical imbalance for most of its years." Six months later she was recovered and on her way to a successful career. "For the first time, I was beginning to find out that I wasn't abnormal and different."[5] (One can only guess what might have happened to her erratic behavior had drugs been used with her as a child.)

Another woman said her reaction to the Tricyclic Elavil was "that of experiencing a miracle, as if I'd been living in a perpetual fog, a drizzle, or wearing misted-over glasses for a long time, which suddenly had been wiped clean. . . . Suddenly things were in place again and not at all overwhelming."

Although we're not quite sure why, antidepressants work better for some people than for others. Barbara, who called WFYR during a radio show on teen suicide, complained that her doctor put her on Elavil, the drug just touted. "All I can say about Elavil is it makes me calmer to plan the suicide. I just think it's a matter of time."[6]

But still, the trend is definitely toward increased use of these drugs and at lower and lower ages. Dr. Barry Garfinkel, a Canadian authority on youth suicide, goes so far as to blame the astronomical rise in the youth suicide rate on ". . . pediatricians and family doctors (who) don't recognize depression in children and are not treating it with antidepressant drugs."

A European study conducted by Swiss psychiatrist Walter Poldinger supports Garfinkel's charge. Poldinger found that suicide rates among young people could be lowered 12–15 percent by using antidepressants.

But these drugs do have side effects—some relatively mild, including constipation, dry mouth, urinary retention, impotence, blurred vision, and dizziness, and some not so mild. The drugs can send the patient into an intense torpor that Wina Sturgeon said turned her into a "zombie for about two weeks," but which passed as soon as her central nervous system adjusted to the medication. "The feeling of torpor is very similar to the feeling you would get if you had taken a sleeping pill, then for some reason had to get up and function," Sturgeon explained. "You would feel as if you were wading through molasses." Her doctor did not advise her to take time off from work when she first started her medication or to avoid driving. He should have. While waiting for a red light to change, she fell asleep. She got so sleepy while driving that she had to open all the windows and shout simple math sums just to stay awake.[7]

One of the reasons why Tricyclics are more widely prescribed today than the older MAO inhibitors is that if the person taking an MAO inhibitor eats certain foods, such as chocolate or beer, or takes certain over-the-counter drugs, such as cold medicines, his blood pressure could rise to a dangerous and even deadly level.

Anyone taking an antidepressant of either type should avoid alcohol completely. These drugs increase the intoxicating effects of alcohol and accentuate alcohol's depressing effect on the central nervous system. Antidepressant users should also avoid all tranquilizers, narcotics, and stimulants. The mix can be deadly.

Similarly, if a doctor switches a patient between a Tricyclic and an MAO inhibitor, he must realize that these drugs can be killers if mixed. It is absolutely essential that the person be free of one type of antidepressant for at least ten days before starting another type. A fourteen-year-old girl, for example, had been taking an MAO inhibitor for three weeks without any discernible improvement. Her mother became impatient and took her daughter to another psychiatrist whom she didn't tell about the first medication and from whom she got a prescription for a Tricyclic. She abruptly switched her daughter's medication, obviously before the

MAO inhibitor had left her system. About a week later, the girl began convulsing and died.

The key to the effectiveness of an antidepressant is the doctor who prescribes it. He must be up to date and experienced in using these drugs. The field of depression drug research is so new (the first antidepressant was discovered thirty years ago) that a doctor who got his degree more than fifteen years ago may have only the most primitive knowledge of antidepressants.

The doctor who has a "feel" for using these drugs, who has a good track record in using them, is most likely to find the right drug for the particular patient the first time—rather than the third or fourth time—around. Considering that most of these drugs take a minimum of two weeks to begin working, and considering that depressed people are often suicidal, wasting time can prove fatal.

Pitfalls await the inexperienced doctor. Erring on the side of caution, he may prescribe too low a dose, which means that the medication will have little or no effect. Valuable time and sometimes a life can be wasted.

And there is another common problem in treating depression. Even if one Tricyclic doesn't work, the patient may react positively to a second or third—there are twelve Tricyclics currently on the market. An inexperienced doctor may stubbornly persist for months with the first drug he has tried. Or he may persist with one class of antidepressants—Tricyclics, for example—when one of the eleven MAO inhibitors currently available might do the trick.

Making the wrong guess several times can consume months of a depressed person's life. The fact that the drugs aren't working may, of course, make the depressed person feel more hopeless than ever.

Although Jonathan's unfortunate visit to a psychiatrist and pediatrician happened six years ago, even today many doctors don't consider antidepressants when faced with a patient complaining of anxiety and sleeplessness. Instead they may prescribe a tranquilizer such as Valium, Librium, or Miltown or a barbiturate such as Nembutal or Seconal. Thus they treat the symptoms of depression without treating the cause, which is comparable to giving a serious gunshot-wound patient a painkiller. It may relieve the immediate distress, but it won't stop the bleeding or the patient's inevitable slide into death.

Tranquilizers and barbiturates not only waste valuable time, but, since they are used to reduce anxiety and induce sleep by depressing the central nervous system, can also make a depressed person more depressed.‡

Shock Treatment

Anyone who read *One Flew Over the Cuckoo's Nest* or saw the movie adaptation cannot forget the awful scenes of forced electroshock treatment—the common name for electroconvulsive therapy (ECT). Introduced about forty years ago, over a decade before antidepressant drugs, there are few medical treatments that elicit such horror. Most people think of ECT as a kind of medieval torture, a primitive and inhumane procedure that should have gone out with leeches.

That is why it surprises people to hear that ECT is a widely used treatment (anywhere from 60,000 to 100,000 persons, almost all adults, undergo ECT every year) that is no more horrifying to watch than the induction of anesthesia. Many experts also believe that ECT is an effective treatment.

However, ECT is certainly not the treatment of choice for a depressed youngster. It is almost always used with adults, usually with elderly patients who have gotten no relief at all from psychotherapy or drugs.

We've included a discussion of ECT here because some parents will be confronted with a doctor asking permission to administer it. There are doctors who believe it is an effective treatment for severely depressed children or adolescents. So it is important to

‡ The number of depressed people being "treated" with tranquilizers and barbiturates is enormous. Valium, for example, is the most prescribed drug. In 1979 doctors wrote 81.5 million prescriptions for tranquilizers. And these sedatives and barbiturates are very often the suicide vehicle. In 1978 more than 1,500 people died in hospital emergency rooms from misuse of tranquilizers. Valium alone was responsible for an estimated 50,000 emergency-room visits that year. In England and Wales in 1968, overdoses of barbiturates accounted for 30 percent of all suicide verdicts and 65 percent of all suicide deaths due to drugs. In a just-published study of 505 suicide attempts among adolescents and children, researchers found that 87.9 percent of the youngsters chose drug overdoses as their method of suicide.[8]

know that this option also exists and to understand how it works.

An ECT session would proceed something like this: The patient is sedated and, via an electrode, current is delivered to the temples, triggering a grand mal epileptic seizure. Because the patient is given a muscle relaxer shortly before the current is activated, he does not experience the muscle contractions characteristic of an epileptic seizure. When the doctor delivers the current, the only noticeable movement is the arm shooting up, the fingers clenched in a clawlike fashion. That is the signal to the doctor that the patient is having a full convulsion. The seizure lasts about forty seconds and the entire procedure takes about fifteen minutes. (Researchers are still not sure just how ECT works. They suspect that the electrically induced seizure alters the balance of neurotransmitters in the brain.)

One session is never enough. For most patients the ECT is given about three times a week over a period of two weeks. Some people have as many as twenty-five treatments.

Studies with adults have shown that antidepressant drugs relieve about 65–70 percent of biochemical depressions. That means that they don't work in about 30 percent of the cases. ECT is normally used among the adults who constitute this 30 percent. The re generally people in middle to later life who suffer from severe depression characterized by vast losses of appetite, sleep, energy, concentration, and memory.

Advocates of ECT point to a study showing that while drugs work in 65–70 percent of cases, ECT works in 90–95 percent. In an eight-year study of ECT at the National Institute of Mental Health, only one of nine severely depressed patients failed to respond. According to Dr. Michel R. Mandel, a member of the American Psychiatric Association, which reviewed the efficacy of ECT, and also director of the Somatic Therapies Consultation Service at Massachusetts General Hospital in Boston, "We're talking about a group of people for whom as a matter of fact, nothing *but* brain stimulation is really going to be of help."

Mandel, and many other psychiatrists, consider ECT the treatment of choice when the risk of suicide is great. The two to five weeks that most antidepressants take to work and the frequent need to try more than one drug constitute too big a risk for the severely suicidal person.

Many psychiatrists who have treated patients with both drugs and ECT claim that there are fewer complications and side effects from ECT than from antidepressants. But because the prospect of ECT so terrifies families, even of the devastatingly depressed, drugs are usually tried first.

ECT has one side effect that particularly and understandably frightens people. There is some memory loss of the hours and days preceding the treatment, although the loss is, for the most part, transitory.

However, if you talk to people who have had ECT, most will report that their depression lifted rather quickly, but they suffered memory losses and "dulling." Wina Sturgeon, who interviewed more than twenty-five people treated by ECT, said she heard two complaints over and over. Their memories, they said, were never as good as before and "they had dulled . . . Yes, there was a serenity that was absent during their depressions, but it was a bland serenity. In one person, whom I had admired for his creativity, the creative spark seemed extinguished. He was normal in the traditional sense of the word . . . but he no longer had the spontaneity that had made him a charming and popular person. Where once he had written moving poetry, he no longer showed any interest in writing. . . . He seemed settled, almost vague."[9]

Depression: Is It Inherited?

That suicide and depression run in families is a clinical fact. Carl Tishler, a psychologist at Children's Hospital in Columbus, Ohio, found, for example, that fathers of suicide-prone teens were more depressed and anxious than fathers of control-group youngsters. Mothers of suicide-prone teens often considered suicide themselves, more so than their husbands or the parents in the other control group.

Child psychiatrists Leon Cytryn and Donald McKnew of the NIMH studied a group of children and grandchildren—aged four to fifteen—of patients admitted to NIMH for treatment of depression. They found that these children also were suffering from depression.

In another study of adolescents who had killed themselves, researchers found that almost all the victims' mothers were themselves depressed and preoccupied with suicide. Cynthia Pfeffer found similar results—mothers of suicidal children are more often depressed than mothers of those who are not. Children of depressed parents are said to be as much as 30 percent more likely to become depressed than children of nondepressed parents. Most interesting, studies have shown that if one identical twin suffers from depression, the other twin has a 60–70 percent chance of also being depressed—even when the two were raised separately.

Based on studies such as these, many psychiatrists believe that a tendency to depression may be passed through families in the same way that hypertension and diabetes are passed through families.

However, what part genetics and what part environment plays in producing depression is not known. Is the child of a depressed parent doomed by his genes or by the household in which he grew up? Does the child identify with his depressed parent? Obviously, the parent who has low self-esteem and low energy is not going to provide a healthy model to his child. Does the depressed child feel responsible for his parent's depression? Is his depression a result of the depressed parent's lack of emotional support? Of the depressed parent's inability to see beyond his own problems?

If depression is indeed genetic, passed from one generation to the next, shouldn't there be genetic markers? Shouldn't we be able to test for depression as we test for diabetes? Shouldn't we be able to warn parents that the genes they're passing to their children may make those children susceptible to depression?

There is mounting evidence that the answers are yes. In November 1981, scientists at the University of Rochester Medical School reported in the *New England Journal of Medicine* that they had located one or more genes that make people susceptible to severe depression. Their discovery should make it possible for doctors to identify couples who are likely to produce children with the affliction.

In May 1982 researchers announced two tests for depression that underscore the physiological and genetic nature of many depressions. A researcher from Northwestern University, using a simple blood test, reported an 80 percent accuracy rate in identifying patients suffering from depression or manic-depression. When results of the blood test were correlated with a patient's family history, the accuracy rate increased to nearly 100 percent. Researchers at the University of Pittsburgh were able to detect depression in 80–90 percent of cases by charting the brain waves of sleeping patients.

Depression Is *An Illness*

Chris's mother talked, on camera, to the producers of a television program on suicide: "Well, since he's dead I realize he was really very depressed the last year of his life, and when he was alive, I didn't realize this so much. So, I never said anything to him about depression. But he didn't smile much, did he? And we used to tease him about that. We'd say, 'Oh, Chris, you'd be happy if you'd look happy and make a better impression.' Well, reading about people who have depression—I-I realize now that's the world's stupidest thing to say to someone who's really depressed, because he probably didn't know why he was depressed, and he couldn't possibly have smiled, and it just wasn't in him."[10]

Chris's mother's analysis, although it came too late, was perfectly correct. Demanding of a very depressed person, "Snap out of it!" or "Cheer up!" is like telling a terminal cancer patient, "Cheer up, things will get better." Such advice is not only *not* going to make the person feel better, it's going to increase his psychic pain because he knows he can't do anything to extricate himself from his awful ordeal.

One of the biggest problems people with depression face is that their friends and relatives and they themselves don't believe they are *really* sick. The person who has pneumonia gets sympathy; the person who has depression gets barely tolerated. He is seen by himself and others as self-indulgent and weak-willed. Depressed young people have a special problem that we mentioned earlier. Their wild, often obnoxious, behavior leaves parents feeling angry instead of sympathetic.

Psychiatrist Ari Kiev, director of Cornell University's Suicide Prevention Center, tells depressed patients and their parents,

"Look, Tommy has a disease just like the Hong Kong flu. Maybe he has the Hong Kong depression. First, he has got to realize he is emotionally ill. . . . Most of the patients have never admitted to themselves that they are sick . . ."

Depression is an illness, but it is not an incurable illness. The youngster must be made to understand this—that he will get better; and that he is, in fact, in good company. Abraham Lincoln, Nathaniel Hawthorne, Winston Churchill, Sigmund Freud, and astronaut Buzz Aldrin are just a few of the famous people who suffered serious bouts of depression and went on to great accomplishments.

What Are the Chances for a Cure?

With the proper treatment, the depressed patient has an 80–90 percent chance for a full recovery. About 50 percent of those who suffer a single attack of depression never suffer one again.

However, the latest estimates from the National Institute of Mental Health indicate that, in the absence of effective treatment, depression becomes a chronic and relapsing disorder in as many as 80–100 percent of patients who are struck with their first episode. Studies show that the person hospitalized for depression at some time in his life is about 30 times more likely to commit suicide than is the nondepressed person.

Although most psychiatric textbooks contain the statement that there is an excellent chance—many experts say as high as a 95 percent chance—of recovery from depression, the sobering caveat "unless suicide intervenes" always follows.

"Unless suicide intervenes"—psychotherapy and drug therapy are obviously treatments that require time. Sometimes there simply is no time. Parents are faced with a child who has made up his mind to kill himself—that evening or the next morning or the next week. What to do in a situation such as this—how to get the child through the suicidal crisis so he can be helped—is the subject of our next chapter.

PART IV

What Parents Can Do

11

The Crisis: What Can You Do?

"What can you do?" The answer to that question is "Plenty." And the answer to its companion question—"When should you do it?"—is "Now."

Our message to parents in this chapter is that, in the moment of crisis, they must do something and do it right away. They must discard their old patterns of relating to the child, especially if those patterns include avoiding confrontation or waiting until the morning. The suicidal child, who typically feels out of control and uncared for, needs someone to take control immediately. By doing so, parents will assuage the child's other fear. They will show their son or daughter that someone does care.

Recently we interviewed friends and family of a girl from the Los Angeles area who, early one Saturday evening in June, jumped out from between parked cars into the path of a speeding van. She lingered in a coma for three days before dying.

In piecing together a "psychological autopsy" of this fifteen-year-old girl, whom we'll call Monica S., it is obvious that in the months before her death she cried for help time and again and never got it. Although some of her cries were oblique, others were quite straightforward.

Caught up in their own problems, Monica's parents didn't hear her—or didn't want to hear her. A month before she died, Monica grilled her mother about what transpired during Mrs. S.'s weekly sessions with her psychoanalyst and whether Dr. R. might also be

able "to help a kid." Mrs. S., who enjoyed talking about the progress of her own analysis, gave Monica a detailed description, but
never asked her daughter, "Why the sudden interest?" She also
didn't pursue the second part of Monica's question. "Would Dr.
R. also be able to help a kid?"

In the days before her suicide, Monica had slept and eaten very
little. When her boyfriend called late Saturday afternoon to make
plans for that evening, Monica asked her father to tell him she
was sick. All of this behavior was totally out of character.

On the night of the suicide, while Mr. and Mrs. S. dressed to go
out, they worried together about the changes in their daughter.
Mr. S. suggested asking Monica straight out if anything was
wrong. But they agreed there was no time for talk if they were
going to make their dinner party on time. They decided to talk to
Monica first thing in the morning "when we're all fresher."

Mr. S. was backing the car out of the garage when Monica
came running and knocked on the car window. "What is it?" Mr.
S. asked, as he pushed the power window button and, reflexively
and impatiently, glanced at his watch. Monica, greeted by a cold
gust of air conditioning, blushed and looked flustered as she answered, "Oh, nothing, I just wanted to say good-bye." She obviously wanted to say much more.

One of the points we have made repeatedly is that people who
attempt or commit suicide are almost always highly ambivalent
about actually killing themselves. Remember, 75 percent of people who commit suicide give repeated warning. Most suicidal people are crying—indeed begging—for help. It is up to their friends,
and especially their families, to give them that help.

When Dr. Louis Wekstein finished writing a scholarly book on
suicide, he sent the manuscript to a colleague who read it and then
asked Wekstein, "After having written this book, what in your
opinion is the greatest single obstacle to a more effective approach
against this needless self-inflicted slaughter?"

Wekstein replied with one word: "Indifference."[1]

We must prove to the suicidal person that we are not indifferent; that we care; that we are willing to become actively involved with him and stay actively involved—even if getting involved means getting into a fight. Anger, after all, is at least a
form of communication. The crucial thing is to connect with that

child in some way. Like Monica, the troubled youngster can sense detachment, and detachment simply confirms his suspicion that no one cares.

"Primarily I learned . . . that all the clichés about tender-loving-care are true," wrote one young woman who flirted with suicide and ultimately backed away. "What I needed was to have people with me, to listen when I needed to talk, to hold and comfort me when I needed to cry, and occasionally to play parent and take things away from me when I was out of control."[2]

Do Something! Now!

The cardinal rule of suicide prevention is Do Something—and NOW. Don't wait to make sure the person is really serious. Don't wait to see if other signs develop. Don't decide to sleep on it, or, as Monica's parents did, to wait until tomorrow morning "when we're all fresher." Tomorrow may be too late.

The most obvious and appropriate first step is to ask your child if he is considering killing himself. Don't worry about putting ideas into his head. The ideas are already there. Putting a fear into words defuses it; transforms it into something tangible that can be dealt with.

You'll show you care by broaching the subject. Too often adults wait for exactly the right opportunity. There is no right opportunity. When you see the need, start talking.

It has happened often enough in my practice to constitute a trend of sorts. Parents who fear their child may be suicidal come to me for advice. When I ask them if they have talked to the child about suicide, they say, "That's too important to talk about."

Obviously, it's too important *not* to talk about. Ask the child straight out, "Are you thinking of suicide?" "Are you feeling depressed enough to want to end your life?" "Do you ever feel there is no hope in life?" "Do you *never* have any fun?" "Do you ever want to hurt yourself?"

If you simply can't be that blunt, if you need to ease into the question, you might say, "I've noticed you stay in your room a lot, you don't talk anymore, you're not eating very much, you're not sleeping. Is something bothering you?" If the child says, "Yes," continue with, "I guess sometimes it seems as though it's not worth it to go on struggling and fighting when so many disappointing things happen to you." If he agrees again, you might ask, "Do you sometimes wake up in the morning and wish you didn't have to wake up, wish you were dead?" If the answer is still yes, then it's time to ask, "Have you been thinking of killing yourself?"

Sometimes it's better to take this more indirect route because asking immediately, "Are you thinking about killing yourself?" can lead to a denial. The child may be too stubborn or embarrassed to back off from the denial. Then both parent and child are stuck with a lie.

No matter the particular words, what's most important is that the lines of communication be kept open. The "conversation without words" that's part of the mother/infant bonding process should come into play again at the time of a crisis. The words themselves are not the major communication. The fact of seizing the initiative, of looking at the child with concern and love, of airing a darkly forbidden subject—this is the real communication.

No One To Talk To

Young people who attempt suicide typically feel they have no one they can talk to. "I didn't like myself at all," Jennifer, who had attempted suicide, explained to a reporter on ABC's "Nightline," "and I didn't feel like there was anybody that if turned to, they'd say 'I care.'"[3]

At a meeting of Suiciders Anonymous in Corona, California, two girls explained why they had attempted suicide. "I got into a fight with my stepmother and I was kicked out of the house," said one girl who had attempted suicide twice, "and I lived by myself for a long time, and I just felt there was nobody around, and I thought that if my father didn't want me there, I wasn't worth being around."

Another girl said, "I didn't think anybody cared for me, and I didn't think I had anything to live for. So, I tried suicide."[4]

In a recent study, when asked to whom they would turn if they were in trouble, over 25 percent of the young people responded that there was *no one* who really cared or would understand them. Most teens are terrified by this isolation.

For a Harvard College course on death and suicide, a young man named Gordon, whose brother committed suicide, described the wake. "What are you all frightened of, you kids?" an uncle asked him. "I don't know," Gordon answered. "I guess, sort of the fear of being rejected by another person, of being humiliated if you ask them for help. Just scared to death of that."[5]

The most important force preventing young people from killing themselves is a warm and dependable relationship with someone who genuinely cares for the young person and can convince him or her that this concern is genuine. In short, someone to *really* talk to—and we emphasize *really* talk. And, even more important, someone who will *really* listen. Far too often, when a parent and a troubled youngster sit down to talk, the conversation turns into a lecture. Talk *with* your child, not *at* him. Listen; don't preach.

Too many conversations turn into converse interchanges—with parent and child going in opposite directions. This happens because the person with the supposed answers gives too many words and too much advice. The best advice is the child's own words coming back to him. It is a common experience in therapy to learn that the less one says the better. Then the patient can come up with his own answers.

So as your child talks about what's troubling him, don't jump in with your recommended solution. Let him vent his feelings. He may sound inarticulate and unintelligible, but let him ramble. Having a compassionate listener who will permit him to express feelings of rage and resentment is the most important thing.

"I was just so happy to get it all out. To have someone put their arm around me and say, 'I really care about you . . .' It made me think again what would happen to me if I really did die . . ." said one girl who decided against suicide.

Calling for Outside Help

There are, of course, families in which parent and child couldn't talk to each other if their lives depended on it. Because they do, the parents should call an outside person for help—immediate help, not an appointment for next week. In Chapter 12, we'll discuss the variety of professionals available in most communities and how to find them. But for now, let's just show how an outsider can mediate when parent/child communication seems utterly impossible.

In the case described below, the outsider is a psychiatrist. A person who is specially trained to help suicidal youngsters should be first on the list of people to call. But sometimes a child will adamantly refuse to talk to a "shrink" or other specialist. In such a case the parent must get the child talking to someone with whom he feels communicative—perhaps a clergyman whom the child trusts, a teacher whom he respects, a favorite uncle, a neighbor to whom the child sometimes talked after school. The outsider also needn't be an adult. If the child refuses to talk to anyone but her boyfriend, then that teenager may be the bridge between life and death. Parents should be sure to have a trained person standing by as a consultant.

What's most important is that the parent not get trapped in the sort of mindless jealousy we've seen repeatedly. "I am the parent here. If my child needs help in a crisis, he'll get it from me."

A North Shore mother called one evening to say she had found in her purse a suicide note from her thirteen-year-old daughter, then crying in her room. Rachel had a history of refusing to talk to her mother but of occasionally confiding in her father. I recommended that Rachel's father talk to her about the note and that Rachel see me at the clinic first thing in the morning.

Rachel sat quietly in the waiting room, shaking her head no to my invitation to come in. I told her I'd be in my room and hoped she'd join me. After fifteen minutes of waiting I went to a typewriter, in full view of Rachel, wrote a brief note thanking her for coming and hoping that next time she would join me. When I took it to her, she read it carefully and, as I turned to leave, tore it up. Then she quietly left the building.

During the next session, Rachel sat with me in my office, but turned forty-five degrees away, offered nothing spontaneously, and answered in short, hostile sentences. However, she stayed for forty-five of the fifty minutes scheduled. In the sketchiest fashion, she shared her concerns about her upcoming bas mitzvah, her feeling that nothing would ever work out, that "shrinks" could never help, and that she did not want to come back to the clinic. She left the interview in a huff, but timed her departure minutes before she knew I would have to prepare to see another patient.

I learned from a teacher that Rachel had been talking about suicide at school and I suggested, with her parents' permission, that the teacher focus a classroom discussion on suicide and encourage students to express their feelings on the subject in poetry or short stories. Several nights later, Rachel left a suicidal poem for her father. Her mother called me for direction. I suggested she let Rachel know she knew of the poem and that, with her approval, both she and I would like to see it.

Two days later, the poem arrived in my mail with a note indicating that Rachel had approved her mother's sending it.

> Outside I'm happy and enjoy life,
> Inside I want to cut my heart out with a knife.
> Outside I'm as happy and funny as can be,
> Inside I seem to be angry at everyone, really me!
>
> People push my buttons to make me work,
> ding—ding—ding—dong.
> I break into little pieces, they try to put me together,
> but they put me together all wrong.
>
> I have two faces like a good actress,
> Happy, the one that's not really me.
> The second is Sad as you can guess,
> That's the one that's me.
>
> I'm going to be an actress,
> and a good one at that!
> No need to be so distressed,
> For I have my two faces.
>
> I'm very good at hiding my feelings,
> I've been doing it all my life,
> And thanks to that I've tried to take away my life,
> by cutting my wrists with a knife.

For the first time, Rachel was putting her random feelings into perspective. With the help of an outsider, Rachel was talking more to her father and also beginning to trust her mother. By communicating with their daughter in a way the girl could accept, Rachel's parents had started her down a nonsuicidal path.

What Not to Say to a Suicidal Teen

Imagine yourself having a conversation with a fourteen-year-old who admits to being on the verge of suicide.

"I am so unhappy," the child complains. "I can't stand it. There's only one thing for me to do and that's kill myself."

How do you respond? Unfortunately, too many parents respond with "That's ridiculous"—a comment that merely intensifies a child's anguish and alienation. Such a response makes him feel totally useless, as if he is never going to be taken seriously, as if he is doomed to be the object of rejection, indifference, derision.

Another common response to such a declaration is kinder, but equally defeating. A child's confession that he is contemplating suicide prompts a parent to pat the young person on the shoulder and assure him, "Everything will be all right." Well, it won't, and the child knows it. Trivial reassurances only confirm the child's fear of not being taken seriously, his fear that nobody will ever be able to fathom the depths of his despair.

"There's nothing to worry about," a parent says, as he dismisses his son's confession that he is so shattered by not being asked to join a club that he is considering suicide. To the adult, the child's problem does seem unimportant. But the parent must understand that to the child the problem is literally a matter of life and death.

This is a lesson that is very hard for parents to learn. Consider the case of Ed Kane. He had two sons who killed themselves, first Tom, age twenty-one, and then Mike, age twenty-four. "Finding out the reason doesn't do a damn bit of good," Ed Kane said after his boys' deaths. "It has no comfort. There's no satisfaction in it at all because the results are just so bloody horrible. It doesn't alter things because even when you know, even when you find out the reason, the reaction is, 'For that? For that stupid reason? For that, this, my beautiful son did himself in?' Christ, *that* we could have taken care of in ten minutes." His sons undoubtedly would have disagreed. They presumably thought their problems could not be "taken care of in ten minutes" or they wouldn't have killed themselves.[6]

If the young person admits he is contemplating suicide, don't try to argue with him about whether he should live or die. One young woman recalled, ". . . when I was feeling suicidal, a friend dealt with it by telling me I didn't really feel that way, and the results were disastrous. I felt guiltier, more isolated, and hence more suicidal than before."[7]

And don't try to convince a suicidal person that suicide is immoral. The suicidal person already feels guilty. Lecturing him on the immorality of suicide only deepens his depression and guilt. Similarly, don't try to induce guilt by telling him that feeling suicidal is selfish, that he should be grateful for what he has because so many others are worse off. If the suicidal person believed that, he would not be suicidal. All you do by making such a statement is add to the person's feelings of guilt, hopelessness, and worthlessness, his belief that nobody understands him and his conviction that he does not deserve to live.

The suicidal young person must sense that he can express his true feelings with impunity—that he can freely show hostility, hate, resentment, vindictiveness, and immorality without a parent piously demanding, "How could you dare think and say such a thing?" In America, suicide has always been viewed as a dishonorable act. The youngster knows this and is terribly ashamed. At the time he needs help most, he knows he risks being treated as an outcast if he asks for it.

Forget moralizing and chastising. This is the worst possible time for it. Instead show your child an unshakable attitude of acceptance, interest, and concern.

Suicide Is Not Painless

The young woman just quoted who overcame her suicidal wishes remembered one friend in particular who helped her immensely by coolly discussing suicide as a practical and impending act. ". . . how was I going to carry it out? Was I sure I could do it without botching it and ending up alive and paralyzed or brain-damaged? Could I do it in such a way that my body wasn't discovered by someone who loved me and would be traumatized for life?

"The discussion may sound heartless, but it was in fact extremely helpful. It demystified suicide, taking it out of the realm of guilt and sentiment and making it what it was: a totally serious and irrevocable decision which I had the right to make but was responsible—both to myself and my friends—for making clear-headedly."[8]

When I have tried psychotherapy with a suicidal patient for a meaningful period of time and we just don't seem to be getting anywhere, I will say directly, "Well, if you are determined to kill yourself then be sure to do a good job. I don't want you brain-damaged or paraplegic." I have no data on whether or not this approach helps, but none of the patients with whom I have used it ever tried suicide again.

Parents should follow this lead and question their child closely and specifically about his suicide plans. When do you plan to do it?—late at night, in the late afternoon, etc.? Where? With what? If pills, what kind and how many? If with a gun, do you have access to one? Will you shoot yourself through the head, the eye, the heart?

Not only will these questions force the suicidal person to look at the suicide act as unromantic, disfiguring, and permanent, they will also provide an accurate indication of just how critical the crisis is. In general, the more specific the plans, the greater the danger of suicide.

"You Won't Always Feel This Bad"

In getting children to understand the reality of suicide, parents must stress what to them seems obvious, but is not necessarily obvious to the child. Suicide is irreversible; but as long as there is life there is always the chance that things will get better. The depression that the child feels is temporary. It will lift.

Tell your child to "hang on." The depressive feelings, the painful feelings, the feelings of utter hopelessness and despair, will pass. He will feel much better. And when he does, he will be glad to be alive.

The annals of suicide research are filled with young people whose attempts were "unsuccessful" and who agree that even if things are still bad in their lives, they're glad to be alive. Mention some of these cases to your child—for example, three of the teens from Omaha, Nebraska, featured in a recent nationally aired television program on teen suicide.

Erin, fifteen, swallowed thirty-six phenobarbital pills, climbed into her locker, and shut the door. If her gym teacher hadn't noticed the edge of her dress sticking out, she would have died. She said later, "I really don't know how to put it in words. I feel that I don't want to die anymore. I feel that committing suicide is very self-centered and it was very foolish because I had a lot of people around me and I should have noticed and thought of them. I never did."

Dan, sixteen, is now in group therapy with other adolescents who have attempted suicide. He said, "Well, I figured it (suicide) would be a way to end . . . all my problems and everything. I felt that there was no other way out of there and tried suicide. Then, suddenly, when I started to get help I came to realize that no, that was not the truth, that I wanted to live."

The third teenager, a boy, slit his wrists and, while bleeding to death, hid from the paramedics, police, and his family. Paramedics found him after thirty minutes and rushed him to a hospital. He said, "Do you know why I'm glad to be alive? I'm very glad. I'm glad I didn't succeed. I tried too—hard. I ran. I ran from the cops. I ran from the ambulance. I ditched in bushes. I sat there and bled to death but they found me. And the funny thing is when they found me I felt pretty damned good about it. What can I say? It's great. Now I got a lot more time to think about what the hell I'm doing. It's good. I'll have a lot more time to think about it."[9]

"You're Not a Freak"

"Sometimes I think that some of the changes I'm going through are unique," said Anita, fifteen. "I feel, 'Does anybody else go through this?' I ask myself if I'm crazy for feeling this way. 'Is there something wrong with me for feeling those desires, for hating my mother so much; for taking all those pills? Do I need to be in a mental institution?' "10

Anita felt hopeless, worthless, utterly alone. Let your child know that he is not alone, that he is not the first to suffer so, that he is not a freak or crazy, that others have been equally or more depressed and have survived.

Take Charge

If you trace the hours before a young person commits suicide, in almost every case you'll realize that the suicide wouldn't have happened had someone stayed with the child—not left him alone, even for a minute.

Mark Cada had been noticeably depressed and had even threatened suicide. His mother recalled that the night before he killed himself, "I had heard some noise during the night and I got up and Mark was still up puttering in the bathroom. And I thought, 'He's going to run away 'cause he's so upset.' And I told him he better get to bed and it was two or three in the morning. And when we got up we were kind of thinking that maybe he was going to do something like that, in a way, not really, but I don't know, it was just a strange feeling."11

The moral to that case is that if you have any suspicions, even a vague hunch that your child is suicidal—which Mark's mother obviously did have—don't, under any circumstances, leave him alone. Don't go to bed. Follow—don't swallow—that strange feeling. Offer hot chocolate and a kitchen table at which to talk.

Don't worry about infuriating the suicidal person who screams, "Leave me alone!" Don't worry about invading his privacy. Don't worry about feeling stupid if your suspicions prove groundless.

You can't take chances with a suicidal person. And you can't take too many precautions. Don't leave any lethal weapons around the house. Clear every room of razor blades, ropes, poisons in the form of household cleaners, medicines, sleeping pills. And don't just hide them. Throw them out or store them in another location to which the suicidal person does not have access.

Parents: The Last Ones to Know

Elizabeth George, a friend of newspaper reporter and suicide victim Frances Kryzwicki's, recalled one afternoon in April. "I found her (Frances) stumbling across her apartment floor loaded with thirty-six sleeping pills. I told Fran I didn't want to write her obituary and took her to a hospital. But I promised her I wouldn't tell anyone what she had done and told them it was bad pork she had eaten." Three months later, Frances, twenty-five, a reporter for the Newport News *Daily Press*, jumped to her death from the Chesapeake Bay Bridge. Frances' parents were utterly confounded by their daughter's suicide. Elizabeth George, also a newspaper reporter, had kept Frances' confidence and not told her parents of the attempt.[12]

Mike Kane, the Baltimore youth who hanged himself halfway through his freshman year at the University of Maryland Law School, told at least seven people of his problems and depression. But he spoke to each in confidence, extracting a promise from each not to reveal the contents of the conversation or to try to get him help.[13]

Vivienne Loomis' best friend, Anne Tucker, recalled, "We used to go on long walks around the campus (of the private high school they attended in Weston, Massachusetts). She told me all about the pills in August (i.e., about her first suicide attempt). I knew from what she told me that she was very, very serious about suicide, but it was sacred, like a secret between us. I could never have betrayed her by telling anyone. It would have been like stabbing her. I had no choice."

Vivienne's sister, Laurel, also decided that her sister's confessions were confidential, not to be shared with their parents. "Sometimes she'd tell me that she'd tried to strangle herself. She swore me to secrecy. . . . It's hard to explain, but it was like a trade-off. She knew about things I was doing that our parents would never approve of, and I trusted her not to tell them. She trusted me too."

Vivienne wrote long letters to her former teacher describing in vivid detail her suicide "rehearsals." She did not try to moderate or disguise her cry for help. She was openly begging him to do something. The teacher, then living in California, did not share his insights and information about Vivienne's anguished existence with her parents. He assumed they were aware their daughter was dangerously suicidal.

By the end of that year, Vivienne was dead, having hanged herself in her mother's silversmith studio. It was only then that Anne, Laurel, and Vivienne's teacher discussed Vivienne's problems with her parents.[14]

Francine Klagsbrun found in her survey of college students that 49 percent answered "yes" to the question, "Do you think suicide among young people is ever justified?" This response seems to show that suicide is not only free of sin in young people's minds, but also a socially acceptable solution to life's problems.[15]

A teacher recently told us of overhearing two tenth-graders talking. One said she had so many problems that she was thinking of either killing herself or visiting a cousin in Colorado. The friend simply nodded understandingly, showing no sign of being the least bit surprised that her friend considered, in the same breath, suicide or a vacation as equally viable means of dealing with problems.

The danger in such an attitude is that young people may feel no moral obligation to let a parent or responsible adult know if a friend confesses to feeling suicidal.

Don't count on your child's friends to take the initiative and warn you of trouble. Many youngsters simply don't consider suicide trouble. Heartbreaking cases of young people who told their friends only to have them say, "Well, if that's what you want, it's your business," show us that suicide, to some teens, has been drained of all stigma and horror.

Consider the case of Michelle, who told a national audience on the "Today Show" of her friends' reaction to her unsuccessful attempt: "I've since been told that if you want to commit suicide slitting your wrists you lay yourself down in warm water and you slit up. You don't slit down. People were very mean to tell me that. Here I wanted help and instead they were telling me this is how you failed. You can succeed better next time by doing this."

"They told you you did it wrong?" Phil Donahue, who was interviewing the girl, asked, appalled. "Yes," Michelle answered. "I was crying for help. I really was. I wanted someone to listen to me and instead this is what I got."[16]

You must aggressively question your children's friends and demand information. Keep asking, pressing until you get answers. Your behavior will undoubtedly infuriate your child. So be it. As we advise in the next section, there are some times when it's best *not* to respect your child's privacy.

"Every one of my child's friends knew of Fred's plans," said one mother whose son drowned himself. "I guessed that things were going badly for him and I knew his friends would know much more than I did, but I felt he would never forgive me if I called any of them. Isn't that silly? He's certainly never going to forgive me now."

Ed Kane said that the loss of two children to suicide has made him and his wife "overly solicitous" of the three remaining children and "more involved in each other's business." Before, Kane said, their attitude was to "trust" their children and to leave them alone to work out their own problems. He now tells his children, "It probably isn't in any way necessary, but don't be insulted if you find me asking very personal questions about you from your friends." He learned the hard way.[17]

When Not to Respect Your Child's Privacy

Just as they would consider calling their child's friend to be spying, many parents would no more read their child's letters or diaries than they would enter his room without first knocking. Some parents respect their children's privacy and make no exceptions.

Such a blanket policy is fine—and admirable—as long as the child seems to be thriving. But if he seems despondent, protecting him is much more important than respecting his rights. One formerly suicidal woman recalled an incident from her childhood, during a period when she was feeling depressed. Her normally nonintrusive father opened a letter addressed to her and wrote on the back, "Opened to see what it said." She said she was first furious but later felt protected.

In talking to parents whose children have killed themselves, we hear one recrimination over and over. "I could have stopped her from killing herself if only I'd read her poetry," said the mother of a sixteen-year-old high school junior who asphyxiated herself in the family garage. "It was all in there, and she used to leave it on her dresser, even on the dining room table. I studiously avoided it. She was asking me to read it."

We hear constantly of the child who orders his parents not to read his private diaries or letters and then leaves them out invitingly in full view, obviously asking that they be read. This is a double message—a message that reflects the great ambivalence of suicide—that parents must learn to read.

In 1980, twenty-one-year-old John Woytowitz—an award-winning chess player, cartoonist, and editor—hanged himself. After his death, his mother discovered that, for days, John had been leaving suicide notes in his bedroom. She had seen but deliberately not read them. "I respected his privacy," she explained. It's likely that John, like the girl described above, was hoping his mother would read the notes and rescue him.[18]

Vivienne Loomis asked her parents not to read her writings, and they didn't. An informal family code of respect for privacy made such an invasion impossible. Mrs. Loomis recalled that they did not read any of Vivienne's poetry, journals, or letters until after her death when they wanted to use something she had written in her memorial service.[19]

Mrs. Loomis also learned the hard way that respect for privacy is a luxury that parents of suicidal children cannot afford.

After the crisis passes, although it is imperative that parent/child communication continue, kitchen conversations over hot chocolate won't be enough. Suicidal children need professional help.

In the next chapter, we discuss where to find this help in emergency and nonemergency situations. Unfortunately, most parents of suicidal children eventually find themselves in the former situation.

And so we will also deal with the problem of a child brandishing a gun at three o'clock on a Sunday morning, threatening to blow his brains out "for sure" if his parents come near. Where do they call for help?

12

Finding Help in Your Community

At 9 P.M., one school night, Rosemarie, fifteen, placed a suicide note on top of the pile of clothes her grandmother always laid out for her to wear the next day. Then she put on her pajamas, crawled into bed, and swallowed about one third of a bottle of barbiturates. When her grandmother came in the next morning to wake her, Rosemarie did not respond to the usual nudge. As Mrs. T.'s voice rose in a scream and as she began rolling Rosemarie from side to side, the girl awoke, groggy but apparently okay. It was then that Rosemarie's grandmother saw and read the suicide note.

Cal M., sixteen, also tried to kill himself with the remainder of a bottle of barbiturates, but he washed them down with straight whiskey. The next morning, when his parents didn't hear the rock music that he always switched on immediately upon awakening, when they didn't hear him slamming doors and drawers, Mr. M. went up to check. Cal was breathing, but unconscious. His only suicide note was the empty prescription bottle on the nightstand and the fifth of whiskey on the bed, its remaining contents spilled on the quilt and carpet.

Scott T., eighteen, who had once attempted suicide, was again threatening to kill himself. After the asphyxiation attempt two years earlier, his parents found him and rushed him to the emergency room where doctors easily revived him. He was hospitalized overnight and a psychiatrist visited him the next morning, but Scott had no intention of continuing to see a "shrink" and his parents, confused and embarrassed by the attempt, wanted to forget the incident. They decided it would be best to simply not talk about it.

But Mrs. T., although she never mentioned it, thought about it constantly. And now she was noticing some of the same behavior—behavior she so frequently relived in her mind. Her son wouldn't eat, he had been up all night the night before, he looked pasty. Although he had stopped threatening to kill himself, he was upstairs cleaning his room and acting in an uncharacteristically determined fashion. In an attempt to cheer up his son, Mr. T. had told him of a fishing trip he was planning for the two of them. Scott's only reaction was, "Naw, I don't think so, Dad." It was 10 P.M. and Scott's mother did not know where to turn.

Rosemarie's grandmother, Cal's parents, and Scott's parents all needed help for their children—but a particular kind of help would have best suited each of these teenagers. Whom should these parents have called?—in an emergency such as Cal's and Scott's or in a nonemergency such as Rosemarie's that, without help, would almost surely have developed into a second, more serious, suicide attempt.

Suicide-Prevention Agencies

Scattered throughout the United States are over two hundred suicide-prevention centers. Almost all offer twenty-four-hour, seven-day-a-week emergency telephone service designed to give help quickly. Some have their own rescue squads to help people *after* they have taken an overdose or slit their wrists. Others are hooked up to emergency services so they can get help to the person in the quickest way possible.

For most people who call these prevention centers contact is limited to the telephone. But some of the centers do have professionals on staff who will counsel the caller in person.

For Scott's parents, given the lateness of the hour, a suicide-prevention center was a good choice. The person who answered the phone (a well-trained volunteer) listened to Mr. and Mrs. T.'s description of their son's behavior and his history. The volunteer assessed Scott's chances of making a second attempt as very high and put his parents in touch with the center's psychiatrist, who was on emergency call.

The psychiatrist gave them specific instructions on how to handle Scott during the crisis. He recommended immediate and intensive counseling and referred Scott to a psychiatrist at a mental health center (described below), who charged according to the family's ability to pay.

Most of the calls to these centers are not from parents, but from the suicidal people themselves. If they call immediately after they have made the attempt—as many do—the volunteer will attempt to assess just how life-threatening the attempt was. Assuming the caller won't give his address, the volunteer will try to keep him on the phone long enough to trace the call and dispatch emergency help.

The typical caller is the person who feels totally isolated, who is contemplating suicide but has not yet made specific plans. He needs the immediate and sympathetic contact the center offers, the anonymity, and the assurance that the volunteer is not going to be judgmental.

Sometimes the ideal helper is a stranger who has been trained to understand the suicidal impulse, who will not moralize, and to whom the suicidal person feels free to really open up, no matter how embarrassing or unattractive his confessions. These prevention centers give the person sanctuary until the destructive impulse —which, studies show, lasts for a brief period of time—has passed.

People who call suicide-prevention centers usually don't know how to find help on their own. The last thing they'd ever do is call a psychiatrist's office for an appointment. They often believe that they are crazy and worthless. Talking to someone face to face would be out of the question.

Many suicide-prevention volunteers report that the person who calls during a crisis continues calling, sometimes for months on end. The voice at the other end may become the only friend he or she has. The volunteer will urge the caller to get professional counseling—either at the center or through some other community agency.

In fact, one of the most valuable functions of the prevention center is referral. Volunteers are equipped with up-to-date files of specialized agencies that handle all sorts of problems—from anorexia to xenophobia. Most volunteers will make the initial contact for the youngster and will also make a follow-up call to be certain the youngster is actually using the resource.

The suicide-prevention center is not new. In 1774, in England, the Royal Humane Society was created to frustrate attempted suicides. In 1906, in New York, the National-Save-a-Life League became the first suicide-prevention agency in this country.*

But the proliferation of these centers is new. If services that are strictly telephone hotlines are added, there are about seven hundred in the United States. In 1960, there were fewer than half a dozen.†

How do you find the closest center? Call 411, "O," 911, or look in the Yellow Pages under "Suicide," "Crisis," "Mental Health," or "Counseling." In some locales, the front page of the phone book gives information on a variety of emergency services including suicide prevention. Also, any police station would have telephone numbers and locations.

There are two suicide-prevention "chains" operating worldwide and spreading rapidly in the United States—Contact (197 centers worldwide; 104 in the U.S.) and The Samaritans (about 215

* The National-Save-a-Life League was founded by Rev. Harry M. Warren, who held services in various Manhattan hotels. One day a woman called the desk and said she wanted to speak to a minister. The clerk was unable to reach Reverend Warren. The woman then tried to kill herself. When Reverend Warren came to her bedside at Bellevue, she told him, "I think maybe if I had talked to someone like you, I wouldn't have done it." She eventually died and Reverend Warren vowed to create a service that would offer, at all times of the day and night, someone to talk to.

† Edwin Shneidman and Norman Farberow, who founded the Los Angeles Suicide Prevention Agency in 1958—the prototype for those that followed—and who spread the notion that suicidal people don't really want to die, are responsible, more than anyone else, for the fact that people in most larger communities have access to a center or a hotline.

worldwide; 6 in the U.S.). If there is a center near you, it would be listed in the white pages under "Contact" or "Samaritans."

In a nonemergency, a good way to find the closest center is to call, during business hours, the American Association of Suicidology at 303–692–0985. An AAS staff member will refer the caller to the nearest center. An annually updated directory of suicide-prevention centers is available for $5 by writing AAS, 2459 S. Ash, Denver CO 80222. (For a list of Contact centers, write CONTACT USA, 900 South Arlington Avenue, Harrisburg PA 17109.)

Community Mental Health Clinics

Rosemarie's grandmother panicked when she read her grand-daughter's suicide note. She could not afford a private psychiatrist and even if she could have, she wouldn't have known how to go about finding one. So she called Rosemarie's pediatrician, who referred her to the mental health clinic serving her county.

These nonprofit, publicly supported centers serve a specific geographic area that may range from a section of a city to several counties. Typically they employ a psychiatrist or two and a number of psychologists, social workers, counselors, and alcohol and drug abuse specialists. Although a child might end up under a social worker's care rather than a psychiatrist's, the psychiatrist supervises most cases and is available to prescribe medication.

Clinics usually set their fees on a sliding scale. This is an important consideration for most families at a time when the median fee for a psychiatrist is sixty dollars per visit and the median for psychologists and other non-physician therapists is forty dollars. (Although insurance policies generally cover psychiatric fees, the services of other mental health professionals are often not covered.) Even on the North Shore of Chicago, which has the highest median income in the nation, about half the residents can't afford outpatient mental health care on a private basis.

It is important to note here that a community mental health clinic would probably have been an even better choice for Scott's parents—assuming that they had called for help during business hours. Scott needed personal, ongoing contact and a mental health clinic is better equipped to offer that than is a suicide-prevention agency, where contact, in the majority of cases, is limited to the telephone. The suicide-prevention agency's major attribute is its around-the-clock, around-the-calendar service, not its capacity to offer intensive therapy.

Had Mr. and Mrs. T. called a clinic they would have been told to bring Scott in immediately. An intake worker, who is trained to quickly assess a problem and assign the patient to a clinician, would have seen him. The clinician to whom the intake worker assigned Scott might not have been a psychiatrist—the crucial need is to get the patient and the professional together without any delay.

The clinic's twenty-four-hour emergency number refers after-hours callers to a crisis intervention center at a nearby hospital, which offers emergency assistance and referral—probably back to the mental health clinic the next day.

Community mental health clinics are listed in the Yellow Pages under "Mental Health." If you have difficulty finding one, contact the National Mental Health Association, 1800 N. Kent Street, Arlington VA 22209, 703–528–6405. A staff member will tell you where the nearest branch is located. For a listing of community mental health centers throughout the country, write National Institute of Mental Health, Public Inquiries, 5600 Fishers Lane, Rockville, MD 20857.

Emergency Rooms

When Cal's father found his son unconscious, he had only one option—to call an ambulance which would transport his son to the nearest emergency room. In general, emergency-room doctors have an excellent record of using the latest equipment and techniques to revive suicide attempters—not surprisingly, considering how much practice they get. In larger emergency rooms, rarely a week passes without at least one suicide-related crisis.

But emergency-room doctors and nurses merely patch up the child and send him home. They repair his body, not his mind. Only a few ERs offer counseling for suicidal children, which is just fine with many parents. They want to get their child home and pick up their lives where they left off. They want nothing—certainly not counseling—to remind them of the recent crisis.

During a suicide attempter's stay in the hospital, which typically is short, he will probably be visited by a staff psychiatrist, psychologist, or social worker. But once the child checks out of the hospital, statistics show that the majority do not seek additional professional assistance. It is up to the parents to make certain the child receives continuing therapy.

Parents should also be warned that emergency-room doctors and nurses, who have seen so many suicide attempters, can be callous and even cruel. Their feelings are understandable. They see hundreds of people who are suffering through no fault of their own. Then they see the suicide attempter who took a perfectly healthy body and tried to destroy it. They find it hard to be sympathetic, to make heroic efforts to save the life of someone who doesn't appear to value it. "I will show you where to cut the artery the next time," an ER doctor told one young patient. "I can't be bothered with them," another doctor said. "They take up my time when I could be helping someone else who really wants to live." One doctor, whose Thanksgiving dinner was interrupted by a call from the emergency room, admitted that as he tried to revive a suicide attempter who had slit his throat, "I fought the urge to raise my fist and bring it smashing down on his face . . ."

Emergency-room doctors and nurses have been known to suture wounds or clean burns without anesthetics in order "to teach them a lesson." Unfortunately, the lesson learned is to make sure the next attempt is fatal, "so I don't have to go through that again," as one young woman put it. "They closed off the possibility of a hospital being a place to get help. The next time I would have done it properly."

Parents must demand humane treatment. They must let the doctors and nurses know that they expect the emergency-room staff to treat the child, not to punish him.

Hospitals

All hospitals that are connected with medical schools and all hospitals that have more than two hundred beds also have departments of psychiatry, social work departments, and frequently adolescent clinics, where youngsters can be treated as inpatients or outpatients. A hospital affiliated with a medical school is a good choice because the treatment approach is likely to be the most up to date. The drawback is that the child will probably see someone in training, although that person would be under the supervision of a certified psychiatrist.

Finding Help—in Canada

Canada, like the United States, has a nationwide network of suicide hotlines. There are, for example, nine in the metro-Toronto area alone. Telephone numbers for these "distress centres," as the Canadians usually call them, are nearly always listed on the inside front cover of the phone book, along with other emergency numbers. (This is not, unfortunately, always the case in the United States, where, typically, numbers for a wide variety of emergency services are listed, but suicide prevention is not among them. For example, in Chicago, numbers for police, fire, ambulance, Coast Guard, FBI, poison control, and Secret Service are given. So are numbers for emergency assistance to the deaf and for tornado reporting, but no number is listed for suicide emergencies.)

It may seem obvious, but it is worth stressing, that in Canada or the United States, the person who does not have a phone book at hand can simply dial "O." By doing so he reaches perhaps the most dependable and accessible of suicide prevention resources. The telephone operator has at her or his fingertips numbers for crisis services of all kinds, including suicide prevention. In the larger population centers of Canada—as in the United States—dialing 911 will quickly connect the caller with emergency services.

For the same reason we did not offer a comprehensive directory of suicide-prevention services for the United States, we will not offer one for Canada. New centers open and existing ones close all the time. Addresses and phone numbers change. Before such a directory could be printed it would be out-of-date. We recommend the much safer and less frustrating course of consulting an up-to-date phone book or dialing "O" or 911.

However we are listing here three established centers that service large population areas.

—Ontario: Toronto Distress Centre
          10 Trinity Square
          Toronto, Ontario
          416–598–1121
—Quebec: Montreal Tel-Aide
          PO Box 437
          Station A, Westmount
          Montreal, Quebec
          514–935–1101
—British Columbia: Vancouver Crisis Intervention and
                   Suicide Prevention Centre
                   1946 W. Broadway
                   Vancouver, British Columbia
                   604–733–4111

In Canada, the Salvation Army operates suicide-prevention agencies. Canada also has branches of The Samaritans and Contact (in Canada called Tele-Care). Check the front of the phone book or the white pages under those names.

In nonemergency situations, a person can find out about the range of suicide-prevention services available or the center closest to his home by calling, during business hours, the local branch of the Canadian Mental Health Association. There are CMHA branches throughout the country, including the remote Northwest Territories and the Yukon Territory.

Unlike the United States, Canada does not have a nationwide system of county mental health clinics. Instead, Canada has Universal Health Insurance, which means that the government pays for treatment of physical *and* mental illness. However, some private practitioners will "overbill" (i.e. charge a fee above the government medical insurance fee), although many psychiatrists and other mental health professionals will accept medical insurance as the whole payment.

The Suicide Information and Education Centre, a comprehensive—international in scope—data bank of articles, books, films, etc. about suicide, has recently opened in Calgary, Alberta. The center is used mainly by scholars and researchers but the public also has access to this wealth of information about suicide. Contact S.I.E.C., Suite 201, 723 14th Street N.W., Calgary, Alberta, 403–283–3044.

How to Find a Good Therapist

There is certainly no shortage of psychiatrists and other therapists of all levels of training and competence (not surprisingly, considering that an estimated 34 million Americans are receiving some sort of counseling). Some of these therapists are excellent, some are barely competent, and others are downright dangerous. How does a parent, especially one who has never seen a psychiatrist or other counselor himself, find a good therapist?

First of all, a parent should look for a therapist who specializes in treating children and adolescents. As anyone who has lived under the same roof with a young person knows, communicating takes a very special talent. The therapist should also have experience working with suicidal youngsters. A therapist who doesn't may feel overwhelmed by fear of a potential suicide. The therapist must be available to the patient on a twenty-four-hour basis. He must be flexible enough to be willing to see the child without an appointment and perhaps for two hours instead of the usual fifty-minute session.

The therapist must be someone with whom both the child and the parents feel comfortable. The family is usually involved to some extent in therapy and a lack of trust means impeded progress.

The family doctor or pediatrician is usually a good source of recommendations. So are clergymen. Parents might also get recommendations by calling a suicide-prevention center, the psychiatric division or adolescent clinic of a local hospital, or the psychiatric department of a local medical school.

Professional associations also encourage the public to call for referrals—The American Psychiatric Association (1700 18th Street, N.W., Washington, D.C. 20009, 202–797–4900); The American Psychological Association (1200 17th Street, N.W.,

Washington, D.C. 20036, 202–833–7600); and The National Association of Social Workers (1425 H Street, N.W., Suite 600, Washington, D.C., 20005, 202–628–6800).

A parent should never hire a therapist without first carefully checking his qualifications. (The easiest place to do so is in the reference room of any public library.) A psychiatrist should be certified by the American Board of Psychiatry. A psychologist should be accredited by the American Psychological Association and a social worker by the Academy of Certified Social Workers.

In *The Great Billion Dollar Medical Swindle,* Keith Lasko, M.D., warned against assuming that a person knows what he's doing simply because he has an impressive title, office, or manner. In Florida, Lasko pointed out, a psychologist by law has only to meet one requirement—the ability to pay the license fee to the city or county in which he wants to practice. Lasko also found that a reporter who had flunked psychology in college became a licensed psychologist. A hamster was licensed as an "animal psychologist" and a chameleon was licensed as a psychoanalyst and sex therapist.[1]

We have discussed above some options parents have in emergencies and near emergencies. Below we will discuss the one resource in every community that parents should take advantage of throughout their child's school years—a resource that, if used properly, may prevent an emergency.

We will also describe resources that are *not* in every community —not by a long shot—but rather only in those very few communities that are taking a leadership role in the fight against suicide. Parents in these communities, and their children, appeared before school boards, village boards, township boards, and county boards. They made a case for drop-in centers and outreach workers and suicide-prevention courses in the elementary and high schools, just as they would have made a case for a new soccer team or increased garbage collection or support for an amateur theatrical production.‡

‡ Chapter 1, on the grim statistics, Chapter 2, on the deadly myths, and Chapter 7, on the problems of growing up in the suburbs would be good sources for the sort of information that should be included in a pitch for suicide-prevention services.

Teachers: An Untapped Resource

Teachers remain the most untapped of suicide-prevention resources. They are such a valuable resource because they spend more hours with the child, day in and day out, than do most parents and are frequently more aware of what the child's life is really like. Is he frequently high on drugs? Is he a loner by choice or by decree of his classmates? Has he seemed suddenly depressed? Has his classroom performance plunged? Is he soaring one day and sinking the next? Does he regularly cut classes?

If a parent suspects that a child is having problems, the teacher should be the first person to whom he turns. Not only is a favorite teacher more likely to be a confidant than is a parent or school counselor (students tend to view counselors as part of the administration, someone who might "turn them in"), but teachers have an incomparable pipeline to students because youngsters often express their anguish in their school work.

Unfortunately, teachers can be as blind as parents to the warning signs of suicide, and so they ignore the evidence that will seem so clear in retrospect. We discuss in the next section the importance of suicide-prevention training programs for teachers. But first, consider why such programs are necessary.

This poem was written by a fifteen-year-old and handed to his English teacher. The teacher did nothing and the boy later committed suicide:

> To Santa Claus and
> Little Sisters
>
> Once . . . he wrote a poem.
> And called it "chops,"
> Because that was the name of
> his dog, and that's what it was
> all about.
> And the teacher gave him an "A"
> And a gold star.

And his mother hung it on the
kitchen door, and read it to
all his aunts . . .
Once . . . he wrote another
poem.
And he called it "Question Marked
Innocence."
Because that was the name of
His grief and that's what it
was all about.
And the professor gave him
an "A"
And a strange and steady look.
And his mother never hung it
on the kitchen door, because
he never let her see it . . .
Once, at 3 A.M. . . . he tried
another poem . . .
And he called it absolutely
nothing, because that's what it
was all about.
And he gave himself an "A"
And a slash on each damp wrist,
And hung it on the bathroom
door because he couldn't reach
the kitchen.

One teacher in a North Shore high school recalled receiving a
poem from a boy just a couple of days before he committed suicide. The poem was about a person who was lost in the woods
after being separated from friends. He called frantically to them
for help. He could hear their replies but he couldn't see them and
eventually their voices faded away. "Obviously it was a call for
help," the teacher said, "but at the time I took it quite literally. I
criticized it rather completely. Of course, had I known what the
situation was, it would have been different."[2]

Diane, a girl who eventually attempted suicide, recalled submit-
ting some death poetry to a teacher. "He said it was a selfish, morbid poem. He said it was one-sided. I mean he was really critical

of it. Those were my feelings. I was hurting and he was being critical of my feelings! I couldn't see anything getting better."

Peter Walker, the Canadian boy whose suicide is described in
Growing Up Dead, submitted to his teacher, shortly before he shot
himself in the head, a short story with the title "Story of Retep
Reklaw" (Peter Walker spelled backward). Retep, the "hero" of
the story, is constantly heckled by his classmates. His poor performance in an important volleyball game costs his team the victory.
He is also having trouble at home. He punches his mother when he
feels crushed by her demands, he hides out in his room, sleeping,
burning incense, and playing the Beatles's "Nowhere Man" ("He's
a real nowhere man, sitting in his nowhere land, making all his nowhere plans for nobody") and "Strawberry Fields" ("Living is
easy with eyes closed, misunderstanding all you see. . . . It's getting hard to be someone, but it should work out, it doesn't matter
much to me."). The story ends when the police break the door
down to find Retep, lying on the bed, "finally at peace."

The only response Peter got from his teacher was a good grade.

A friend of Peter's complained after his death, "And I know a
lot of teachers were upset when he died, but I can't remember any
of the English teachers being upset. They get so many essays and
poetry, so many different messages that it just goes right through
them!"[3]

A nine-year-old boy wrote a school essay describing the murder
of a family and the suicide of the murderer, the family's nine-year-
old son. The teacher missed the warning and soon after the boy
executed the crime he had earlier described.

Making Teachers More Sensitive

In a few communities across the country—unfortunately, very
few—parents and administrators and community groups have decided that there have been enough Peter Walkers and Dianes. In
the Cherry Creek School District south of Denver, for example,
teachers are trained to recognize distress signals. They are taught
how to approach the suicidal child, how to assess his potential to
commit suicide.

School counselors and nurses are also included in the training sessions. After twelve suicides in eighteen months, parents are now demanding that counselors do more than advise students on which college to attend and that nurses do more than baby-sit for a sick child until his mother picks him up.

After a Student Commits Suicide

On Chicago's North Shore, the Irene Josselyn Clinic sponsors suicide-prevention workshops for teachers, counselors, and administrators. One of the key topics is how to reach out to students after a classmate commits suicide.

We have described in Chapter 8 the phenomenon familiar to any child psychiatrist—that one teen suicide in a school frequently triggers others.

If school administrators are not smart enough to realize the trauma that students—especially friends of the victim—suffer at the loss—especially by suicide—of one of their own, then parents must demand meetings where students can air their grief and their guilt. They must demand that teachers devote classroom discussion to the subject. They must demand that therapists and members of the clergy circulate throughout the school to talk to students, that school counselors emerge from their offices to mingle in the lunchrooms and corridors. They must demand that administrators not do what one North Shore superintendent did after a suicide—sent a directive from the administration to teachers to act as if nothing had happened.

In one Chicago-suburban high school, after two students killed themselves within a four-day period, the principal talked "at" students in their homerooms over the public address system. That, apparently, was his notion of discussion. He told them that if they "had any problems" they should make an appointment with a counselor. "The kids wanted to talk about the death of their classmates," a social worker said, "and there were people who said, 'I am afraid I may be the next one.' Many, many kids have had that thought in their mind, and now it comes back again."

In a suburb of New Jersey, it wasn't until the second suicide in less than a week that the administration directed counselors and teachers to talk about what happened. A social worker in that community recalled, "Many of the kids needed assurance that they would not kill themselves. Even though they had no real intention of committing such an act, the boundaries between thought and actions were blurred under such circumstances. Many kids were frightened." When the administration finally offered help, nearly half of the school's 1,600 students asked for it.

After that second suicide, counseling centers were set up at several locations in the high school so students who wished to talk to professionals could do so at any time of the day. The homeroom period was extended to allow for discussion. Clergymen came into the school to support members of their congregations and anyone else who needed comfort and assistance.

Outreach Workers and Drop-in Centers

For several years now on the North Shore, outreach programs (funded by the township and the suburbs) have sent young social workers into the schools and community hangouts to meet teens on their own turf. These social workers, who don't look much different from the high school students they serve, hang out in the student smoking lounge, in the local McDonald's across from the railroad tracks. As one twenty-three-year-old outreach worker said, "We do have offices, but we try not to use them."

The great advantage of having these young social workers in the schools and in the community is that they offer on-the-spot help. They get the kids where they live. They connect with young people who may be contemplating suicide but would never consider approaching a teacher or counselor or parent.

As Vivian Lerner, one of the social workers, put it, "Most people here are brought up to think they should take care of their own problems. They would never call a therapist for an appointment. That's why it's so good that I can go to them. I'm on their turf. They get to check me out through time, to get to know me, to feel safe. Kids hear about me through other kids. There's a big difference talking to them in the high school's outside smoking area. Inside in an office they would clam up."

Most of the North Shore suburbs also have established and funded drop-in centers, staffed usually by young social workers with occasional help from college students. Youngsters might "drop in" to talk to staff members or to relax over a game of foosball, to listen to music, or to do their homework. What's important is that the staff people get to know the adolescents, to observe them over an extended period of time. It might take months for a child to start talking, but in most cases, he eventually does. "The first step is to be available," said one social worker. "You learn a lot over a game of cards and it gives the kids a chance to know me. Most won't make a commitment to therapy twice a week. But in a crisis they'll talk to me for two hours straight."

These drop-in centers are valuable because they tend to attract the students who feel that they have no place else to go. These are often the teens whose parents are in the process of getting divorced. They do not have a sense of community at home, or in school. These are often the teens who know they aren't going to make the varsity football team or cheerleading squad or get a good part in the school play or an editor's job on the paper. As a twenty-three-year-old social worker, wearing her work uniform of jeans and a T-shirt, put it, "This is a great place for kids who feel alienated from school, who aren't in the in-crowd."

Teaching Courses in Suicide Prevention

The Cherry Creek School District, mentioned earlier, trains students—as well as teachers—in suicide prevention. A psychologist who directs the district's Suicide Prevention Project developed the idea of offering a course on the subject when he talked to an eighth-grade class shortly after a ninth-grader committed suicide.

Young people are hungry for information on suicide, but the few courses available are almost all offered in colleges. For many students, they come too late.

The demand for these college courses is extremely heavy. When suicidologist Edwin Shneidman taught a class on death at Harvard

University it was scheduled for a room with twenty chairs. Over two hundred students came to the first session. The largest registration ever recorded for a noncredit course sponsored by Wayne State University, the University of Michigan, and Eastern Michigan State was for "Psychological Studies of Dying, Death and Lethal Behavior."

Ideally, suicide-prevention courses should start in elementary school. Schools should also offer special courses to prepare youngsters for major passages in their lives—for example, graduation from high school, typically one of the most stressful passages of adolescence.

At a high school on the North Shore, after two students killed themselves within three months of graduation, a course—the 3D's of College (disillusionment, doubt, and depression)—was developed.

The course focuses, in part, on what it will be like to go away to college. The teen will experience disillusionment with new peers who have different values and different notions of privacy. Doubt —self-doubt, really—refers to their anxiety about meeting their own and their parents' expectations. Depression refers to the intense feelings of loss they may suffer after moving away from family, friends, a familiar home, high school, and neighborhood.

The course also helps students deal with their current feelings of fear and depression—to realize that "senior slump" is a normal reaction to the prospect of separating from an institution that has become familiar. It is, in fact, a process of denial. The student doesn't really want to leave and so becomes apathetic and even hostile toward everything connected with his school.

Ben Wheatley, who designed and taught the course, warned students that they would find themselves in more arguments with parents and friends. This is a way of loosening the ties and lessening the pain of leaving. It is normal—and so is the familiar complaint that all their friends seem to be drifting away, no longer working at friendship or taking it seriously. "Every kid thinks, 'My God, there's something wrong,'" Wheatley explained. "Friends who used to be so intimate aren't anymore."

Wheatley advised students to "pay attention" to the emotional support system that they use in their everyday lives, which will be temporarily lost to them when they go to college. They should try to duplicate the system as quickly as possible. Otherwise they may suffer from strong feelings of loss and loneliness.

Some of Wheatley's specific suggestions include getting immediately involved in activities, eating with the same group of friends (at all costs avoiding eating alone), developing a series of routines and activities that create a sense of belonging in the new environment, talking to others about feelings of fear or sadness, calling home often. "Mother Bell is the best umbilical cord available."

Working with the Police and Paramedics

The suicidal child, especially the one suffering from masked depression, will sometimes, as we explained in Chapter 10, get in trouble with the police. For example, in Northfield (one of the North Shore suburbs), the police recently stopped one teenage boy for driving at ninety miles an hour through the business district of a sleepy neighboring suburb. Another boy was picked up for walking across three lanes of an expressway.

In most communities, the police would have simply labeled these young people "crazy kids" and released them to the custody of their parents. Case closed. That's how it was in Northfield as well, until the police chief realized that some of these youngsters who seemed simply reckless were actually suicidal. Staff members of the clinic met with the police chief and with the paramedics who work under him. Today police alert us when any child is picked up for extreme recklessness. At least we can now identify those youngsters who are publicly and unlawfully "rehearsing" their suicides.

Paramedics also wanted to get involved. So now they tell us every time they respond to an urgent plea to revive a young suicide attempter. Village officials are also looking at a plan, adopted by many police departments, to dispatch a social worker, along with paramedics, to suicide emergencies.

An alliance among paramedics, police, and mental health workers is a natural. Although their approach varies, they are all in the business of handling emergencies.

College Counseling: Don't Depend on It

Even though a high school student may feel miserable and lonely, at least he suffers in familiar surroundings. Parents must never forget that it is easier for a child to find help when he is living at home than when he is living in a dormitory. And even if the child attempts suicide and doesn't want to be discovered, chances are much better that he will be discovered if he makes the attempt in his bedroom than if he makes it in his dorm room. Far too often a college student who kills himself is discovered days or even weeks later. No one misses him.

Counseling services at most colleges range from uneven to inadequate. It is the rare student who knows such services exist and the rarer one who has the courage to use them. (Will the fact he saw a counselor be noted in his records and hurt his chances of getting a good job or getting into law or medical school?)

College counseling centers also tend to be badly understaffed. John Woytowitz went with his girlfriend to see a counselor on campus. The counselor told the couple, "We're too busy. Is it an emergency?" They said no and made an appointment for a few days later. John was dead the next day. His suicide note began, "I feel so lonely now. No one wants to talk to me."[4]

Because mental health counseling is not a service that will be high on the list of student demands, it is up to parents to insist that colleges offer adequate counseling—and that they advertise this service in places students are likely to look, such as on bulletin boards, in the campus newspaper, in dorm snack bars, and in fraternity and sorority dining rooms. (On one midwestern campus, students complained that an ad for a "help line" appeared for the first time in months beside a news story reporting the suicide death of a freshman.) Parents must also insist that counseling services be strictly confidential, that all records be destroyed when the student graduates, and that he be assured that the fact he saw a counselor will never be released to graduate schools or employers.

These are all policies that are difficult to implement—especially for parents who live hundreds of miles away. So perhaps the most important point to be made here is that parents must realize that going away to college is an experience that can be fraught with difficulties; that parents cannot sit back and figure that their child is being protected, that *in loco parentis* extends to matters of mental health.

The "7 Warning Signs" of Suicide

Scott T., one of the boys described at the opening of this chapter, killed himself about an hour after his father had tried to raise his son's spirits with the promise of a fishing trip. At the moment Scott shot himself, his parents were worrying separately downstairs, still unable to admit—even to each other—their gut feeling that their son was about to make a second suicide attempt.

Five years after Scott's death, his father, by then divorced, became a leader in a community effort to raise money for suicide-prevention efforts. It was only then that he learned about depression and warning signs and deadly myths. It was only then that he learned what to do in a crisis and, at his psychiatrist's urging, devoted his spare time to sharing this information with other parents.

At a community meeting after the death of another boy from the same subdivision, Mr. T. was admitting how ignorant he was about depression during his son's last year; how futile it was to expect Scott to "snap out of it" by promising him a fishing trip.

"But really, how was I supposed to know? I was raised in an era when mental illness was shameful, something to be hidden. All I can say is that it is criminal that in this supposedly enlightened day and age, that the tragedy of suicide is still in the closet. If a physical disease were destroying our children at the rate of suicide, there would be a massive public outcry, and a national campaign infused with huge amounts of private and government donations to study suicide and to develop programs to prevent it."

Why, parents should ask, has there never been a public campaign against suicide as there has been against other less easily preventable forms of death? Most childhood diseases have been eradicated, while suicide rates continue to climb.

Mass campaigns that stimulated private donations and federal support helped to rid us of such childhood scourges as smallpox. Who ever heard of a charity ball or a door-to-door fund-raising campaign to rid us of suicide? There are organizations to fight cancer and heart disease and muscular dystrophy and birth defects. Where is the well-publicized organization to fight suicide? (Who ever heard of the American Association of Suicidology?) And where is the public money?

In 1976, for example, Congress appropriated almost $744 million for research into cancer but only slightly more than $5 million for research into depression, although depression affects many more people. The tragedy of youth suicide needs to be recognized, researched, and attacked as a major public health problem—it needs the movers and shakers in communities across the nation to take it up as their cause.

Consider how effective the publicity campaign against cancer has been. Once cancer, like suicide, was something to be hidden, a family secret. But because of the "7 warning signs" campaign, people learned to recognize symptoms and get early treatment. Why not a campaign to recognize the warning signs of suicide? Unlike some cancer patients, the suicidal person is never terminal or hopeless. He can always be helped.

We must never forget the real dimensions of the public health problem suicide poses. It affects many more people than just the person who hangs or gases himself. It affects the entire family— and frequently destroys their lives with guilt that simply refuses to be assuaged.

If a family member dies of cancer or heart disease, his relatives grieve but, with the help of sympathetic friends, usually put their lives back together. For the family of a suicide, the grief never ends and even the most sympathetic of friends can't help but wonder, "What did those parents do to cause their child to commit suicide?"

In the final chapter we shall deal with this most pathetic of suicide's legacies—the survivors.

13

Helping the Survivors

"I'd find myself driving to work in the morning and all the sudden just breaking out into tears," said Ernie Fluder, whose eighteen-year-old daughter Teresa hanged herself in her Northern Illinois University dorm room.

The pain on their faces was striking as two fathers told parents at a meeting of LOSS (Loving Outreach to Survivors of Suicide) about struggling to come to terms with their sons' suicides the year before. "He's the first thing on my mind when I wake up and the last thing when I go to sleep," said one. "It took me the longest time, especially during the day when I was off and Mary was working for me to stay home because I felt scared, I felt nervous," said another. "I just didn't want to stay in the house . . . because you had visions . . . when I pulled the pins on the door upstairs and I see Mike hanging and I cut him down and I said, 'Why, why did you do something like that?' . . . I was so stunned that I was holding Mary and the one son and I didn't even know where the other son was. He was crying in the bedroom . . . It's hard to get over something like that."[1]

Several years ago in West Linn, Oregon, a nineteen-year-old honor student fatally shot his parents, his younger brother, and, finally, himself, leaving behind a note which read, "I am not in any way upset with my family. I am simply sparing them the tremendous grief I know my death would have caused them."[2]

Fortunately, most young people who commit suicide leave their relatives behind. But they leave behind families who are scarred as if hit by a nuclear bomb. Natural death carries its share of torment, but suicide creates grief that is magnified to unbelievable and unbearable levels. For added to grief is crushing, relentless guilt—guilt of such prodigious proportions that perhaps only someone who has experienced the death of a child by suicide can begin to understand it. (Hence the value of parent support groups, such as LOSS described below.)

Very few parents can escape this guilt. In many cases they see the suicide as a direct result of something they did or, more likely, didn't do. "To think she killed herself with my medication. Why didn't I lock it up?" a father agonized. His only child had threatened suicide for months. He and his wife had not taken Meg seriously until the school principal suggested that she see a psychiatrist. The doctor had urged hospitalization. The parents said no, insisting Meg's "condition" was not that serious. Now she was dead. She had died on the same intensive-care unit that had saved her father's life six months earlier.

"Your daughter was found in Wisconsin, in a state park. She apparently hanged herself. We'll need you at the autopsy," the coroner, calling long distance, told Lindsay's stunned parents. How does a parent survive such a call? How do the parents and the girl's brothers accept the fact that this child, this sister, is no longer alive, growing, challenging, changing with the years? What happens to the hopes, the fantasies, the expectations for this eldest of five children?

Lindsay had been the gem in her mother's crown. She had just been accepted by an Ivy League college that would open not only intellectual doors but social ones as well. Mother's frustrations at having to settle in a midwestern city after her marriage would now be offset by her daughter's opportunity. Father had never quite understood his wife's social ambitions, and now he could not help but think, "It's all her fault."

But at the same time he wondered, "How will we tell her brothers? What will we tell the neighbors? Will it be in the papers? Together the parents found their way to the autopsy to identify their dead daughter but each was so absorbed in private anguish that they barely spoke to each other.

What did I do wrong as a parent? What could I have done to prevent it? For months and for years after a child commits suicide those questions return. Why? What? What might have been different? The question remains, hanging, unanswered: What went so wrong? How could anything have been so bad that suicide was the only answer? For the survivors, life becomes a hauntingly unanswered question.

"Nothing can assuage such anguish," Vivienne Loomis's father concluded. He knew what it was, he added, to feel "just utterly damned."[3]

Describing the problems that plague survivors of suicide could fill another book—the suddenness and finality of the separation, for example, the lack of an opportunity to resolve differences, to express love or remorse. As Bill, whose son killed himself, put it, "You're prepared for the death of a parent, but you're not usually prepared for the death of a child. The suddenness . . . there's no chance to say good-bye."[4]

No tragedy has so giant-sized a stigma attached to it as suicide. Added to grief is extreme social humiliation, for even the most enlightened people blanch in the face of suicide. When Paulette Loomis was asked on "Good Morning America" why she agreed to talk about Vivienne on network television, she said that the decision to appear had been excruciatingly difficult to make. Shortly after arriving at the studio, she and her son were seated with other guests. When one guest, making polite conversation, asked Paulette what she would be talking about, Paulette answered, "Suicide." The conversation suddenly stopped. The questioner was embarrassed into silence. "What to say to the mother of a girl who killed herself?"[5]

The stigma is never completely forgotten or forgiven. "I read something after Shaun's death," said Bill Casey, the father of a seventeen-year-old who committed suicide. "Everybody has a skeleton in their closet. A suicide is a person who leaves his skeleton in somebody else's closet."[6]

For parents and for siblings, the unrelenting horror of the suicide of a loved one does more than weaken and often destroy ongoing relationships. It also colors all future relationships, often culminating in a lifelong mistrust of intimacies. When something so drastic goes wrong with a basic family tie, there is no firm foundation upon which to form subsequent ties.

In the middle chapters of this book we addressed ourselves to the reasons why young people kill themselves. We emphasized that they felt like status symbols, rather than beloved children. We noted that meaningful communication was lacking. We detailed their feeings of rootlessness and valuelessness. We clarified the role of unbearable loss. Those same problems batter the survivors of a suicide—and they strike simultaneously. With the act of suicide the adolescent fires a volley that makes the family lose status, freeze in communication, feel rootless and valueless, and face an unbearable loss.

But in spite of this tremendous stress, survivors can use it to master conflicts and grow with the process, provided they get help.

Get Help—Now!

In Chapter 11 we asked, "What can be done to help a suicidal adolescent?" The answer was, "Plenty" and the answer to its companion question, "When should you do it?" was "Now!" If we now ask, "What can be done to help the family after an adolescent kills himself?" the answers are the same: "Plenty" and "On the double!"

Every family of a suicide must be viewed as "at high risk." Such a family is one which, without help, will likely become nonfunctional, unable to care for itself as a family and as individuals, except in the most marginal way.

What kind of help do survivors of suicide need? That will vary, depending on the individual, from neighborhood supports to the clergy to support groups to mental health professionals. What is vital is that relatives, friends, and professionals recognize that the family is at high risk until proven otherwise. Often in psychiatry we wait to see. With the survivors of suicide we must act and support, backing off only when the family is clearly making it on its own.

In Chapter 8 we detailed the suicide of Sandy, the salutatorian of her high school class. Her family's reaction to her death, described below, is a good example of what usually happens when a family shuns help. Each member suffered alone, storing inside his guilt, hurt, and humiliation. In contrast, the book's final section contains some "happy endings"—families that did get help and not only survived but went on to really live again.

At their fifth high school reunion, several of Sandy's classmates called on her mother. She had become a recluse since her daughter's death. She had obviously not wanted to see the girls during the reunion and had made it difficult, but the friends insisted and eventually she relented. But she kept mumbling, almost as if in a trance, "I still can't believe it." It was impossible to help her move beyond that stricken stance to the recall of specific memories. She seemed to resent the reveries of the friends as they asked to see some of Sandy's mementos. When her friends laughed at the collective memories, she winced.

During their visit, Sandy's father never came into the living room. He had done no productive research since his daughter's suicide. Sandy's brothers had gone to medical school, but they seemed colorless. For this family, life had stopped with Sandy's suicide. The parents had been so stricken they could no longer catalyze a life for their other children. Sandy had, in fact, taken them with her on her plunge from a hotel roof.

Sandy's family reflects the rigidity and inhibition that often occurs when no one accepts responsibility for directing a family struggling with suicide. Each family member tried to cope with his guilt on his own. Their pattern of limited expression became even more stunted and the sharing of emotions was nil. Little wonder that Sandy's mother did not want the three friends to visit. Their recollections made it more difficult for her to keep on the lid. Father couldn't even risk coming into contact with the memories.

Counseling—A Family Affair

Hours before Teresa Fluder hanged herself, her parents and her older sister Elaine drove her from their home in suburban Hoffman Estates to Northern Illinois University. They left her in her dorm room in what they thought was the typical anxiety of a girl away from home for the first time at a big university. After asking the dorm resident to check on Teresa that evening, the parents left. Elaine stayed behind to have dinner with Teresa. After dropping Teresa back in her room at 10 P.M., Elaine headed for home. At 11, the dorm resident knocked on Teresa's door. No response. The door was locked. When her roommate returned from Chicago the next day, she found Teresa hanging from a hook in her closet.

"When I left, she was crying," Elaine recalled, "and I was upset because she was crying and I almost went back and I told myself as I was leaving, 'No, she'll be able to handle it. She'll do fine.'" Several minutes later, Elaine's thoughts returned to that night. "I regret it. I wish I had gone back. I had stopped the car, I was on my way out on the road and I had stopped the car and was going to turn around on the highway and I stopped and I thought for a minute and I went on."[7]

Siblings of suicide victims usually need as much help as their parents. Counseling should be a family affair—not necessarily as a group, not necessarily with the same clinician, but counseling is a must. As we discuss later in the case of Nellie, those who don't work through their grief and guilt at the time, find that guilt coming back to haunt them—and perhaps their own children—years later.

Elaine Fluder's year-and-a-half-long counseling helped. ". . . one of the most important things I learned was that the decisions we make at the time are what we think are best, and that I just have to assume that what I did at the time was the best that I could." Laura, another of Teresa's sisters, fought back tears as she described a family in which suicide and the resulting counseling seems to have fostered a new closeness. "My relationship with my family was no where's near as close as it is today. I was more concerned with myself and having fun and that kind of thing. And since then my whole attitude has changed and my family life and what I do with myself. I'm a lot closer to my parents. . . . Not that I've enjoyed losing her but she's really changed our whole family."[8]

Siblings who disliked or teased or were jealous of the dead child

What Parents Can Do

suffer special guilt. They must struggle with the fear that their wishes caused the suicide. A clinician who can recognize and interpret this fear may open the door to family discussion.

When anxiety about a second suicide in the family permeates the household, still another complication arises. This constant expectation, verging on paranoia, that a second child is "going to do it" can poison family life. Again, a clinician will probably be the only one in a position to stop such a potentially deadly pattern.

A boy whose brother hanged himself in his college room recalled his first realization—at the wake—of how suicide would completely change his life. Gazing out the window, he suddenly had the urge to see the street below. He restrained himself, because he couldn't do so without opening the window and leaning over the edge. ". . . someone in the room might think I was trying to jump. Those possibilities were no longer out of the question, whereas no one would have conceived of them before. Before. I wonder if I would only measure time from then on as before or after . . . it."[9]

Some parents compound their children's problems by paying a consuming amount of attention to and overidealizing the dead child. They may handle their grief by extolling the virtues of the dead child and, in the process, forget the other children. The surviving children may feel like orphans. Often if the guilt is unusually great, if the parents feel that they did indeed drive the child to suicide, they will create unusual symbols of commitment to the deceased, such as inappropriate memorials or scholarships. Such acts may cover guilt rather than express love. The remaining children may feel even more demoted and unimportant to the parents.

The parents, generally, are unaware of the hurt they're inflicting. They need someone to stop them before the damage becomes too deep to reverse.

Anniversary Reaction

"How long should a family remain in counseling?" That depends on the individuals—perhaps six months in some cases, a year in others, and years and years in others. But survivors of suicide must accept the answer to the companion question. "How long does it take to recover from a suicide?" In two words, *probably forever*.

For every year on the anniversary of the suicide, anger, grief, and loneliness, as well as depression and anxiety will be back. With each suicide, as with each loss by death, a process is started in the psyche that we call the anniversary reaction. Without our consciously remembering the fact of a significant anniversary, these emotions are triggered simply by the passage of time and the return of the calendar date.

A grandmother wrote to a psychiatrist seeking help for her hospitalized granddaughter. When the correspondence became somewhat involved, the psychiatrist asked what had prompted the inquiry in the first place. Only then did the woman realize that her son had committed suicide in that very month. Perhaps the date had sparked her concern for her granddaughter. It soon became clear that she herself needed an opportunity once again to work through her grief about her son. She finally described the ways in which she had locked that loss inside her, rarely sharing anything about him, yet steeping in guilt through the years.

Families should mark their calendars with dates of significant losses, not because anyone needs to be reminded, but so time can be allocated for talking about them. The family needs to take on the task of working through the mutual loss. They need to select a clinician who can help them accept the loss as an emotional trauma. They need to be urged to express their feelings about an anniversary, a family holiday such as Christmas, or a milestone such as graduation. Otherwise, as in the case of the woman just described, the pain can be needlessly prolonged.

Onward Bound

The survivors of a suicide must accept the fact that theirs is a fight for survival and that techniques for survival are different from techniques for living. There is no alternative but to use survival techniques. In a sense, the survivors are experiencing an Outward Bound survival test. Just as candidates for the wilderness

experience can be taught techniques and then muster the courage
to pursue their course, so can suicide survivors be taught that the
future can bring resolution to what seems an inextricable plight.
But it takes time, hard work, and, almost always, professional
help before the bereaved can move beyond survival to reintegra-
tion and learning to live again.

Nellie R. had been riding her bicycle on a fast-moving highway
after supper. She was reported to have lost her balance and
swerved into oncoming traffic. She was hit by three cars and
thrown into the path of a fourth. The newspapers called it an accident.

Nellie's teachers and her friends had seen the newspaper pictures. It was an accident, all right, proof that one should not ride
on that highway, or any highway. The police used the picture for a
seminar on highway safety. The children planted a tree in Nellie's
memory. They were ready to put it to rest as God's will. The children at this Catholic school were troubled but accepting.

Mrs. R. made an appointment with a psychiatrist to talk it over.
She didn't believe, she said, that Nellie's death had been an accident. She described her daughter's increasing withdrawal from
friends during the preceding four months. She described school
grades dropping, her menstrual periods becoming irregular, her
previous interest in helping around the house vanishing. Mother
had been worried. Father had dissuaded her from seeking help or
even from talking it over with Nellie. "Let well enough alone," he
urged. Now it was too late.

She told the doctor something she had never discussed with
anyone before. Her beloved brother Greg had hanged himself at
age sixteen. Her parents had insisted that it was an accident. She
had known how depressed and discouraged Greg had been. They
had talked of it openly, but she had never warned her parents. She
realized now that, after the suicide, she and her parents had never
communicated their feelings, sadness, confusion, and guilt over
Greg's death. Similarly, she had never talked of it with her husband, Nellie, or the other children. She felt too guilty.

With tears in her eyes, she sadly shook her head and said, "I
should have known about Nellie. She must have known about my
brother." She explained that Nellie was always perusing old picture albums and talking to her grandparents, who probably hinted
at Greg's suicide.

The psychiatrist urged her to come in regularly but after that first visit she disappeared. Three weeks later she was back, looking almost immobile. Slowly she creaked out the statement, "I am curdled with grief." She seemed to age twenty years in the next two. She remained bereft for months, even as she tried to cooperate with the therapy. She refused medication, saying that she knew the source of her depression. She just needed to come to grips with it. Slowly she came to understand that it was not only the loss of her daughter that had so shattered her. It was also the guilt, that she and her parents never worked through, over the suicide of her brother. She was convinced that her guilt had been telegraphed to her daughter and that in killing herself Nellie had expressed her mother's anger and confusion over the loss of her brother.

Ever so slowly during the fifth year of therapy she began to smile; she found new interests. She survived at great cost to her energies but significant gain in her self-understanding and in her capacity to relate herself to life instead of to loss.

Group Grief

Six couples sat around a church lounge in a suburb of Chicago. They might have been members of a bridge club or a homeowners organization. They instead belonged to a much more exclusive club. They came to this meeting of LOSS because each had a son or daughter who had committed suicide.

"One of the things we do at LOSS here," one father said to new members of the group, "is to seek out, to find how other people have dealt with the suicide. What could we have done? . . . Did we do the proper thing? Well, it seems . . . listening to you folks, that you did everything we thought we should have done and in spite of that you were not able to prevent the child from taking their own life. And how that helps in LOSS, I think, is that a lot of us feel guilt. And those women and men who feel guilt about their child's suicide should listen to your stories and that's where LOSS helps us."

A mother added, "LOSS gives us hope that we need so desper-

ately and I urge all parents to come to that first meeting because
here you'll find hope."[10]

LOSS, sponsored by Catholic Charities, has counterparts in
most areas of the country. Why are these self-help groups valuable
for most parents? Sitting around a room with other parents, they
can finally drop the feeling that they are monsters and look
around them to see that suicide happens to average people from
average families.

Most important, they can finally talk—to others who understand, who will not be moralistic or impatient, who will not urge
them to, forget about it already or put it behind you. Father
Charles Rubey, director of mental health services for Catholic
Charities, explains that a month or so after the suicide, friends and
family often no longer want to hear about it. "I remember
one couple saying they were talking to their immediate family and
it was only a month or six weeks after and the immediate response
was, 'Aren't you over this? That was six weeks ago.' "[11]

Not only can they talk to other parents but they can begin talking to each other. Marriage can endure no stress greater than the
suicide of a child. Parents often withdraw, as Sandy's did, each
into a state of his own agonized silence. Marriage turns into a
series of misunderstandings, recriminations, angry outbursts over
trivial matters rather than about the mutual loss, the blame, about
what's really bothering husband and wife. The sense of community, of hope that parents find in these groups will probably extend
beyond the meetings, to the home.

Beyond Survival—Some Happy Endings

"I notice that I am occasionally thinking of something else, not
the hanging," said the father of a boy who had hanged himself in
the bathroom. The psychiatrist felt relieved and able to breathe a
little easier.

"Today I smiled. It surprised me. I didn't know I could anymore," said a mother whose daughter had drowned on a lonely
beach early in the morning. "I have blamed myself for all these
months for not picking up the meaning of her reading Virginia
Woolf. Now finally I have stopped blaming myself all of the time.

She could have shared more and tried to help herself," the mother added. The social worker nodded assent. Mother was beginning a new life.

"I finally had a good night's rest," said the brother of an adolescent who had shot himself through the mouth. "For months I have relived that scene I didn't see. Thank God for some rest finally." The psychologist relaxed somewhat too.

The period of feeling momentarily relieved of responsibility is a blessed comfort to those who have been survivors. It is as if the hiatus will never come, and then one day, after months of travail, there it is. The person suddenly begins to uncoil, his self begins to emerge again. Friends sense a return. The psychiatrist sees for the first time an untroubled and somewhat relaxed person, very different from the tight, guilty, depressed, and shocked person he first saw.

"What do you know? I'm getting married," said the mother of a seventeen-year-old boy who shot himself. Both patient and psychiatrist beamed with delight. Both remembered the years this mother struggled to work through the guilt she felt because her son killed himself just at the time she was about to remarry.

After the suicide she was too shattered to think of marriage. It was all she could do to keep going to work. Her friend understood, but fifteen weary months of her depression and withdrawal left him wondering if the marriage would be a mistake. The psychiatrist had explained that survival guilt was a special brand of turmoil and urged him to be patient. Finally, two and a half years after the suicide, and hundreds of psychiatric hours later, Mother had made her announcement. Tears came to the eyes of the patient and her doctor.

The father of a daughter who killed herself with *his* medication settled into the chair in the psychologist's office. "I finally have enough self-respect to take a new job." He explained the internal steps that seemed to occur during the last few months. He was thinking more clearly, he was coming up with some new ideas, and he was challenging his boss more directly. "I guess I am ready to go on living after all these months of being stopped in my tracks. It's a good feeling. Not that I'll ever forget, but perhaps I have learned to forgive myself." The psychologist felt as if he had delivered a new baby. The handshake after that hour was more vigorous than usual.

There does come a time when life begins again. It may be two months or two years after the suicide but it does come. Having survived, having worked hard on understanding what made it all happen, having struggled to improve communication within the family and within himself, the survivor finally arrives at the new beginning. When it happens the survivor has reached a depth of sensitivity he has not previously had. The suicide has destroyed one life but helped build another.

Lindsay's parents and brothers went to the autopsy, all six of them. The boys played catch in the park while the parents identified the body. Lindsay looked normal except for the neck. It was their daughter all right. What had happened to the charming, outgoing young lady heading for college?

After Lindsay's death, Mother became passive, guilty. Father immersed himself even more in his work. Laird, who started seeing his school counselor regularly, kept asking questions of his parents and his brothers. He wrote a junior paper on the sociology of suicide. His counselor kept urging him to "talk." And talk he did. He learned about recovering feelings and memories, and he sternly expected the others in his family to do likewise. They began to call him the analyst. Mother said he made her cry. Laird said, "Good" and kept talking and questioning. Laird's brothers became sold on the value of sharing their questions, their feelings, and, eventually, their insights about their sister's suicide.

With the first anniversary of the hanging, Laird suggested going to the state park where Lindsay had died. Mother shuddered but went. Father stayed home to attend to business. Laird bothered the sheriff until he found the exact tree. Mother vomited and then sobbed when they found it. The brothers all cried together. As they turned into the driveway, they were worn out, but they had a sense of family. They had been there together and they were surviving as a group. "It was a terrible day but it was right," Laird said.

Four times this family had an outing of remembrance on Lindsay's anniversary. On the fifth, Father joined them. They went to the duck pond where the parents had taken them as little children. Father sensed their unusual closeness and commented on it. Laird smiled and said, "I guess we have begun to live again." For the first time, Father wept openly in front of the family. Mother hugged him and on the way home they sang. Lindsay was finally at rest.

Nellie's parents began to share their feelings and to smile again. Father began to travel more for business reasons and Mother joined him. The trips took them to New Mexico, then Mexico. Both became interested in archaeology and Mother enrolled in the university. She even began to wonder if Nellie would have shared the interest. When they visited Chichen Itza she said spontaneously to her husband, "Nellie would have liked that." Father wondered how she knew, but agreed.

They both noticed that they had become more interested in each other than they had been for years. "I think you have finally put the past to rest," said Father. Nellie's mother agreed and smiled the most tender-eyed smile he had seen in many years.

For three years, Meg's mother and father seemed to do nothing but fight. Neither of them slept well, they both lost weight. After much pushing from their family doctor and their priest, they agreed to see a psychiatrist. The doctor pointed out that the fighting was merely a way to cover their mutual depressions and that they needed to share instead of hide their true feelings. In twelve sessions focused on their depression, they cried, questioned, and remembered, prodded by the therapist. He seemed ruthless but somehow they knew his prodding was the only stimulus that would force them to share their guilt.

During the final session, the parents expressed their sadness at ending the treatment. It had become important in its own right, not just because it made them talk about Meg. "You know," said the father, "Meg has served as a bridge for Mary and me to get closer. Perhaps that is her gift to us, hidden in all the grief."

It took another year for the parents but they finally found a new level of companionship. At Christmas of that year, surrounded by their nieces and nephews, they were able to say a toast to Meg: "To Meg, who in death, has brought us all closer." The younger children did not understand, but they sensed a room full of love.

Notes

Chapter 1 The Grim Statistics

1. Truman E. Dollar and Grace H. Ketterman, *Teenage Rebellion,* Revell, 1979.
2. Daniel Offer, Eric Ostrov, and Kenneth I. Howard, *The Adolescent: A Psychological Self-Portrait,* Basic, 1981.
3. James Wechsler, *In a Darkness,* Norton, 1972.
4. "She tried to grow up too fast, and now she's dead too young," Chicago *Tribune,* November 7, 1981, by Jane Fritsch.
5. "Children Who Want to Die. Their Suicide Attempts and Depressions Concern Researchers," *Time,* September 25, 1978.
6. Francine Klagsbrun, *Too Young to Die: Youth and Suicide,* Pocket, 1981.
7. "Suicide Belt: Rates Up for Affluent Teens," *Time,* September 1, 1980.
8. "In Loveland, U.S.A.: Study of a Teenage Suicide," "Directions," ABC-TV, produced and written by Herbert Danska, December 13, 1981, second of two-part series.
9. Chicago *Sun-Times,* June 18, 1979.
10. John E. Mack and Holly Hickler, *Vivienne: The Life and Suicide of an Adolescent Girl,* Little, Brown, 1981.
11. WFYR, Chicago, October 25, 1981.

Chapter 2 The Deadly Myths

1. Francine Klagsbrun, *Too Young to Die: Youth and Suicide,* Pocket, 1981.
2. "The Alarming Rise in Teenage Suicide," *McCall's,* January 1982, by Mary Ann O'Roark.
3. Ibid.
4. Chicago *Sun-Times,* November 21, 1981.

5. "In Loveland, U.S.A.: Study of a Teenage Suicide," "Directions," ABC-TV, produced and written by Herbert Danska, December 13, 1981, second of two-part series.

6. Ibid.

7. Mira Rothenberg, *Children with Emerald Eyes,* Pocket, 1978.

8. Edwin S. Shneidman, ed., *Death and the College Student,* Behavioral Publications, 1972.

9. "Suicide Ends Four Young Lives," *Baltimore Magazine,* June 1980, by Jon Reisfeld.

10. John E. Mack and Holly Hickler, *Vivienne: The Life and Suicide of an Adolescent Girl,* Little, Brown, 1981.

11. "Teenage Suicide: Don't Try It," Alan Landsburg Productions, 1981.

12. John E. Mack and Holly Hickler, *Vivienne.*

13. WFYR, Chicago, October 25, 1981.

14. A. Alvarez, *The Savage God: A Study of Suicide,* Bantam, 1973.

15. John E. Mack and Holly Hickler, *Vivienne.*

16. "In Loveland, U.S.A.: Study of a Teenage Suicide," ABC-TV.

17. "Deadlines and demons send reporter to death," Chicago *Tribune,* August 17, 1980, by Michael Sneed.

18. "Suicide Ends Four Young Lives," *Baltimore Magazine.*

19. "Airing the anguish of loneliness and despair," Chicago *Tribune,* November 14, 1979.

20. A. Alvarez, *The Savage God.*

Chapter 3 Distress Signals

1. "Her suicide wouldn't die," Chicago *Sun-Times,* August 12, 1979, by Zay N. Smith.

2. "Good Morning America," ABC-TV, October 29, 1981.

3. "Teenage Suicide: Don't Try It," Alan Landsburg Productions, 1981.

4. "NBC Nightly News," with Bob Jamieson, May 2, 1981.

5. "Teenage Suicide," "Directions," ABC-TV, Correspondent Herbert Kaplow, December 6, 1981, first of two-part series.

6. A few of the facts in this case are taken from, "Teenage suicide on the rise," *The News,* New Trier Township High School, February 5, 1982.

7. Herbert Hendin, *The Age of Sensation: A Psychoanalytic Exploration of Youth in the 1970s,* McGraw-Hill Paperback, 1977.

8. "Teenage Suicide: Don't Try It," Alan Landsburg Productions.
9. Sylvia Plath, *The Bell Jar,* Bantam, 1972.
10. Judith Guest, *Ordinary People,* Ballantine, 1977.
11. Beatrice Sparks, ed., *Jay's Journal,* Times, 1979.
12. "Teen Suicide and the North Shore Connection," Chicago *Tribune Magazine,* July 27, 1980, by April Olzak.
13. Edwin S. Shneidman, ed., *Death and the College Student,* Behavioral Publications, 1972.
14. "Donahue," Multimedia Program Productions, transcript #08150.
15. Aimee Liu, *Solitaire,* Harper/Colophon, 1980.
16. Chicago *Tribune,* November 3, 1981.
17. *Newsweek,* November 23, 1981, Beth Clewis, Durham, North Carolina.
18. "In Loveland, U.S.A.: Study of a Teenage Suicide," "Directions," ABC-TV, produced and written by Herbert Danska, December 13, 1981, second of a two-part series.
19. "Suicide Ends Four Young Lives," *Baltimore Magazine,* June 1980, by Jon Reisfeld.
20. Maggie Scarf, *Unfinished Business: Pressure Points in the Lives of Women,* Doubleday, 1980.
21. Beatrice Sparks, ed., *Jay's Journal.*
22. "A Brilliant Student's Troubled Life and Early Death," New York *Times,* August 25, 1981, by William Robbins.
23. John E. Mack and Holly Hickler, *Vivienne: The Life and Suicide of an Adolescent Girl,* Little, Brown, 1981.
24. "Airing the anguish of loneliness and despair," Chicago *Tribune,* November 14, 1979.
25. John E. Mack and Holly Hickler, *Vivienne.*
26. Sylvia Plath, *The Bell Jar.*
27. "In Loveland, U.S.A.: Study of a Teenage Suicide," ABC-TV.
28. "Suicide Ends Four Young Lives," *Baltimore Magazine.*
29. Sylvia Plath, *The Bell Jar.*
30. "Teenage Suicide: Don't Try It," Alan Landsburg Productions.
31. John E. Mack and Holly Hickler, *Vivienne.*
32. *The Collected Poems: Sylvia Plath,* Harper & Row, 1981.
33. Anne Sexton, *The Complete Poems,* Houghton Mifflin, 1981.
34. James Wechsler, *In a Darkness,* Norton, 1972.
35. "In Loveland, U.S.A.: Study of a Teenage Suicide," ABC-TV.

Chapter 4 A Child's View of Death

1. Edwin S. Shneidman and Norman L. Farberow, eds., *Clues to Suicide: an Investigation*, McGraw-Hill Paperback, 1957, Chapter 2.
2. Ibid., Chapter 1.
3. "Nightline," ABC-TV, April 24, 1981.
4. "In Loveland, U.S.A.: Study of a Teenage Suicide," "Directions," ABC-TV, produced and written by Herbert Danska, December 13, 1981, second of two-part series.
5. "Teenage Suicide: Don't Try It," Alan Landsburg Productions, 1981.
6. "Nightline," ABC-TV.
7. "In Loveland, U.S.A.: Study of a Teenage Suicide," ABC-TV.
8. *Paturot à la recherche d'une position sociale*, 1844. Quoted in A. Alvarez, *The Savage God*.
9. Edwin S. Shneidman, ed., *Death and the College Student*, Behavioral Publications, 1972.
10. Eliot Asinof, *Craig and Joan*, Viking, 1971.
11. Brenda Rabkin, *Growing Up Dead: A Hard Look at Why Adolescents Commit Suicide*, Abingdon, 1979.
12. Edwin S. Shneidman, ed., *Death and the College Student*.
13. Ibid.
14. John E. Mack and Holly Hickler, *Vivienne: The Life and Suicide of an Adolescent Girl*, Little, Brown, 1981.
15. Edwin S. Shneidman, *Voices of Death*, Bantam, 1982.
16. "Nightline," ABC-TV.
17. Ibid.
18. Antoine de Saint-Exupéry, *The Little Prince*, Harcourt Brace Jovanovich, 1943.
19. John E. Mack and Holly Hickler, *Vivienne*.
20. "Suicide's horror: Facing the reality," Chicago *Tribune*, October 24, 1979, by Jack Mabley.
21. "The Alarming Rise in Teenage Suicide," *McCall's*, January 1982, by Mary Ann O'Roark.
22. A. Alvarez, *The Savage God: A Study of Suicide*, Bantam, 1973.
23. "Teenage Suicide: Don't Try It," Alan Landsburg Productions.

Chapter 5 Children as Status Symbols

1. "Suicide Belt: Rates Up for Affluent Teens," *Time,* September 1, 1980.
2. Francine Klagsbrun, *Too Young to Die: Youth and Suicide,* Pocket, 1981.
3. "In Loveland, U.S.A.: Study of a Teenage Suicide," "Directions," ABC-TV, produced and written by Herbert Danska, December 13, 1981, second of two-part series.
4. Herbert Hendin, *The Age of Sensation: A Psychoanalytic Exploration of Youth in the 1970s,* McGraw-Hill Paperback, 1977.
5. "Today Show," September 3, 1980, first of two-part series by Phil Donahue on college student suicides.
6. "Suicide Ends Four Young Lives," *Baltimore Magazine,* June 1980, by Jon Reisfeld.
7. "Donahue," Multimedia Program Productions, transcript #01161.
8. Sylvia Plath, *The Bell Jar,* Bantam, 1972.
9. "Suicide Ends Four Young Lives," *Baltimore Magazine.*

Chapter 6 Blocked Communication

1. "Nightline," ABC-TV, April 24, 1981.
2. "In Loveland, U.S.A.: Study of a Teenage Suicide," "Directions," ABC-TV, produced and written by Herbert Danska, December 13, 1981, second of two-part series.
3. "Teenage Suicide: Don't Try It," Alan Landsburg Productions, 1981.
4. "In Loveland, U.S.A.: Study of a Teenage Suicide," ABC-TV.
5. "Teenage Suicide: Don't Try It," Alan Landsburg Productions.
6. WFYR, Chicago, October 25, 1981.
7. "In Loveland, U.S.A.: Study of a Teenage Suicide," ABC-TV.
8. "Teenage Suicide: Don't Try It," Alan Landsburg Productions.
9. Louis Wekstein, *Handbook of Suicidology: Principles, Problems and Practice,* Brunner/Mazel, 1979.
10. Beatrice Sparks, ed., *Jay's Journal,* Times, 1979.
11. "Suicide Ends Four Young Lives," *Baltimore Magazine,* June 1980, by Jon Reisfeld.

12. "Nightline," ABC-TV, April 24, 1981.
13. WFYR, Chicago.
14. John E. Mack and Holly Hickler, *Vivienne: The Life and Suicide of an Adolescent Girl*, Little, Brown, 1981.

Chapter 7 Feeling Rootless and Valueless

1. "Teenage Suicide and the North Shore Connection," Chicago *Tribune Magazine*, July 27, 1980, by April Olzak.
2. Ibid.
3. Ibid.
4. "Suicide Belt: Rates Up for Affluent Teens," *Time*, September 1, 1980.
5. Jane Norman and Myron Harris, *The Private Life of the American Teenager*, Rawson, Wade, 1981.
6. Maria W. Piers and Genevieve Millet Landau, *The Gift of Play: And Why Young Children Cannot Thrive Without It*, Walker, 1980.
7. "Boy found hanged in closet," Chicago *Tribune*, December 21, 1980.
8. "The nanny network," *Chicago*, November 1981, by Connie Fletcher.
9. "Troubled Teenagers," *U.S. News & World Report*, December 14, 1981.
10. "In Loveland, U.S.A.: Study of a Teenage Suicide," "Directions," ABC-TV, produced and written by Herbert Danska, December 13, 1981, second of two-part series.
11. "Growing Up Faster," *Psychology Today*, February 1979, by David Elkind.
12. "Teenage Suicide: Don't Try It," Alan Landsburg Productions, 1981.
13. "Donahue," Multimedia Program Productions, transcript #01161.
14. "Youth's Suicide May Lead to Help for Other Children Who Are Brilliant but Troubled," New York *Times*, September 21, 1980, by William Robbins.
15. "Donahue," transcript #01161.
16. "Childhood's End," *Harper's*, May 1979, by Scott Spencer.
17. "A Nation of Runaway Kids," *Newsweek*, October 18, 1982, by Lynn Langway.

Chapter 8 An Unbearable Loss

1. "Nightline," ABC-TV, April 24, 1981.
2. "Teenage Suicide: Don't Try It," Alan Landsburg Productions, 1981.
3. WFYR, Chicago, October 25, 1981.
4. Herbert Hendin, *The Age of Sensation: A Psychoanalytic Exploration of Youth in the 1970s,* McGraw-Hill Paperback, 1977.
5. "The nanny network," *Chicago Magazine,* November 1981, by Connie Fletcher.
6. Herbert Hendin, *The Age of Sensation.*
7. "The nanny network," *Chicago.*
8. Truman E. Dollar and Grace H. Ketterman, *Teenage Rebellion,* Revell, 1979.
9. "Nightline," ABC-TV.
10. "In Loveland, U.S.A.: Study of a Teenage Suicide," "Directions," ABC-TV, produced and written by Herbert Danska, December 13, 1981, second of two-part series.
11. "Teenage Suicide: Don't Try It," Alan Landsburg Productions.
12. Edwin S. Shneidman, ed., *Death and the College Student,* Behavioral Publications, 1972.
13. "Suicide Ends Four Young Lives," *Baltimore Magazine,* June 1980, by Jon Reisfeld.
14. Ibid.
15. "How Publicity Affects Violent Behavior," *Psychology Today,* January 1981, by Sheila Mary Eby.
16. "Deadlines and demons send reporter to death," Chicago *Tribune,* August 17, 1980, by Michael Sneed.
17. "Suicide Ends Four Young Lives," *Baltimore Magazine.*
18. Karl Menninger, *Man Against Himself,* Harvest/Harcourt Brace Jovanovich, 1938.

Chapter 9 The Key to Good Mental Health

1. Silvia Feldman, *Choices in Childbirth,* Grosset & Dunlap, 1978.
2. Ashley Montagu, *Touching: The Human Significance of the Skin,* Harper & Row, 1972.

3. "Nobody Home: The Erosion of the American Family," *Psychology Today*, May 1977, by Urie Bronfenbrenner.

4. Benjamin Spock, *Raising Children in a Difficult Time*, Norton, 1974.

5. "Should You Stay Home with Your Baby?" *Young Children*, November 1981, by Burton L. White.

6. Ibid.

7. "Billy: Psychological Intervention for a Failure-to-Thrive Infant," by Selma Fraiberg. In *Maternal Attachment and Mothering Disorders: A Round Table*, October 1974, Johnson & Johnson.

8. Herbert Hendin, *Suicide in America*, Norton, 1982.

9. John E. Mack and Holly Hickler, *Vivienne: The Life and Suicide of an Adolescent Girl*, Little, Brown, 1981.

10. John Killinger, *The Loneliness of Children*, Vanguard, 1980.

11. Bruno Bettelheim, *The Uses of Enchantment: The Meaning and Importance of Fairy Tales*, Knopf, 1976.

12. "You'll Be Sorry When I'm Not Here Anymore!" *Good Housekeeping*, by Alice E. Chase.

Chapter 10 Depression: It Strikes Children, Too

1. "The Alarming Rise in Teenage Suicide," *McCall's*, January 1982, by Mary Ann O'Roark.

2. "Airing the anguish of loneliness and despair," Chicago *Tribune*, November 14, 1979.

3. Sylvia Plath, *The Bell Jar*, Bantam, 1972.

4. "Airing the anguish of loneliness and despair," Chicago *Tribune*.

5. Wina Sturgeon, *Conquering Depression*, Cornerstone/Simon & Schuster, 1981.

6. WFYR, Chicago, October 25, 1981.

7. Wina Sturgeon, *Conquering Depression*.

8. H. G. Morgan, *Death Wishes? The Understanding and Management of Deliberate Self-Harm*, Wiley, 1979.

9. Wina Sturgeon, *Conquering Depression*.

10. "Teenage Suicide: Don't Try It," Alan Landsburg Productions, 1981.

Chapter 11 The Crisis: What Can You Do?

1. Louis Wekstein, *Handbook of Suicidology: Principles, Problems and Practice,* Brunner/Mazel, 1979.
2. "Rx for Depression: One Friend Every 4 Hours," *Ms.,* June 1979, by Karen Lindsey.
3. "Nightline," ABC-TV, April 24, 1981.
4. "NBC Nightly News," with Bob Jamieson, May 2, 1981.
5. Edwin S. Shneidman, ed., *Death and the College Student,* Behavioral Publications, 1972.
6. "Suicide Ends Four Young Lives," *Baltimore Magazine,* June 1980, by Jon Reisfeld.
7. "Rx for Depression: One Friend Every 4 Hours," *Ms.*
8. Ibid.
9. "Teenage Suicide: Don't Try It," Alan Landsburg Productions, 1981.
10. Jane Norman and Myron Harris, *The Private Life of the American Teenager,* Rawson, Wade, 1981.
11. "In Loveland, U.S.A.: Study of a Teenage Suicide," "Directions," ABC-TV, produced and written by Herbert Danska, December 13, 1981, second of two-part series.
12. "Deadlines and demons send reporter to death," Chicago *Tribune,* August 17, 1980, by Michael Sneed.
13. "Suicide Ends Four Young Lives," *Baltimore Magazine.*
14. John E. Mack and Holly Hickler, *Vivienne: The Life and Suicide of an Adolescent Girl,* Little, Brown, 1981.
15. Francine Klagsbrun, *Too Young to Die: Youth and Suicide,* Pocket, 1981.
16. "Today Show," September 3, 1980, first of two-part series by Phil Donahue on college-student suicides.
17. "Suicide Ends Four Young Lives," *Baltimore Magazine.*
18. Ibid.
19. "Good Morning America," ABC-TV, October 29, 1981.

Chapter 12 Finding Help in Your Community

1. Keith Lasko, *The Great Billion Dollar Medical Swindle*, Bobbs-Merrill, 1980.
2. "Teenage suicide on the rise," *The News*, New Trier Township High School, February 5, 1982.
3. Brenda Rabkin, *Growing Up Dead: A Hard Look at Why Adolescents Commit Suicide*, Abingdon, 1979.
4. "Suicide Ends Four Young Lives," *Baltimore Magazine*, June 1980, by Jon Reisfeld.

Chapter 13 Helping the Survivors

1. "The Loss of Teresa," "Channel 2—The People," WBBM-TV, Chicago, June 19, 1982, Bruce DuMont, Producer.
2. "Murder-suicide: the most tragic of family affairs," Chicago *Tribune*, January 7, 1979, by Ann Marie Lipinski.
3. John E. Mack and Holly Hickler, *Vivienne: The Life and Suicide of an Adolescent Girl*, Little, Brown, 1981.
4. WFYR, Chicago, October 25, 1981.
5. "Good Morning America," ABC-TV, October 29, 1981.
6. "Donahue," Multimedia Program Productions, transcript #01161.
7. "The Loss of Teresa," June 19, 1982.
8. Ibid.
9. Edwin S. Shneidman, ed., *Death and the College Student*, Behavioral Publications, 1972.
10. "The Loss of Teresa," June 19, 1982.
11. Ibid.

Selected Bibliography

Books

Alvarez, A. *The Savage God: A Study of Suicide.* Bantam, 1973. (Generally on suicide, specifically on the suicide of poet Sylvia Plath and the suicide attempt of the author.)

Anderson, D., and McClean, L. *Identifying Suicide Potential.* Behavioral Publications, 1971.

Asinof, Eliot. *Craig and Joan.* Viking, 1971. (The true story of two teenagers who killed themselves to protest the Vietnam War.)

Brazelton, T. Berry. *On Becoming a Family: The Growth of Attachment.* Delta, 1982.

Cain, A. Editor. *Survivors of Suicide.* Thomas, 1972.

Giovacchini, Peter. *The Urge to Die: Why Young People Commit Suicide.* Macmillan, 1981.

Grollman, Earl A. *Suicide: Prevention, Intervention, Postvention.* Beacon, 1971.

Guest, Judith. *Ordinary People.* Ballantine, 1977. (Novel about the suicide attempt of a suburban teenager and the effect on his family.)

Haim, A. *Adolescent Suicide.* IUP, 1974.

Hendin, Herbert. *The Age of Sensation: A Psychoanalytic Exploration of Youth in the 1970s.* McGraw-Hill, 1977. (Based on interviews with Columbia University students. Includes chapter on suicide.)

———. *Suicide in America.* Norton, 1982.

Killinger, John. *The Loneliness of Children.* Vanguard, 1980.

Klagsbrun, Francine. *Too Young to Die: Youth and Suicide.* Pocket, 1981. (Originally published in hardcover in 1976.)

Liu, Aimee. *Solitaire: A Young Woman's Triumph Over Anorexia Nervosa.* Harper/Colophon, 1980.

Mack, John E., and Hickler, Holly. *Vivienne: The Life and Suicide of an Adolescent Girl.* Little, Brown, 1981.

Mahler, Margaret S.; Pine, Fred; and Bergman, Anni. *The Psychological Birth of the Human Infant.* Basic, 1975. (A classic on mother/infant bonding.)

McCoy, Kathleen. *Coping with Teenage Depression: A Parent's Guide.* NAL, 1982.

McIntire, M., and Angle, C. *Suicide Attempts in Children and Youth.* Harper & Row, 1980.

Piers, Maria W., and Landau, Genevieve Millet. *The Gift of Play: And Why Young Children Cannot Thrive Without It.* Walker, 1980.

Plath, Sylvia. *The Bell Jar.* Bantam, 1972. (Originally published in England in January 1963, a month before the author killed herself. This is a fictionalized but strongly autobiographical account of poet Sylvia Plath's first suicide attempt, made when she was twenty.)

Rabkin, Brenda. *Growing Up Dead: A Hard Look at Why Adolescents Commit Suicide.* Abingdon, 1979. (Originally published in Canada in 1978. Focused on the suicide of a Canadian teenager.)

Reynolds, D., and Farberow, N. *Suicide, Inside and Out.* University of California, Berkeley, 1976.

Shaffer, David, and Dunn, Judy. *The First Year of Life . . . Psychological and Medical Implications of Early Experience.* Wiley, 1979.

Shneidman, Edwin S. *Voices of Death.* Harper & Row, 1980.

———. Editor. *Death and the College Student.* Behavioral Publications, 1972. (Essays written by students in Shneidman's course on death and suicide.)

———, and Farberow, Norman L. Editors. *Clues to Suicide: An Investigation.* McGraw-Hill, 1957.

Sparks, Beatrice. *Jay's Journal.* Times, 1979. (The journal of a teenage boy who eventually killed himself.)

Stern, Daniel. *The First Relationship: Mother and Infant.* Harvard University Press, 1977.

Wechsler, James. *In a Darkness.* Norton, 1972. (The author describes the mental illness of his son and the boy's eventual suicide.)

White, Burton. *The First Three Years of Life.* Prentice-Hall, 1975.

Zusman, J., and Davidson, D. Editors. *Organizing the Community to Prevent Suicide.* Thomas, 1971.

Articles

Felsenthal, Carol Greenberg. "Teen Suicide: What to Do When a Friend Is in Trouble." *Seventeen*. April 1979.

Jerome, Jim. "Catching Them Before Suicide." New York *Times Magazine*. January 14, 1979.

Langone, John. "Too Weary to Go On." *Discoverer*. November 1981.

Marano, Hara Estroff. "Biology Is One Key to the Bonding of Mothers and Babies." *The Smithsonian*. February 1981.

O'Roark, Mary Ann. "The Alarming Rise in Teenage Suicide." *McCall's*. January 1982.

Quinn, Susan. "The Competence of Babies." *Atlantic Monthly*. January 1982.

Reisfeld, Jon. "Suicide Ends Four Young Lives." *Baltimore Magazine*. June 1980.

Spencer, Scott. "Childhood's End." *Harper's*. May 1979. (Novelist Spencer laments that the current crop of parents, unlike their parents and grandparents, seem to place a low priority on children; to be unwilling to genuinely sacrifice for them.)

Index

Kovacs, Maria, 11
Kryzwicki, Frances, 33, 178–79, 259

"Lady Lazarus" (Plath), 72
Landau, Genevieve Millet, 135
Landers, Ann, 14, 20
Lasko, Keith, 274
Leibrecht, Walter, 105
Lennon, John, 179
Lerner, Vivian, 279
Levi, Stanley A., 131
Lewis, Michael, 194, 195
Lifton, Robert Jay, 38, 172
Lincoln, Abraham, 244
LINKS, 41–42
Lithium, 235
Litman, Robert, 110
The Little Prince (Saint-Exupéry), 87
Liu, Aimee, 53
The Loneliness of Children
    (Killinger), 203
Loomis, David, 209
Loomis, Laurel, 209, 259, 260
Loomis, Paulette, 209, 262, 288
Loomis, Rob, 41, 122
Loomis, Vivienne, 25–26, 29, 31, 41,
    65, 69, 85, 122, 209, 259–60,
    262, 288
Los Angeles County Suicide
    Prevention Center, 145, 267 n
Los Angeles *Times,* 177
Loss
    death in family, 166–73
    of identity or status, 163–66
    of important person or thing,
    66–68
Lourie, Reginald, 61
Love, parental, and suicide, 155–59
Loving Outreach to Survivors of
    Suicide (LOSS), 286, 295–96

McIntire, Matilda, 9
Mack, John, 122 n
McKnew, Donald, 11, 79, 241–42
Man Against Himself (Menninger),
    181

Mandel, Michel R., 240–41
MAO inhibitors, 234–35, 237–38
Materialism, as way of life, 130–32
"Me and Bobby McGee" (song),
    138
Menninger, Karl, 49, 181
Mental health clinics, community,
    268–69
Metro-Help, 157
Meyers, Peter, 6 n
Miller, Derek, 147 n
Mobility, of families, 129–30
Monroe, Marilyn, 179 n
Montagu, Ashley, 193
Montreal Tel-Aide, 272
Mood-swings, as distress signal,
    60–61
Mooney Problem Checklist, 219
Moore, Mary Tyler, 8
Moss, Leonard M., 170
Mothers
    liberated, 94–97
    as natural bonders, 200–1
    working, 159–63
    See also Children; Family;
    Parents
"Mourning and Melancholia"
    (Freud), 181
Myers, Cynthia, 157
Myths
    that failed suicides will eventually
    succeed, 21
    that few people under psychiatric
    care commit suicide, 27–28
    that pain and shame stop failed
    suicides from trying again,
    30–31
    that suicide attempts stop when
    depression ends, 32–34
    that suicide occurs out of the blue,
    28–30
    that suicide runs in families,
    37–38
    that suicides are insane, 30
    that suicides are old, 37

A CRY FOR HELP

Mary Giffin, M.D., and Carol Felsenthal

The statistics are tragic. Every day, somewhere in the United States, eighteen teenagers take their own lives. Today, suicide ranks as the third leading cause of death among young people.

In A CRY FOR HELP, psychiatrist Mary Giffin and journalist Carol Felsenthal review actual case histories as Dr. Giffin shares everything she has learned about the suicide-prone teenager: just who is likely to attempt it, who will succeed, and why. The authors alert parents to warning signals — specific behavior changes and mood swings — which are the cries for help that most often precede suicide. Dr. Giffin focuses on the single most common cause of teenage suicide — adolescent depression — and explains both its symptoms (loneliness, despair, and a feeling of worthlessness) and its cure. Most important, Dr. Giffin tells parents exactly what to do — and what not to do — in an acute suicide crisis, and advises them of suicide hotlines and prevention centers they can call on in an emergency.